Archaeological Survey of the Lower Kennet Valley, Berkshire

by S.J. Lobb and P.G. Rose

Archaeological Survey of the Lower Kennet Valley, Berkshire

by S.J. Lobb and P.G. Rose

with contributions from
Michael J. Allen, P.A. Harding, Lorraine Mepham, and M.R. Trott

Illustrations by S.E. James

Wessex Archaeology Report No. 9
Wessex Archaeology 1996

Published 1996 by the Trust for Wessex Archaeology Ltd, Registered Charity No. 287786
Portway House, Old Sarum Park, Salisbury, England, SP4 6EB

Copyright © 1996 Trust for Wessex Archaeology Ltd
All rights reserved

British Library Cataloguing in Publication Data
A catalogue record for this book is available from the British Library

ISBN 1–874350–14–0
ISSN 0965–5778

Produced by Wessex Archaeology
Printed by Henry Ling (Dorset Press) Ltd, Dorchester

Editor: Melanie Gauden
Series Editor: Julie Gardiner

The publication was funded by English Heritage

Front cover: Typical view of the present day River Kennet, near Thatcham, Berkshire
Back cover: Donnington Castle with Civil War defences in the foreground. Cover photographs by Elaine Wakefield

Contents

List of Figures v
List of Plates vi
List of Tables vi
Contents of Microfiche vi
Acknowledgements vii
Abstract vii

1. Introduction

Introduction to all Surveys and to the Evaluation 1
History of Previous Work 3
Summary of Archaeological Knowledge 5
The Major Monuments of the Area 5
Radiocarbon Calibrated Dates 6

2. The Survey Area

Location and Geology 7
    Topography 7
    Soils 7
    Landuse 7
Threats to the Archaeological Resource 10
    Gravel Extraction 10
    Forestry 10
    Agriculture 11

3. 1976–77 Survey, *by P.G. Rose*

Aims of the Survey 12
Strategy 12
    Air Photography 12
    Documentary Evidence 12
    Fieldwork in Woodland, Heath, and Plantation 13
    Fieldwalking of Cultivated Land 13
    Finds Analysis 13
Results 13
    Air Photography 13
    Documentary Evidence 13
    Earthworks 14
Fieldwalking, Finds Analyses 14
    Worked Flint 14
    Burnt, Unworked Flint 17
Pottery 18
Discussion 22
    Appraisal of Fieldwalking Methods and Results 22

4. Surveys 1982–87

Extent and Aims of the Surveys 24
Strategy 24
    Field Survey 24
    The Transect 24
    The Burghfield Area 24
    Excavation 26
Methods 26

Fieldwalking. 26
Phosphate Survey 27
Woodland Survey. 27
Finds Analysis 27
Results. 29
Woodland Survey. 29
Phosphate Analysis, *by M.R. Trott and S.J. Lobb* 30
Finds Analyses (the Transect). 30
Other Finds, *by Lorraine Mepham* 37
Pottery 40
Tile 45
The Burghfield Area 47
Other Finds, *by Lorraine Mepham* 48
Tile. 53

5. Kennet Valley Survey Middle, 1988–89

Extent and Aims of the Survey 54
Strategy and Method 54
Finds Distributions. 54
Flint 54
Burnt Flint 56
Pottery 57
Tile 57
Pilot Auger Survey, *by Michael J. Allen* 58

6. Synthesis 62

7. Evaluations Within the Survey Area

Results. 68
Comment 69

8. The Development of the Landscape

Lower and Middle Palaeolithic. 70
Mesolithic 73
Early Neolithic 75
Late Neolithic/Early Bronze Age 77
Later Bronze Age 79
Iron Age. 82
Romano-British. 86
Post-Romano-British to Medieval 92

9. Review

Summary. 100
Floodplain. 100
River Gravels 101
Valley Side (London Clay, Bagshot Beds, and Plateau Gravel Edge) 101
Plateau (Plateau Gravel). 101
Conclusion. 102

iv

10. Appendices

Appendix 1: 1976–77 Survey: New Air Photographic Sites 103
Appendix 2: 1976–77 Survey: Field and Place Names 104
Appendix 3: 1976–77 Survey: Earthwork Sites in Woodland, Heath, and Plantation 105
Appendix 4: 1976–77 Survey: Fieldwalking Results from Cropmark Sites. 106
Appendix 5: 1976–77 Survey: Pottery Find Spots/Sites 107
Appendix 6: 1976–77 Survey: Recommendations 109
    Environmental Work. 109
    Fieldwalking. 109
    Survey of Earthworks 109
    Air Photography. 109
    Geophysical Survey 109
    Watching Briefs 110
    Excavation 110
    Preservetion and Management. 110
    Presentation. 110
Appendix 7: 1982–87 Surveys: Transect, all Finds. 111
Appendix 8: 1982–87 Surveys: Burghfield Area, all Finds. 114
Appendix 9: 1988–89 Survey, all Finds 115
Appendix 10: Summary of Archaeological Evaluations in the Survey Area 117

Bibliography 122
Index 129

List of Figures

Figure 1   The Kennet Valley Survey area
Figure 2   Location of the survey areas
Figure 3   Extent of the major features and monuments visible on the air photographs
Figure 4   Drift geology
Figure 5   Modern landuse
Figure 6   1982–87 Surveys: transect, location of fields walked
Figure 7   1982–87 Surveys: Burghfield area, location of fields walked
Figure 8   1988–89 Survey Middle, location of fields walked
Figure 9   Location of pilot auger survey
Figure 10   Axonometric auger survey
Figure 11   Location of evaluations within the survey area

Figure 12   Distribution of Palaeolithic finds from the survey area
Figure 13   Distribution of Mesolithic sites and finds from the survey area
Figure 14   Distribution of Neolithic–Early Bronze Age sites and finds from the survey area
Figure 15   Distribution of later Bronze Age sites and finds from the survey area
Figure 16   Distribution of Iron Age sites and finds from the survey area
Figure 17   Distribution of Romano-British sites and finds from the survey area
Figure 18   Distribution of Saxon sites and finds from the survey area
Figure 19   The medieval landscape within the survey area

List of Tables

Table 1   1976–77 Survey: flint clusters
Table 2   1976–77 Survey: flint densities by geology
Table 3   1976–77 Survey: percentages of areas walked not producing flints
Table 4   1976–77 Survey: concentrations of burnt, unworked flint
Table 5   1976–77 Survey: summary of Iron Age finds from fieldwalking
Table 6   1976–77 Survey: summary of Romano-British pottery from fieldwalking
Table 7   1976–77 Survey: size of Romano-British sites on valley side and valley floor
Table 8   1976–77 Survey: summary of medieval pottery distribution
Table 9   1976–77 Survey: size of medieval 'sites' on the valley side and valley floor
Table 10   1976–77 Survey: comparison of Romano-British and medieval findspots
Table 11   1976–77 Survey: percentage change in number of findspots, Romano-British to medieval
Table 12   1982–87 Surveys: summary of excavation and watching briefs
Table 13   1982–87 Surveys: phosphate survey, summary of results
Table 14   1982–87 Surveys, transect: flint clusters

Table 15   1982–87 Survey, transect, burnt flint concentrations
Table 16   1982–87 Surveys, transect, pottery clusters and scatters
Table 17   1982–87 Surveys, transect: location and density of pottery by period
Table 18   1982–87 Surveys, transect: Romano-British tile occurrences
Table 19   1982–87 Surveys, Burghfield Area: flint clusters
Table 20   1982–87 Surveys, Burghfield Area: burnt flint concentrations
Table 21   1982–87 Surveys, Burghfield Area: pottery clusters and scatters
Table 22   1982–87 Surveys, Burghfield Area: pottery by geology through time
Table 23   1982–87 Surveys, Burghfield Area, Romano-British tile occurrences
Table 24   1982–87 Surveys: flint clusters
Table 25   1988–89 Survey: burnt flint concentrations
Table 26   1988–89 Survey: pottery clusters and scatters
Table 27:   The Kennet terrace sequence, nomenclature and suggested date

Contents of Microfiche

Figure Mf. 1: 1976–77 Survey: new earthworks and air photo sites A2–3
Figure Mf. 2: 1976–77 Survey: histogram showing density of all worked flints A4
Figure Mf. 3: 1976–77 Survey: Mesolithic flints A5–6
Figure Mf. 4: 1976–77 Survey: Neolithic/Early Bronze Age finds A7–8
Figure Mf. 5: 1976–77 Survey: later Bronze Age pottery A9–10
Figure Mf. 6: 1976–77 Survey: Iron Age pottery A11–12
Figure Mf. 7: 1976–77 Survey: Romano-British pottery A13–14
Figure Mf. 8: 1976–77 Survey: medieval pottery B1–2
Figure Mf. 9: 1982–87 Surveys, transect: flint blade material B3–4
Figure Mf. 10: 1982–87 Surveys, transect: flint flake material B5–6
Figure Mf. 11: 1982–87 Surveys, transect: flint cores B7–8
Figure Mf. 12: 1982–87 Surveys, transect: flint tools B9–10
Figure Mf. 13: 1982–87 Surveys, transect: burnt flint B11–12
Figure Mf. 14: 1982–87 Surveys, transect: prehistoric pottery B13–14
Figure Mf. 15: 1982–87 Surveys, transect: Romano-British finds C1–2
Figure Mf. 16: 1982–87 Surveys, transect: medieval pottery C3–4
Figure Mf. 17: 1982–87 Surveys, transect: post-medieval pottery C5–6
Figure Mf. 18: 1982–87 Surveys, transect: tile: Fabric A C7–8
Figure Mf. 19: 1982–87 Surveys, transect: ceramic building materials C9–10
Figure Mf. 20: 1982–87 Surveys, Burghfield Area: flint blade and flake material C11–12
Figure Mf. 21: 1982–87 Surveys, Burghfield Area: flint cores C13–14
Figure Mf. 22: 1982–87 Surveys, Burghfield Area: flint tools D1–2
Figure Mf. 23: 1982–87 Surveys, Burghfield Area: burnt flint D3–4
Figure Mf. 24: 1982–87 Surveys, Burghfield Area: prehistoric pottery D5–6
Figure Mf. 25: 1982–87 Surveys, Burghfield Area: Romano-British finds D7–8
Figure Mf. 26: 1982–87 Surveys, Burghfield Area: medieval pottery D9–10
Figure Mf. 27: 1982–87 Surveys, Burghfield Area: post-medieval pottery D11–12
Table Mf. 28: 1982–87 Surveys, Burghfield Area: post-medieval tile concentrations D13

vi

Figure Mf. 29: 1982–87 Surveys, Burghfield Area: ceramic building material E1–2
Figure Mf. 30: 1988–89 Survey, Middle: flint blade and flake material E3–4
Figure Mf. 31: 1988–89 Survey, Middle: flint tools E5–6
Figure Mf. 32: 1988–89 Survey, Middle: burnt flint E7–8
Figure Mf. 33: 1988–89 Survey, Middle: pottery E9–10
Figure Mf. 34: 1988–89 Survey, Middle: post-medieval pottery E11–12
Figure Mf. 35: 1988–89 Survey, Middle: ceramic building material E13–14
Table Mf. 36: 1988–89 Survey, Middle: post-medieval tile concentrations F1

Acknowledgements

The structure of the initial report owes much to the efforts of John Coles. Andrew Lawson has read various drafts of the report and his discussions and suggestions were much appreciated. Comments on various parts of the final report were provided by Grenville Astill, (medieval) and Mark Corney (Iron Age and Romano-British). Grenville Astill, Richard Bradley, and Michael Fulford all commented on earlier drafts of the report and we are grateful for their constructive criticisms. We are particularly pleased to acknowledge the help and support of Paul Chadwick of Berkshire County Council.

The project was financed by English Heritage and Berkshire County Council. The finds and archive will be deposited in Reading Museum and Art Gallery.

We are grateful to the many landowners and tenant farmers for their cooperation and patience in allowing us to examine their fields over so many years. A survey of this size owes much to the fieldwalkers who carried out the groundwork, generally at the most inclement times of year, and we are grateful to all those who assisted with the various surveys. Jo Mills, Christine Jones, and Sarah Wyles (among others) dealt efficiently with the finds and subsequent analyses. Christine Butterworth worked on the project over several years and guided the fieldwork of the middle survey. A special debt is owed to Lorraine Mepham for her help in pulling together the archive and to Liz James who spent much time grappling with the often large distribution plans.

Abstract

The archaeological survey of the Lower Kennet Valley, Berkshire arose out of the need to assess the archaeological resource of an area that has seen considerable development pressure within the past two decades and to respond to the consequent threat to it. The survey area encompasses approximately 22 km of the lower part of the Kennet Valley in west Berkshire between the Newbury district and Reading.

This report presents the results of field surveys undertaken in 1976–77 and 1982–87 by the Berkshire Archaeological Unit, and in 1988–89 by Wessex Archaeology, and reviews the evidence for all periods of occupation in this area. In addition the results of evaluations carried out by Wessex Archaeology in the Kennet Valley between 1985 and 1989, are briefly presented and discussed. Several excavations and watching briefs were carried out in the survey area during the second period of fieldwalking and these are reported on separately in Excavations in the Burghfield Area, Berkshire, by C.A. Butterworth and S.J. Lobb (Wessex Archaeological Report 1, 1992).

Through air photographic evidence, documentary sources, and field walking, each survey studied the archaeological potential of areas of mixed geology, including both river and plateau gravels, floodplain, and valley side in order to assess the potential of each topographic zone within its context. The methods themselves are also assessed and discussed.

The individual surveys highlighted a recurring theme in the archaeology of the Lower Kennet Valley, which was the way in which the pattern of settlement and the character of landuse relate to the valley's topographical and geological diversity.

The Kennet Valley Survey has confirmed the considerable human impact on the landscape of the Kennet Valley and also the great potential remaining within zones as yet little explored or exploited. The data presented in this report will be crucial in the development of strategies appropriate to the management of the remaining archaeological resource.

1. Introduction

Introduction to all Surveys and to the Evaluation

A traveller crossing the Lower Kennet Valley in the middle of the 18th century would have seen a countryside little changed from its character of the previous centuries. Subsequent traffic (perhaps along the Kennet and Avon canal, the Great Western Railway, or the Bath Road) will have seen the progressive dismantling of this landscape. During the 18th and 19th centuries, the open fields on the river gravels of the valley floor were enclosed and much of the common heathland on the plateau gravels was enclosed and afforested. In this century, great blocks of the river and plateau gravels have been quarried away to feed the expansion of construction in southern England. Also in the present century large areas of the remaining heath have disappeared under defence establishments (Greenham Common, Aldermaston Weapons Research Establishment). These more recent developments of the historic landscape, gravel quarry, motorway, and missile base, are as much a testimony to the character of society today as the Bronze Age barrow is for that of the 2nd millennium BC and they demonstrate also how national and international, as well as local factors, now play a role in the shaping of the countryside.

The Lower Kennet Valley has come under increasing pressure for change over the past 15 years. Berkshire has become one of the fastest growing counties in England (Berkshire County Council 1988) and the demand for gravel, housing, industrial development, and associated infrastructure has placed in jeopardy the survival of the entire landscape between Reading and Newbury. The Kennet Valley Survey arose out of the need to assess the archaeological resource of the area and to respond to the consequent threat to it.

This report presents the results of field surveys carried out in 1976–77 and 1982–87 by the Berkshire Archaeological Unit, and in 1988–89 by Wessex Archaeology, and it reviews the evidence for all periods of occupation in this area. In addition, the results of evaluations carried out by Wessex Archaeology in the Kennet Valley between 1985 and 1989, are briefly presented and discussed. Several excavations and watching briefs were carried out in the survey area during the second period of fieldwalking and these are reported on separately (Butterworth and Lobb 1992; Lobb *et al.* 1991; Lobb and Mills 1994; Lobb and Morris 1994). The 1976–77 survey, commissioned by the Department of the Environment (latterly English Heritage), was carried out by P.G. Rose; the 1982–87 survey, also funded by English Heritage, was carried out by several teams of people under the management of S.J. Lobb; the 1988–89 survey (Kennet Valley Survey Middle) was funded by Berkshire County Council and English Heritage and carried out under the management of J.C. Richards. (For location of the survey areas, including excavation sites, *see* Fig. 2).

A draft report of the 1976–77 survey was completed and submitted to the Inspectorate of Ancient Monuments in January 1985. The publication of this report was delayed to such an extent that as the 1982–87 survey was nearing completion and because the two surveys shared the same broad aims, it seemed exped-

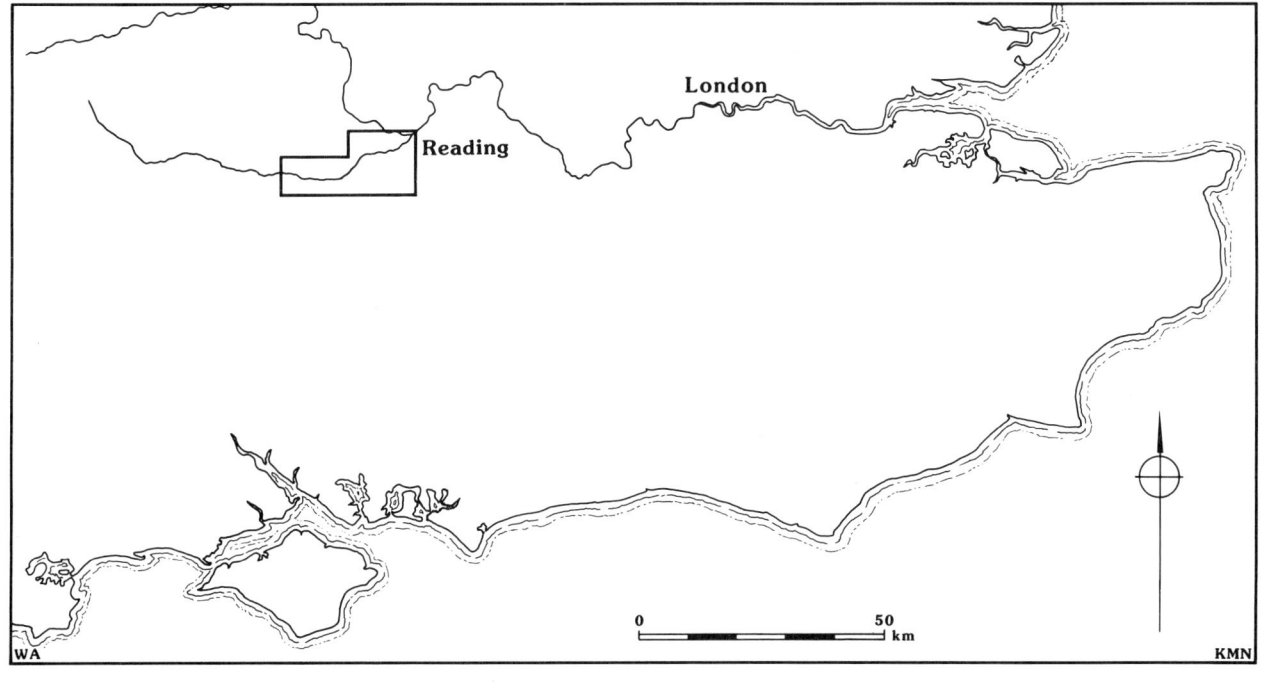

Figure 1   The Kennet Valley Survey area

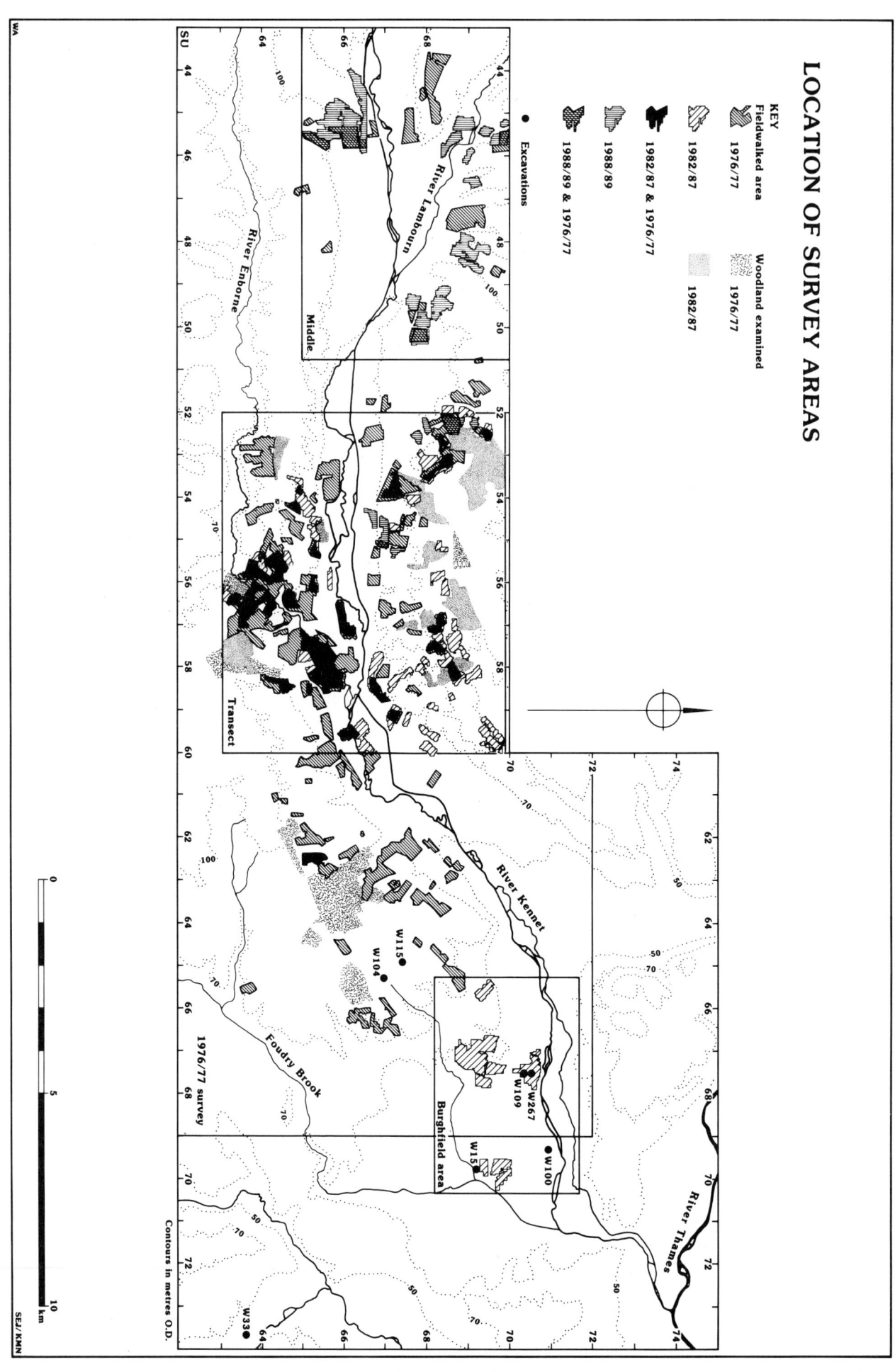

Figure 2 *Location of survey areas*

ient to publish the two together. Subsequently the Kennet Valley Survey Middle (1988–89) was carried out within the area of the previous surveys, although with different aims, and it seemed appropriate to include the results of this survey in this volume. Rose's draft text forms the basis of most of this report, in particular the introductory and discussion chapters, which have been expanded to include more recent information and interpretations.

History of Previous Work

The Lower Kennet Valley has attracted much archaeological, geological, and botanical interest, especially in recent years. The archaeological record for the Lower Kennet Valley is largely made up of chance finds made during mineral extraction or construction work and is consequently biased towards the lower gravel terraces and, to a lesser extent, the plateau gravels and the urban centres. However, a number of local surveys, research projects, and excavations have been carried out in the region which go some way to redressing the balance in certain areas and provide useful background information.

The gravels and terraces of the Lower Kennet Valley have been the subject of several research studies (Bryant et al. 1983; Cheetham 1975; Chartres 1975; Thomas 1961) and are of particular relevance to the Palaeolithic period. The soils and sediments of the floodplain and lower terrace have been studied by Chartres (1975) and Holyoak (1980) and their theses have established a framework for the Late Pleistocene period. Environmental evidence for this period has been provided by specific site studies at Thatcham in conjunction with the excavations of the Mesolithic site (Churchill 1962) and at Theale (Willkinson 1985), and a more general assessment by Holyoak (1980).

The large number of Mesolithic find spots and sites known in the area between Newbury and Hungerford is a reflection of the surface collection work and excavations by Froom in the 1960s and 1970s (Froom 1963; 1965; 1970; 1972a; 1972b) and the Sheridan brothers (Berkshire Sites and Monuments Record (SMR)). Excavations have been carried out on Mesolithic sites at Thatcham Sewerage Works (Peake and Crawford 1922; Wymer 1962), Greenham Dairy Farm (Sheridan et al. 1967) and Wawcott (Froom 1976).

The Kennet Valley Research Committee was established in 1971 to coordinate existing research in the Late glacial Mesolithic and (possibly) Neolithic periods in the valley, concentrating on the area between Hungerford and Thatcham. The main role of this committee has been to provide advice and specialist support to research projects in the area and the three theses carried out by Cheetham, Chartres, and Holyoak were done under its umbrella.

The archaeology of the later prehistoric and historic periods has been investigated in a more haphazard way. Prior to the middle of this century, archaeological fieldwork was largely restricted to a few small-scale exploratory excavations. By contrast, the Roman town of Silchester, on the fringes of the survey area, has been extensively excavated in the 19th and early part of this century (Fox 1892; Fox and St John Hope 1890; 1894; Joyce 1881; Karslake 1910; 1914; Maclauchlan 1851; St. John Hope 1906; 1909; St. John Hope and Stephenson 1910), in the 1930s (Cotton 1947), the 1950s (Boon 1969, 1974), and more recently in the 1970s and 1980s (Fulford 1984; 1984a; 1985; 1987; 1989). The occupation at Silchester in the Late Iron Age and Romano-British periods inevitably had a great influence on the organisation of the contemporaneous landscape and the results of the excavations provide an important chronological framework for these periods.

In the 1960s and 1970s, several large-scale excavations were carried out on cropmark sites on the gravel terrace initiated by increasing pressure from the construction industry (Lobb 1985; Manning 1974; Anon 1964, 190). With the establishment of the Berkshire Archaeological Unit in 1974, gravel extraction was monitored more closely and rescue excavations and salvage recording carried out at several sites (Bradley et al. 1980; Bradley and Richards 1979–80; Cowell et al. 1978; Johnston 1985; Lobb 1978; Lobb and Mills 1994). Similarly, small-scale excavations were carried out in advance of development at one or two sites (Astill 1979–80).

For the later historic period, excavation has largely been confined to the towns. In Reading, small-scale rescue excavations were carried out at Reading Abbey between 1964 and 1976 (Slade 1971–72; 1975–76), and more recently a programme of evaluation and large-scale excavation and watching briefs on development sites in the Abbey precinct and in the town (Vince et al. 1981–2; Hawkes 1986–90; 1991; Hawkes and Fasham in prep; Fasham and Stewart 1986–90). In Newbury, excavations in the 1970s were restricted to properties on the two main roads leading southwards from the medieval market place (Ford 1976; Vince 1980; Mepham (in prep.). Very little investigation of the contemporary landscape has taken place and includes small-scale excavation at Southcote Manor (Slade 1977–78) and occasional features found by chance on other excavations. Gelling's study of the place names of Berkshire (1976) is an important source of information for this period.

The Department of the Environment commissioned a number of surveys to review the state of archaeology in Berkshire. Astill's review of the historic towns in Berkshire (1978) includes the Kennet Valley settlements, while Richards' survey of the Berkshire Downs (1978) provides comparative data for an area bordering the present survey area. Gates's survey collated and presented the evidence available through aerial photography for the river gravels, including most of the survey area (Gates 1975), and this has formed the basis for subsequent surveys in the Kennet Valley. The air photo information has subsequently been updated (during the later survey) as part of an SMR enhancement programme.

Two undergraduate dissertations undertaken at Reading University have been concerned with aspects of the survey area. An intensive fieldwalking survey was carried out in the immediate vicinity of an earlier prehistoric cropmark complex at Theale (Ford 1977) and produced a concentration of worked flint. A survey of the parish of Ufton Nervet reviewed the evidence for the

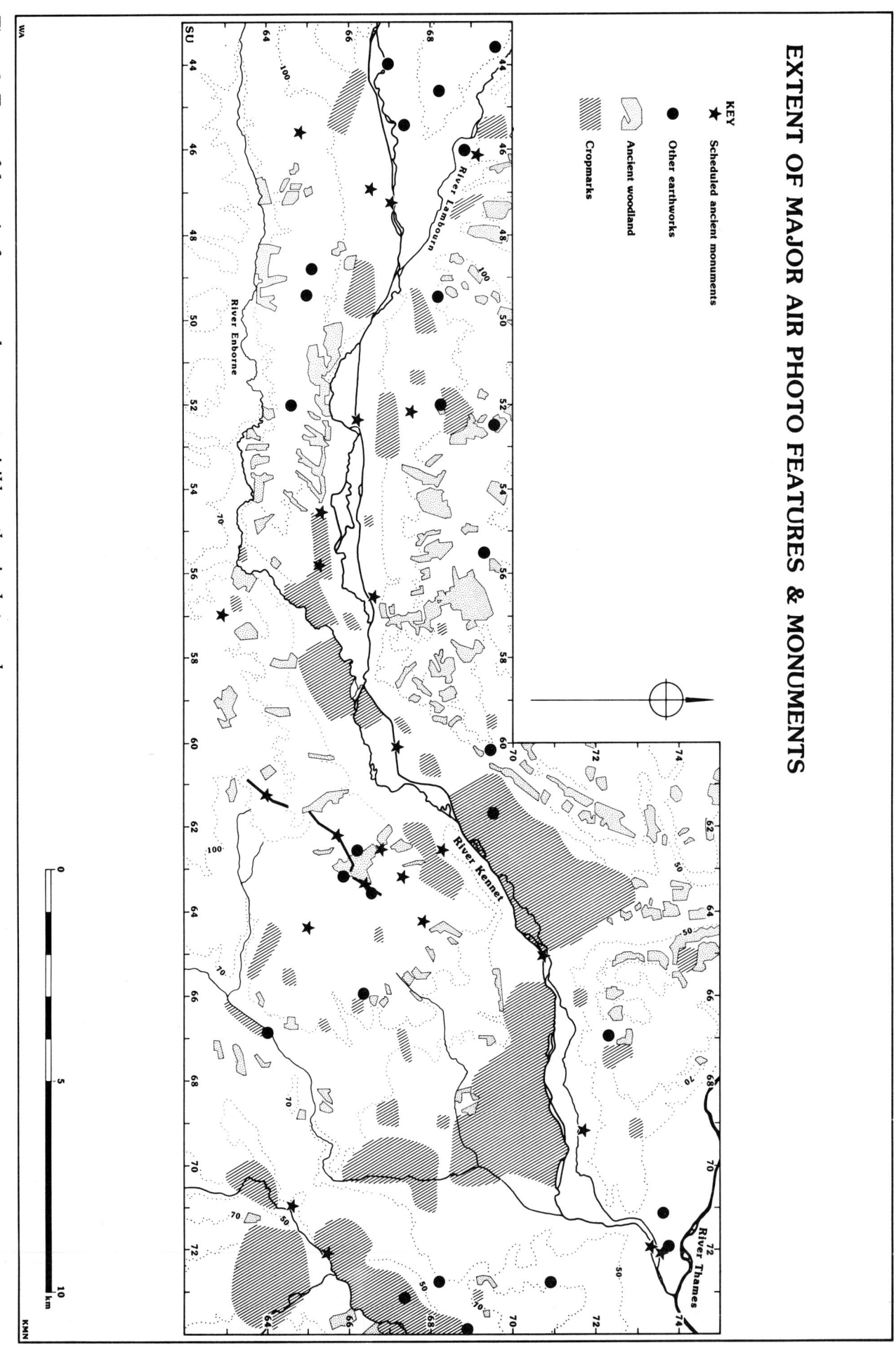

Figure 3 Extent of the major features and monuments visible on the air photographs

prehistoric and historic periods and included some documentary research and fieldwalking on the gravel terrace to the north, and the valley side to the south of the river (Wilkey 1977).

During the course of the later Kennet Valley project, responsibility for the Sites and Monuments Record was taken on and computerised by the County Council. This included a reassessment and updating of the existing record for the survey area; this information has been used extensively in the discussion sections.

Summary of Archaeological Knowledge

From the above review it can be seen that our knowledge of the archaeology of the study area is patchy and in places very sketchy. The lack of surviving earthworks (*see below*) and systematic fieldwork has meant that site discovery has depended on chance finds, largely from development sites, and aerial photography. Because of the modern landuse and vegetation, large areas are not available for this method of detection and effective air photo coverage is almost exclusively restricted to the river gravel terrace. Even in this area, sites do not always appear on aerial photographs; in parts of the floodplain and the lower terraces, deep alluvial deposits and soils have accumulated which may mask archaeological features. The evidence is consequently biased towards the built up areas, old gravel pits, and the valley floor.

Many of the geological, palaeo-ecological, and archaeological studies carried out in the area have contributed much information about the Palaeolithic and Mesolithic periods. These studies have concentrated on the lower terraces of the valleys and have capitalised on exposures provided by gravel extraction and other chance disturbances. Similarly, most of the excavations carried out in recent years have been of sites which were generally located on the gravel terraces. Many of these sites date to the later Bronze Age and the Romano-British periods and it is possible to suggest a broad chronological and social framework for landuse patterns in these periods. In contrast, evidence for the Neolithic, Iron Age, and Saxon periods is scarce; this could signify periods of decline, or simply imbalances in the state of our knowledge for the area. The excavations in Reading and Newbury have enabled some reconstruction of the development of the two towns in the Saxon and medieval periods, although evidence for the earlier period is rather insubstantial. However, the relationship between these market centres and the countryside, and the organisation of the contemporaneous rural landscape, has been little explored by excavation and fieldwork.

Interpretation of environmental change is hampered by poor survival of the evidence. Many of the excavated sites are in areas which are dry, well drained, and well above the level of the river, or in areas which are prone to seasonal flooding and drying out. Plant and faunal remains on these sites have survived only in deeper features where waterlogged conditions prevail or where they have been burnt. Although the data sources tend to be restricted in area, there is ample environmental evidence for the period up to the end of the Mesolithic, whereas the information for the later periods is fragmentary, providing a less coherent overview. However, this position is gradually changing as more sites on the floodplain are investigated.

The Major Monuments of the Area

In contrast to the well preserved monuments in the Avebury area of the Upper Kennet Valley, very few earthworks survive in the Lower Kennet Valley (Fig. 3). The latter area has not been systematically searched and more earthworks may exist but they are likely to be of a fairly ephemeral nature. Within the survey area, there are 31 scheduled monuments or groups of monuments, encompassing 51 individual earthworks and buildings. Over half of these are medieval or post-medieval in date. They are almost exclusively found on the valley sides, on the plateau gravel, or in the towns.

The monuments of the valley gravels survive only as cropmark sites or occasionally as very slight earthworks of which none is scheduled. The lack of excavation of these sites makes definition difficult but Gates classified the sites he identified into three categories on the basis of perceived archaeological value: complexes of the first category were deemed worthy of preservation, while those of category 2 should either be preserved or excavated on a large-scale; category 3 sites should be surveyed before destruction and recorded by watching brief. Gates examined only part of the survey area (as far west as the 55 easting line) and identified two category 1 sites, and two category 2 sites. One of the category 2 sites has subsequently been destroyed. Further west, very few cropmark complexes have since been identified (information from Berkshire County Council SMR).

The wealth of Mesolithic sites in the area and recent work on later prehistoric sites on the floodplain, bear witness to the existence of well preserved monuments on the floodplain but these sites have no visible surface characteristics. Morphologically there are no obvious monuments among the recorded cropmark sites of the earlier Neolithic period, although recent excavation has indicated that some of the ring-ditches in the area may date to the later Neolithic. The earliest prehistoric monuments are represented by three barrow cemeteries, including mixed barrow types and a few isolated barrows all on the higher ground, largely to the south of the river. Even within these cemeteries, some of the barrows have been destroyed either in antiquity or by recent forest working and disturbance. The large number of ring-ditches recorded on aerial photographs perhaps suggests that only a small percentage of these monuments survive as earthworks and that they were originally more widespread. A few of these survive as very slight mounds. A site at Marshall's Hill, Reading (SU 72807100), near the confluence of the Thames and Kennet, was first thought to be a disc-barrow but a recent reinterpretation suggests that this may have been the site of a high status Late Bronze Age circular enclosure (Bradley 1986); the site is now entirely built over.

A number of hillforts in the area are sited on plateau gravel ridges or spur ends: south of the Kennet, Pond Farm (SU 627631); north of the river, Ramsbury Hillfort (SU 524696) and just outside the survey area, Grimsbury (SU 512722), Bussock Camp (SU 467725), and possibly Borough Hill Camp (SU 440725) to the north of the Lambourn, although no earthworks survive here. Grims Bank consists of a series of linear earthworks which runs along the plateau gravel ridge to the south of the river. The date and function of these earthworks is not certain, although they are generally ascribed to the Late Iron Age, Romano-British, and post-Romano-British periods (Astill 1979–80). The landscape at this time was dominated by the Iron Age *oppidum* and Roman town at Silchester, which lies on the fringes of the survey area in Hampshire, and the associated road system survives as earthworks in parts of the survey area. Many of the cropmark complexes on the river gravel terraces are likely to date to the Iron Age and Romano-British periods.

The most obvious surviving monuments of the Saxon and medieval periods are the urban centres, including the Saxon royal estates and subsequent boroughs of Aldermaston, Newbury, Thatcham, and Reading; Bucklebury, on the northern fringe of the survey area, was a royal manor and centre of a *Domesday* hundred which did not develop into a town, and Speen was a medieval village with a market (Astill 1978). Very little of the early fabric of these towns remains. In Reading, parts of the Benedictine Abbey survive as ruins and a circular mound within the abbey precincts may be the remains of the castle motte. Reference is also made to a castle in Newbury but no evidence for this remains. The ruins of the castle at Donnington, constructed in the 14th century, occupy a commanding position on the northern side of the river just outside the survey area but still clearly visible from some distance away down stream. In the countryside the many villages and hamlets of the area, 11 moats and 14 fishponds, as well as many churches, chapels, and manorial centres, are believed to date from this period; although now considerably altered they give some indication of the well populated settlement pattern. Traces of ridge and furrow field systems are visible in some areas of the survey area but they are poorly preserved except for the scheduled earthworks at Woolhampton on the floodplain terrace.

Radiocarbon Calibrated Dates

All radiocarbon dates have been calibrated with the 20 year atmospheric calibration curve using CALIB 2.0 and are expressed at the 95 % confidence level with the end points rounded outwards to 10 years following the form recommended by Mook (1986).

Determinations in the Late Glacial period are beyond the spectrum of bristle cone pine. Such determinations presented for this period by Quaternary scientists are consistently given as uncalibrated dates BP, and thus to facilitate comparison within this timescale (ie pre 10, 000 BP) all determinations here are presented likewise.

2. The Survey Area

Location and Geology

The survey area encompasses approximately 22 km of the lower part of the Kennet Valley in west Berkshire between the Newbury district and Reading (Fig. 1). The 1976–77 survey set as its limits the 43 easting line to the west of the confluence of the Kennet and the Lambourn rivers, and the 69 easting line in the west. While the later survey (1982–87) examined two specific localities, the survey area, in the broadest sense, extended from Thatcham (the 52 easting line) and the confluence of the Kennet and Thames, although the most easterly stretch of the Kennet is within the conurbation of Reading and was not available for survey. The 1988–89 survey examined specific areas under potential threat from redevelopment in the Newbury environs (Fig. 2).

The Kennet rises on the Marlborough Downs and passes in an easterly direction across the west of Berkshire to Reading where it joins the Thames. The two main tributaries in the survey area are the Lambourn, which drains from the Berkshire Downs to the north, and the Enborne, which drains from the Eocene upland to the south. Lying at the western fringe of the London Basin, the valley encompasses a narrow belt of deposits, c. 9–16 km wide, between the Berkshire Downs and the Hampshire Downs. Chalk outcrops in the north-west of the area but this dips to the south-east beneath the later marine deposits of the Eocene Beds. These are, in increasing order of age, the Lower Bagshot Beds (sands with seams of clay), London Clay (blue–grey marine clay), and Reading Beds (variable from pebbles to sands and clays). It is through these deposits that the Kennet and its tributaries have cut (Fig. 4).

The Pleistocene deposits include a series of gravel terraces, mostly of flint derived from the chalk, with the so called plateau gravels at the beginning and the floodplain gravels at the end of the sequence. Towards the end of the Pleistocene period, some of the terraces were capped by silty deposits of loess (Chartres 1975). Similar deposits on the lowest terrace may be largely riverine in origin (Jarvis 1968, 44), beginning to accumulate at the end of the last glacial period (Chartres 1975). Subsequently, parts of the lowest terrace have been sealed by flood loams and marls of the floodplain, but loams, silts, marls, and peat are found in various combinations according to local conditions. While the alluvium of the Kennet Valley is largely clayey, in the Enborne Valley it is largely loamy.

Topography

At its simplest the relief is in a clear three-fold division: valley top, valley floor, and valley sides. The gravel plateau of the valley top is, for the most part, flat and featureless. Although in some localities the gravel has been heavily eroded and dissected, in places it remains very extensive, notably south of the Kennet between Mortimer and Newbury and north of the Kennet on Bucklebury Common. The presence of a spring line between the Eocene Beds and the capping of the gravel has aided erosion in the form of gullies of varying sizes, dissecting the plateau and slopes. Consequently, for the most part, the slopes descend in the form of more or less pronounced spurs, more usually in a series of steps than at an even gradient. The valley floor, comprising floodplain and lower terrace, is on average about 2 km wide. The terrace is of subdued relief, though slightly convex in places, and is separated from the floodplain by a bluff of about 2–3 m.

Soils

The soils of the district have been considered in some detail (Chartres 1975; Jarvis 1968; Jarvis et al. 1979). The majority of the soils formed are acid to a greater or lesser extent, particularly on the plateau gravels. There the rather acid soil tends readily towards podzolisation. Virtually all the land that was formerly heath and is now plantation has developed podzols; but brown earths have formed where the plateau gravel is cultivated. These soils are mostly free-draining, except for those formed on loams towards the centre of the plateau, which are waterlogged for much of the year (Jarvis 1968).

On the valley slopes the soils have formed mostly on Eocene sands and clays but also on gravelly drift from the plateau gravel and are generally heavy soils poorly or imperfectly drained. There is considerable local variety on the floodplain: loamy clay over gravel, loam over peat, gleys on marls, and surface peat. These soils are almost invariably poorly drained. The ground-water level is usually very close to the surface.

The gravels of the lower terrace, on the other hand, are mostly free-draining, whether the soils are formed in the loamy drift covering parts of the terrace (Hamble Series) or on the stony gravel surface (Sonning Series). The loamy, clayey or peaty alluvial soils of the floodplain are affected by high ground-water levels and periodic flooding.

Landuse

The lower gravel terraces provide the best agricultural land in the district (mostly classified Grade 2 on the land classification map) and are consequently almost entirely under cultivation (Fig. 5), just as during the medieval period they formed the common fields of the rural land, approximately 50% of this topographic zone is given over to cereal cultivation, while c. 19% is cultivated from time to time and c. 22% is under permanent pasture (Jarvis et al. 1979, 102). The floodplain, which floods at least once a year, has traditionally been meadowland and is used for summer grazing, though some is now arable (c. 12–5% with c. 22% temporary grassland and 57%

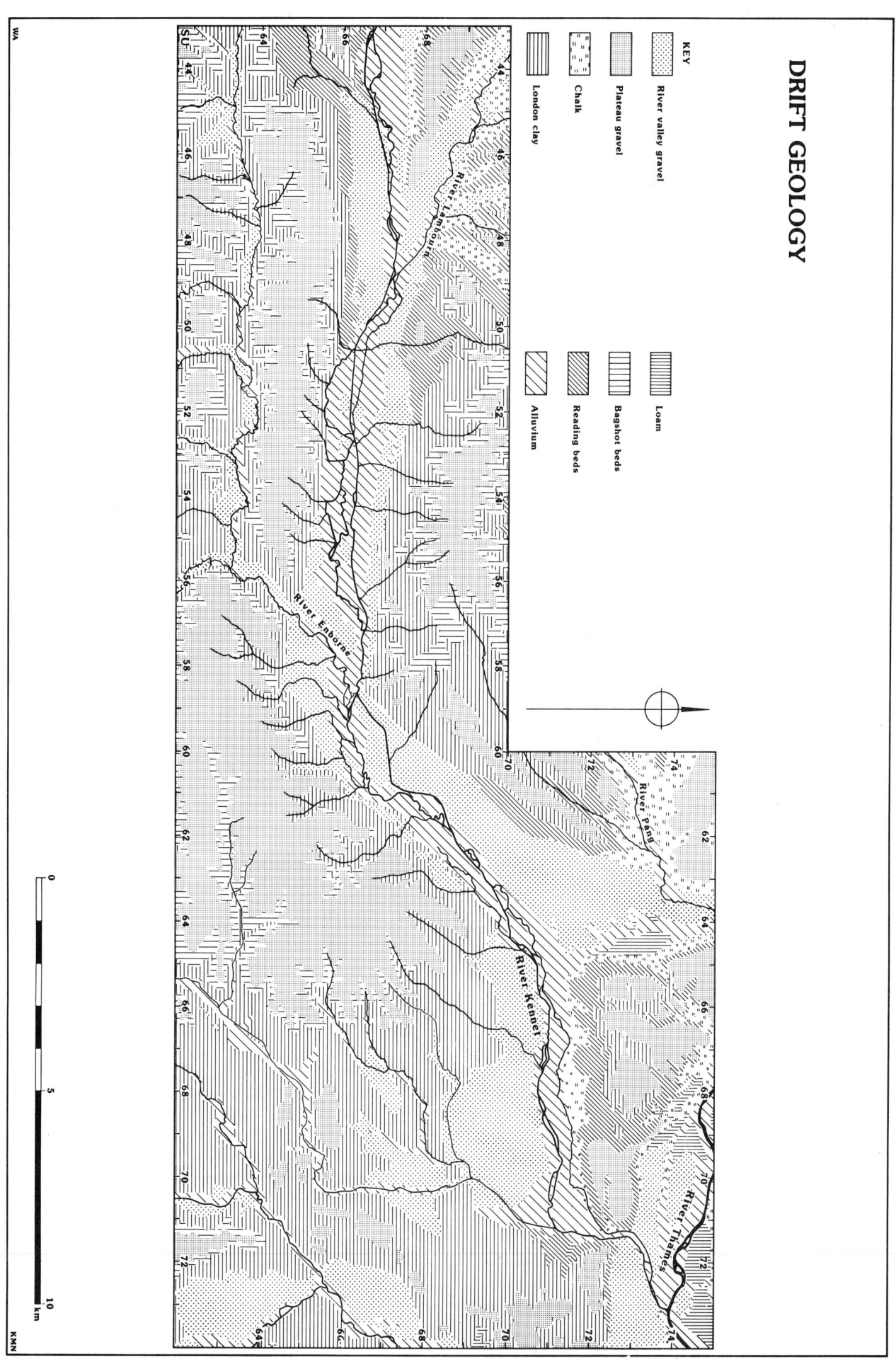

Figure 4 Drift geology

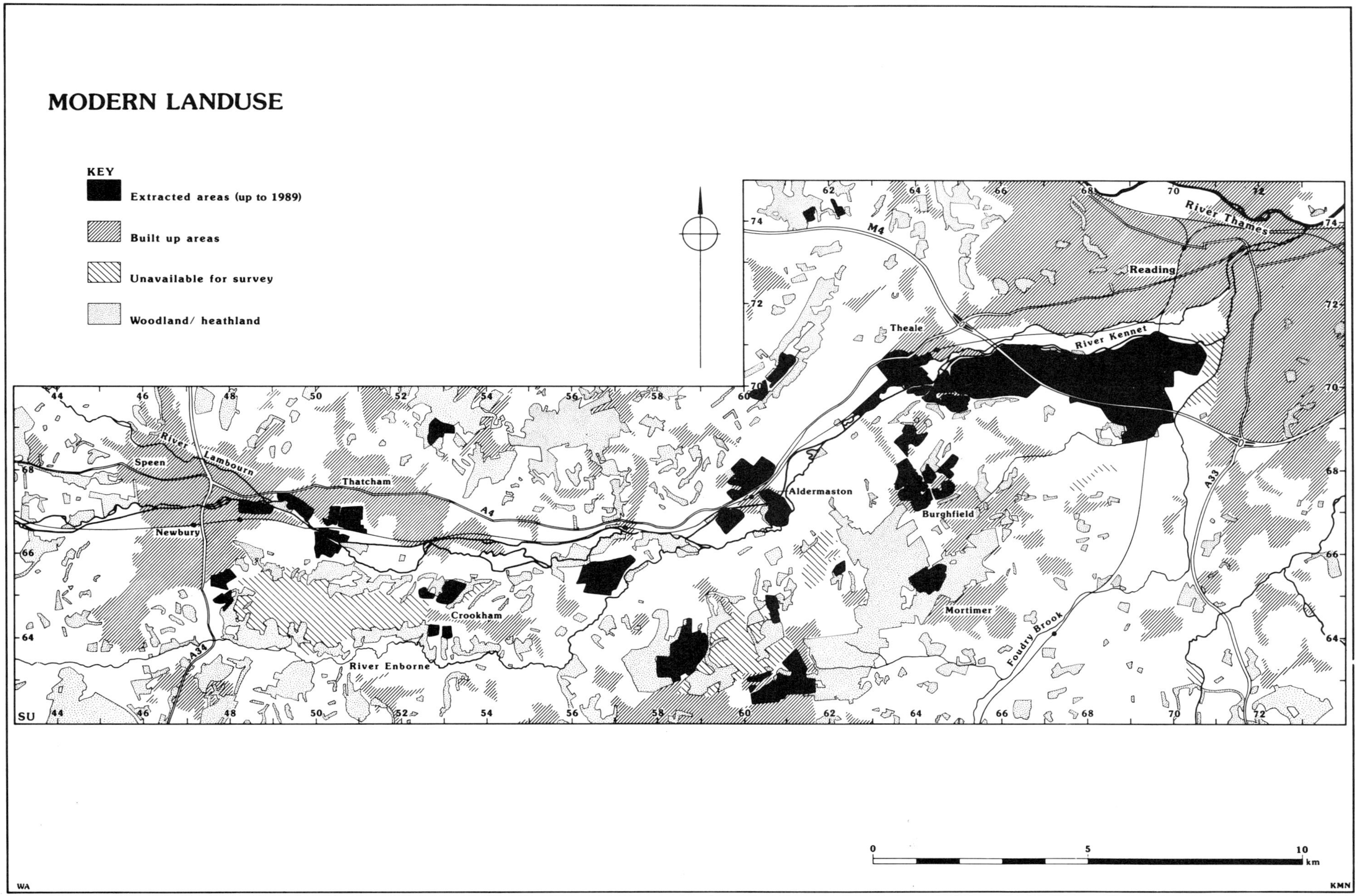

Figure 5 Modern landuse

permanent pasture (Jarvis *et al.* 1979, 102). Water-meadows were constructed over large areas in the 18th and 19th centuries, although these were mostly abandoned in this century. During the same period, extensive areas of peat, especially between Thatcham and Newbury, were cut, the peat used as fuel, or when burnt, as fertiliser (Peake 1935).

The valley sides are more wooded than the other topographic zones in the valley and woodland is found mostly, but not exclusively, in the gully bottoms and on the steeper slopes. Certainly when looking from the valley floor, the valley sides still preserve a wooded appearance. The remainder of the valley side is predominantly grass rather than arable. Drainage can be a problem. During the 18th century, the greater proportion of the plateau gravel supported only common or heath, though a considerable part was arable or grassland around the fringe of the plateau (Rocque 1761). Of the rural land in this area, *c.* 39% is now cultivated for cereals, *c.* 6% is temporary grassland, and 18% is under permanent pasture (Jarvis *et al.* 1979, 102). The former heathland, for the most part, supports conifer plantations, following the enclosures of the late 18th and early 19th centuries.

Most of Berkshire was largely deforested by the time of the *Domesday* survey and the tract of the Forest of Windsor in the Kennet Valley was cleared by Charter in 1226; however, Mavor (1809) refers to the best woodland in the county being to the south of the Kennet (cited in Jarvis *et al.* 1979, 134). Today, small areas of ancient woodland to the south of the river, represent the survival of this forest and woodland; more extensive areas of ancient woodland survive on Bucklebury Common to the north of the river (information from Berkshire County Council).

Threats to the Archaeological Resource

With development and road construction, the gradual erosion and dramatic destruction of archaeological remains is general throughout Britain, but in some areas this is occurring so rapidly through large-scale developments and changes in landuse, that the situation is particularly acute; the Lower Kennet Valley is one such area. This is clearly reflected in the *Replacement Berkshire Structure Plan* and the *Berkshire Minerals Local Plan* (Royal County of Berkshire 1988). 'Berkshire is one of the fastest growing and most densely populated shire counties in Britain, with a population increase of 7% between 1976 and 1982' (1988). The large Area of Outstanding Natural Beauty in the west and north-west of the county and the Green Belt, and already built-up area of the east, effectively rule out new large 'green field' developments in these areas, leaving an area from Newbury to Bracknell open to development (ibid., 1988). Between 1982 and 1996, Newbury District was earmarked for 90,000 new houses and 91 hectares of industrial development (ibid., 83 and 79).

Gravel Extraction

This threat has already been highlighted to some extent by the survey of the archaeological sites on the gravels in the county (Gates 1975, 51–3). The demand for gravel from Berkshire remained constant throughout the 1970s and 1980s but, because of the county's proximity to London and the declining resources further east, the gravel resources within the county have come under increasing pressure (Royal County of Berkshire 1984, 17). *The Berkshire Minerals Local Plan* (1984) groups sand and gravel deposits into four classes according to the likelihood of obtaining planning permission for extraction: Areas of Maximum Objection, Restricted Areas, Prospect Areas, and Preferred Areas. Within the Prospect Areas, the Preferred Areas are those where planning permission is most likely to be granted. Within the Kennet Valley, the area between Newbury and Theale is defined as a Prospect Area and includes 13 of the 18 defined Preferred Areas. In addition, outside the Preferred Areas, some extraction of poor quality gravel from the plateau gravels is likely to be allowed and the most suitable area is identified as the area between Crookham Common and Burghfield Common in the survey area; some plateau gravel reserves are also to be found to the north of the river in this area. (ibid., 44–5). Figure 5 maps those areas which had already been extracted (to end 1988) and gives an idea of the potential threat to the remaining archaeology in the Lower Kennet Valley.

One of the constraints included in the definition of Restricted Areas includes 'sites of archaeological importance which are not at present scheduled as Ancient Monuments' (ibid., 29). This designation does not guarantee that permission will be refused where sites of archaeological importance have been identified but, at a minimum level, it should ensure that consideration is given to the recording of mappable archaeological deposits. However, large parts of the Preferred Areas are on the floodplain or on the plateau gravels where, because of the present landuse, normal survey methods may not be applied to identify archaeological sites but where sites of archaeological importance are likely to exist. In recognition of this policy, EN26 of the *Berkshire Structure Plans* takes account of archaeological sites and monuments of unknown importance and areas of high potential and refers to the need to consider appropriate action when assessing planning applications.

Forestry

Forestry will have had its most serious effect on archaeological remains in the 18th and 19th centuries when large areas of the heath or grassland of the plateau gravels were enclosed and planted. Either then or subsequently, some areas have been disturbed by ploughing or trenching to break up the clay pan and improve drainage, providing a ridge to lift the roots above the water. Increased afforestation on any large-scale is not expected. In replanting, it is now normal to simply dig a shallow hole and plant the tree without further preparation. Damage tends to be gradual or piecemeal.

Although the roots of the softwoods spread outwards rather than downwards, they will still disturb archaeological deposits and damage earthworks. Further damage is caused by the use of heavy machinery, for example, when stands are cleared or roads and firebreaks cut. Even relatively obvious monuments, such as scheduled barrows, can be very vulnerable when heavy machinery is being used by someone who is unaware of their archaeological significance or of their statutory protection. In addition, there are likely to be many more subtle earthworks which have yet to be identified.

Agriculture

Apart from the woodland and heath and areas of the floodplain, most of the agricultural land is regularly ploughed or has been in the recent past. The damage caused by ploughing is difficult to assess. Of sites excavated in the area, none has any horizontal stratigraphy surviving and, although other factors such as erosion may be significant, this is in part likely to be due to plough damage. Normally, only features cut into the subsoil are likely to survive, particularly where the land has been ploughed for centuries, as on the gravel terraces. At Aldermaston Wharf, for example, the foundations of a Romano-British building had been ploughed away to leave only the bases of the hypocaust system (Cowell *et al.* 1978). Subsoiling and pan-busting, though practised, are not general in the area but there is some deep ploughing on the heavier soils (information from various farmers).

At present, the greatest damage will be caused when change of landuse brings land under the plough for the first time. Most serious is the increasing cultivation of the valley sides which contain slight earthworks which would be destroyed immediately by ploughing. In the long term, plough damage may be almost as effective as gravel extraction in the destruction of archaeological sites. Although gravel extraction involves the complete and often immediate destruction of archaeological sites, it is at least subject to statutory planning procedures which ensure that the effect on archaeological sites can be monitored. Agricultural developments are not subject to the same procedures.

3. 1976–77 Survey,

by P.G. Rose

Aims of the Survey

A survey to assess the archaeological potential of parts of the Lower Kennet Valley, commissioned in 1976 by the Department of the Environment, was carried out by P.G. Rose for the Berkshire Archaeological Unit in 1976 and 1977. The archaeological potential of the extensive plateau gravels, which are generally less susceptible to air photographic investigation but are equally affected by gravel extraction, remained obscure; this survey was commissioned primarily to complement Gates's work by looking in detail at an area of the higher gravel terraces in the valley. This objective was substantially modified, largely because of the need to appreciate the role of the plateau gravels within the valley as a whole. Consequently, the survey was a study of the archaeological potential of an area of mixed geology, including both river and plateau gravels and Eocene Beds in order to assess the potential of each topographic zone within its context. The area examined comprised about 150 km^2 of the Lower Kennet Valley between the western environs of Newbury and Theale (Fig. 2).

The report of this survey was intended, partly, to describe the results of fieldwork, principally fieldwalking carried out by Rose; to assess these results in the light of existing knowledge of the area; and to establish a framework for further work in the Lower Kennet Valley.

Strategy

The strategy adopted was largely decided by the nature of the available sources of information, together with the character of the present landuse and the limited time available for the survey. From Figure 5, it is apparent that much of the land was not available for survey having already been disturbed by building developments (notably Newbury, Thatcham, and Burghfield Common), by gravel extraction, and by other factors such as the Greenham Common Airfield and the Aldermaston Weapons Research Establishment, both of which are on plateau gravel. North of the Kennet, Bucklebury Common was also disturbed by military installations during World War II. Other constraints on the survey were imposed by large areas of woodland and grassland and by the clayey soils which have traditionally been less susceptible to cropmark formation.

Air photographs were examined but, at the time, the cover was of only limited value for much of the area. Documentary work was restricted to a rapid trawl through Tithe and Inclosure maps, particularly to examine the evidence available from field names. The greater part of the survey involved the fieldwalking of cultivated land and, to a lesser extent, fieldwork in areas of plantation and heath.

Air Photography

Effective coverage in the area was almost exclusively restricted to the river gravels. Cropmarks in the Lower Kennet Valley east of Thatcham had been plotted by Gates (1975). Photographs available in the Air Photography Unit of the National Monuments Record (NMR) were examined. The other main source was the series of photographs taken in 1963, 1969, 1971, and 1976 by Fairey Surveys Ltd for Berkshire County Council. Although these provide complete vertical coverage of the county at 1:10,000 scale, even known cropmark sites rarely show because almost all the flying was done in March or April. Only a very few soilmarks, cropmarks, or earthworks were noted. One flight was undertaken across the area by the Berkshire Archaeological Unit early in August 1977 but with little success.

Documentary Evidence

Tithe, Inclosure and estate maps, and the associated field names, were examined for evidence of medieval settlement patterns and traces of the open fields. Field boundaries on these maps were compared with numerous soilmarks on the air photographs which appeared to be of relatively recent date. Estate maps of the second half of the 18th century exist for four complete parishes (Midgham, Wasing, Ufton Nervet, and Enborne) and about five maps of the same period cover smaller parts of some parishes. There are Inclosure awards for another seven parishes (Aldermaston, Beenham, Brimpton, Burghfield, Sulhamstead, Thatcham, and Greenham) and the rest are covered by Tithe awards, or copies of Tithe maps. Some of these maps show considerable areas of fields in a strip system, some merely show a few strips in each field as relevant to the estate described, and others only name the open fields. It is possible to gain at least some idea of the areas that were open fields in the medieval period, though probably not their full extent. The medieval settlement pattern is more difficult to infer. Many of these maps deserve much more detailed attention. The Estate maps of Enborne, for example, show field patterns which have since been radically altered; close study would reveal a great deal about the medieval and post-medieval topography.

Field names, as well as providing a guide to local landuse and topography, can sometimes reflect the presence of a feature of antiquity. Frequently, the evidence of the name itself is ambiguous. Potential sites identified by field names were examined in the field. For a convincing correlation these sites must be identified in the field but this was not usually easy.

Other primary sources were not consulted but the *Victoria County History* was found to be a valuable guide for parish and manorial histories.

Fieldwork in Woodland, Heath, and Plantation

With a large proportion of the area, particularly the plateau gravels, covered by woodland, it was clearly important to examine its archaeological potential; however, this proved difficult. Even during the winter and early spring, the density of vegetation and the covering of leaf mould hindered observation, and survey in many areas could not be attempted.

The areas examined (Mf. 1) were walked at intervals of between 50 and 100 m in blocks defined by pathways and drainage ditches. Possible sites were plotted on 1:10,000 maps in relation to these mapped boundaries and sketch plots produced. A list of sites discovered appears in Appendix 3. These mostly include low banks, mounds, and hollow-ways, although one sub-rectangular enclosure at Padworth could prove interesting. Seen in isolation interpretation of these monuments is very difficult.

Fieldwalking of Cultivated Land

Nearly 1400 ha were examined between November and early June in 1976 and 1977. The main aim was to investigate the archaeological potential of the whole range of geologies and topographies in the Lower Kennet Valley, as suggested by the distribution and concentrations of surface finds. Over much of the area (but with notable exceptions) most previous archaeological work had been limited to the recording of chance finds and so the apparent archaeological blanks needed to be checked and redressed by systematic fieldwork. Five of the new sites identified by the air photograph search and 10 sites shown by Gates were included in the fieldwalking programme (Appendix 4).

So as to appreciate the context of the material recovered, adjoining fields were walked where possible. The large area of woodland and long ley grassland meant that the fields available for walking tended to be widely scattered. A statistically based selection of fields would therefore have been inappropriate and was not considered. Almost all the fieldwork was carried out solo by the writer; whilst acknowledging the limitations of field-walking in general, this will have imparted a degree of consistency to the results. For further consistency, the fields were walked to the same system. Within modern field boundaries, transects, generally across the short axis of the field, were examined at intervals of approximately 45–55 m. This provided a fairly low level of surface cover but was chosen as a compromise between the need to retrieve as much material as possible while covering as large an area as possible. The grid selected

was intended to provide a framework which was sufficiently refined to identify a majority of 'sites' and test the changing densities of material recovered, whilst at the same time, covering a broad sample of the survey area.

The fields were numbered by parish. Finds were recorded by field and run number and find spots marked by eye on the 1:10,000 map. Each field walked was given a Primary Record Number (PRN) in the old SMR, held by the Berkshire Archaeological Unit, and cross-referenced to a file of field cards in the archive which list the finds and describe the condition of the fields when walked. The information has now been transferred to the computerised Sites and Monuments Record, compiled and maintained by Berkshire Council, but for ease of reference, the original PRNs which occur in the archive have been used in this report.

Finds Analysis

Initially, the flint from 109 of the fields was scanned by Richard Bradley and divided subjectively into the four groupings adopted by Richards for the Berkshire Downs 1978, 19). The pottery was scanned and spot-dated by Grenville Astill, Richard Bradley, and Michael Fulford.

Results

Air Photography

Twelve new sites observed on the aerial photographs were examined (Fig. 3), three soilmarks and nine crop-marks (Appendix 1). Many examples of removed hedges were identified; used in conjunction with the Tithe maps this can be useful in reconstructing relatively recent landscapes which are likely to be at least partly medieval in origin. Limited areas of ridge and furrow were also noted. This is almost invariably straight and, where checked on the ground (eg Newbury, SU 45106348), the ridges are 3–5 m wide. The areas of ridging have not been included in Appendix 10 but there is a list with the archive.

Although the river gravel terraces have received considerable attention in the past, the presupposition that the rest of the area is unsusceptible to site identification by air photography is largely untested because of the, as yet, limited flying time devoted to the heavier Eocene Beds and to the plateau gravels. The present landuse rules out cropmark identification for much of these areas but it is clear that the plateau gravels can produce good cropmarks; Silchester, just over the county boundary in Hampshire, is a fine example (Boon 1974, pl. 8, 9).

Documentary Evidence

Very few sites were identified or strongly suggested by field name evidence; those of possible archaeological significance are listed in Appendix 2 in groups sharing a common element. Where the site was visited this is indicated.

The two suggested moats at Burghfield and Wasing are unconfirmed and the name 'Mill Field' at Brimpton (3578, Appendix 2) is of particular interest as it hints strongly at the function of the site implied by the concentration of medieval pot found next to a former stream. Names with a possible *burgh* element are common, particularly in the form 'Berry', but their actual meaning is usually ambiguous or obscure. Other than the two names referring to known sites (Ramsbury Hillfort, Thatcham, and Bury's Bank, Greenham), three examples were visited but without result. Some of the other names in this class may, however, be relevant; certainly the 'Oldbury' names at Burghfield ought to be significant, although no site is known there as yet. Whether Gelling's explanation for *wicham* place names (1967; 1977) can be extended to field names, and in particular to the examples in the appendix which have no early forms, is far from certain. Proximity to a Romano-British settlement need not be of relevance in an area where any field name is likely to be within 1 km of such a site.

Nevertheless, it was clear that the Wickham Fields at Woolhampton and Burghfield required fieldwalking. In 1994, work in advance of the construction of a new motorway service area on the M4 involved area excavation of Wickhams (*sic*) Field. This produced evidence for Early Iron Age domestic and and possibly industrial activity. Excavation further confirmed the presence of a Romano-British settlement here and three pits and two wells of Saxon date were also recorded (Andrews and Crockett 1996).

Earthworks

A small number of earthworks were observed (Mf. 1, Appendix 3) and include hollow-ways, low mounds, including a possible pillow mound at Padworth, a small sub-rectangular enclosure in the same parish, and various banks and ditches; one apparently associated with Grim's Bank. Where there are plantations, the ground has sometimes been disturbed by blocks of straight ridges and furrows about 2–4 m wide. These were presumably made when the common was enclosed in order to provide drainage and to raise the roots above water that in places stands on the surface for much of the year. This practice will have removed any low earthworks. Although a large number of banks and ditches were observed, their almost invariable steep profile suggests that most are relatively modern.

The low level of survey carried out has done little more than scratch the surface. Detailed field investigation in these areas, plus large-scale measured survey is required to make a full record of any remains and to tackle the problem of their function, context, and date. The woodland, heath, and plantations need very close and careful study to appreciate their potential. Areas where earthworks survive must be accorded particular importance, not least because they are likely to seal environmental evidence.

Fieldwalking — Finds Analyses

Worked Flint

Methods
Flint artefacts were found in 175 of the 242 fields walked. The quantities found were usually small. The classification of the flint (Richards 1978, 19) provided a broad chronology and general character for the material: Group 1 — Mesolithic; Group 2 — Early Neolithic; Group 3 — Late Neolithic/Early Bronze Age; Group 4 — later Bronze Age. Fields with one or two flint artefacts were largely not classified.

Group 1 flint was represented by 16 find spots, Group 2 by 38, Group 3 by 99, and Group 4 by 30. Finds of Group 2 and Group 4 material were almost invariably in small quantities and associated with Group 3. However, this division of the material is now not felt to be satisfactory for this survey, except perhaps as indicating the general character. In particular, the quantities of the flints (mostly waste flakes) are generally small and contain little that is diagnostic. Secondly, the surface collection from a field might be of more than one period which will confound attempts to regard it as a unity.

It is doubtful how far the surface collection of flint can be used to identify later Bronze Age sites in the survey area, at least at the level of intensity employed here. Attention has been drawn to the rarity of flints from excavated later Bronze Age sites in the Lower Kennet Valley at Aldermaston Wharf and Knight's Farm (Bradley *et al.* 1980, 288–9), in contrast to broadly contemporaneous sites on the Berkshire chalk at Rams Hill and Beedon Manor Farm (Bradley and Ellison 1975; Richards 1984). At Beedon Manor Farm, the excavated site was adjoined by an extensive scatter of flints classified as mainly of Group 4 (Richards 1984). Most, if not all, of the Group 4 material collected during the survey is therefore likely to be the cruder elements of Late Neolithic/Early Bronze Age industries rather than later Bronze Age.

Metrical analysis of assemblages of flint flakes can be used to give an indication of their date; work elsewhere in England has demonstrated that, in comparison with Early Neolithic industries, the Late Neolithic/Early Bronze Age industries tend to have a higher proportion of broad, squat forms and fewer long blade-like flakes (although this is not always as marked as has sometimes been suggested (Farley 1979)). The material recovered by fieldwalking during this survey is not very well suited to this type of analysis, partly because it does not come from a single excavated context and also because the quantities of flint are very low. The length of flakes may also have been affected by plough damage. Nevertheless, breadth:length ratios were determined for flints from the 11 fields where the density of material was higher than three per hectare (*see* below and Table 1) although, even with these, the totals are not large. The details of the analysis are in the survey archive.

15

Table 1 1976–77 Survey: flint clusters of greater density than three pieces per hectare

PRN	NGR	Parish	Total	Field	Density	Geol.	Topography	Flint groups				% Blades
								1	2	3	4	
3613	473687	Donnington	129	6.75	19	C+G	Bottom and sides of dry valley	/	*	/	–	2–4
3614	474692	Donnington	214	16	27	"	of dry valley	/	*	/	–	2–4

Note: flint density diagrams for above two fields suggest possibly two sites centred on 472687 and 472691.
NB. Fields 3614 was walked at 100 m intervals

PRN	NGR	Parish	Total	Field	Density	Geol.	Topography	1	2	3	4	% Blades
3612	487697	Donnington	80	5.7	14	C	Bottom of dry valley	/	*	–	–	2–4
3660	457676	Speen	80	5.75	14	C+ RB	Gentle slope down to gravel terrace	/	/	*	/	10
3661	453676	Speen	161	9.34	17	C+ VG	Gravel terrace slope	/	/	/	–	2–4

Note: flint density diagram suggests concentration centred on 454676

PRN	NGR	Parish	Total	Field	Density	Geol.	Topography	1	2	3	4	% Blades
3713	533673	Thatcham	25	2.75	9	G+ LC	Edge of floodplain adj. gully	/	*	–	–	–
3615	480688	Donnington	81	19.25	8.4	C	Slope	*	/	–	–	–
3710	500678	Thatcham	36	5.7	6	RB+ G	Slope	/	*	*	–	–
3712	497676	Thatcham	13	3.8	3	RB	Slope	/	*	*	–	–
3610	456699	Donnington	45	11	4	C	Side of spur	/	*	–	–	2–4
3739	628685	Ufton Nervet	24	5.7	4	G	Terrace edge above floodplain	–	*	*	–	–
3602	662670	Burghfield	15	4.75	3	PG	Headland	*	*	–	–	14
3690	552653	Thatcham	20	6.25	3	G	Terrace	/	*	–	–	–
3547	602649	Aldermaston	5	0.8	5	PG	Near head of gully	*	–	–	–	–

* = dominant group / = present

Density

It is clear from Figure Mf. 4 that Neolithic/Early Bronze Age activity, as indicated by discarded flint artefacts, was widespread throughout the survey area. The density of flints for each field has been roughly calculated on the basis of number of flints collected and the area of the field, although this does not take into account the number and spacing of the collection units. The overall results are illustrated in Figure Mf. 2. The main contrast seems to be between densities above and below one flint per hectare with most fields (49%) falling in the lower category; 17% of fields contained between one and three flints per hectare and 6% three or more. This may distinguish more intensive Neolithic/Early Bronze Age activity from the background noise of less intensive activity or casual loss over a wide area. Areas of higher densities, arbitrarily defined as those with three or more flints per hectare, are listed in Table 1.

Distribution

Mesolithic

Sixteen find spots of Mesolithic material were noted (Mf. 3) but mostly in very small quantities; much of this material is defined on the basis of the narrow blade component with no other diagnostic material present and could equally be Early Neolithic in date. The assignation of probable or possible was adopted to indicate the degree of confidence of the classification. The only concentration of material, producing two cores and 14 flakes, including blades, was situated on the edge of the floodplain terrace overlooking the River Enborne (3588).

Table 2 1976–77 Survey: flint densities by geology

Geology	Area walked	(ha)	Average density per ha.
Alluvium	149	0.29	–
River gravel		301	2.47
Plateau gravel		399	0.60
Bagshot Beds		106	0.60
London Clay		318	0.74
Reading Beds		53	4.97
Chalk	38	14.12	–

Table 3 1976–77 Survey: percentages of areas walked not producing flints

Chalk	0%	Plateau gravel	19%
Reading Beds	6%	Bagshot Beds	19%
River gravel	10%	Alluvium	48%
London Clay	13%		

The material appeared to be confined to an area of approximately 25 x 50 m, spread along the edge of the terrace.

The limited distribution indicates a preference for the floodplain terrace, although there were six find spots on the London Clay and two on the plateau gravel. The drift geologies are referred to here, more to give an idea of the location, rather than to suggest that they were necessarily relevant to the Mesolithic ecology. It is perhaps surprising that more material and more concentrations were not found in similar locations to those described by Froom. This could be because they are sealed beneath floodplain deposits.

Only seven of the 11 high density fields had any flints of a blade-like character (Table 1), as indicated by a 2:5 breadth:length ratio, although in most cases these were a low percentage of the total flint population of the clusters. In only one case was this percentage higher than 2–4%; the scatter at Speen (3660) with 10% was the only scatter in this group which was felt to have a Mesolithic element. The figure for PRN 3602, Burghfield of 14% should be treated with some caution as it is derived from a total of only 15 flints. All of these scatters were on chalk, except for one (3602, Burghfield) which was on plateau gravel.

Neolithic–Early Bronze Age

The proportions of blade-like flakes can be seen to be low and this is in keeping with the subjective view of the general character of the mass of the material from the survey which seems to show a predominance of squat forms. Off the chalk this might, to some extent, reflect the limitation of quality of the raw material, but it is not known how far this might be a factor. As yet, there is a lack of excavated Neolithic material in the Lower Kennet to demonstrate the character of industry that can be expected here, but if the material can be compared to sites on the chalk downlands and elsewhere (eg Smith 1965; Wainwright and Longworth 1971), it can be suggested that the bulk of the material is likely to be Late Neolithic/Early Bronze Age, rather than Early Neolithic in date.

The distribution of this material is plotted in Figure Mf. 4. There was a marked contrast between the densities on the chalk and those in the rest of the area. The most notable clusters occurred on the chalk; elsewhere the densities are considerably lower and the concen-

trations less marked. Table 2 shows the average densities of flints related to geology (based on the Institute of Geological Sciences Drift editions, sheets 267 and 268). Distinctions were blurred to some extent because the averages were derived from calculations of the density of flints per hectare over the whole of each field; in the cases where fields cover more than one geology, the same average has been applied to each geology but only part of the area has been covered by a soil survey (Jarvis 1968).

Twenty-eight per cent of the fields produced no flints at all and in many others the densities were very low. In Table 3, the areas of fields producing no flints have been converted into a percentage of the total area of each geology. In spite of the limitations of this method, it confirms the picture presented in Table 2, indicating a contrast between the river gravels and the plateau gravels and Bagshot Beds, but it also places more emphasis on the use of the London Clay than was previously suggested. As on the Berkshire Downs (Richards 1978, table 4), flints were found on all the fields on chalk that were walked. The high percentage of alluvium producing no flints is particularly noteworthy.

Discussion

The contrast between the chalk and the valley deposits reflects either the different patterns of landuse or the availability and suitability of raw material: or more likely a combination of both of these factors. Subjectively, it was felt that the character of the raw material is the overriding factor and, for this reason, the results on chalk cannot be compared unreservedly with the results on other geologies when considering how the densities relate to landuse.

In both areas, the raw material is available in abundance on the surface, as nodules and smaller fragments on the chalk, and as flint gravels and nodules on the gravels, although sizeable nodules are far more frequent on the chalk. The immediate availability would have depended on how the material was exposed. Presumably, it would have been picked from the surface of cultivated fields or collected from river banks. If flint from the chalk was preferred, then one might expect to find working sites on the chalk edge which would also increase the densities of flints found. This might be one aspect of the sites revealed during the survey near the edge of the chalk. In the later Bronze Age, there is certainly a contrast in the quantity of flints on excavated sites on the chalk and gravels; it has been suggested that this is because of the greater availability of metalwork in the Thames Valley (Bradley et al. 1980, 288–89), but the character of the raw material deserves further consideration. A study is required to assess more objectively the potential of the different raw materials and their use; for example, there may well be rather more chalk flint in the material collected from fieldwalking than was initially identified.

The apparent preference for the chalk may also reflect relatively intense activity here. Away from the chalk, the main observations are firstly, the low figure for the alluvium and secondly, the contrast between slightly higher densities on the river gravels and broadly similar figures for the other geologies (Table 2). It is interesting to see such similar densities on London Clay, Bagshot Beds, and plateau gravels.

The higher densities off the chalk were not apparent as concentrations. It is useful here to consider the results from the intensive collection survey carried out on the river gravels in the area surrounding the ring-ditches at Theale (Ford 1977). The 13 fields walked (131 hectares) using a 10 m grid had an average density of 19 flints per hectare, with a range from 5–35 flints per hectare. Although comparatively large numbers of flints were found (2510), Ford noted that, even at this level of intensity, very localised concentrations were difficult to pinpoint. At first the densities seem markedly higher than the results from the present survey, but when the figures are crudely converted (along the lines suggested below), the average becomes five flints per hectare with a range of one to eight. This is broadly comparable with some of the higher concentrations defined by this survey off the chalk and is most useful in indicating the potential importance of these otherwise rather insignificant looking densities.

Simple calculations can convert the densities to very approximate figures that can be compared with different intensities of fieldwalking elsewhere. For example, if a field is typically 300 m long, with seven 'runs', there will be on average 2.4 runs per 100 m (this allows for a statistical bias produced by having a traverse at the beginning of each field). If each run covers a width of 1 m, then the *total collection* per hectare should equal 100/2.3 x collected total. This would convert a density of 1 flint per hectare to 43 per hectare; 3 per hectare to 129; 19 to 817 per hectare.

On re-examining the fieldwalking data, it was found that of 33 fields which included an area of alluvium, in only 10 or 11 were flints actually found on the alluvium (a total of 20–30 flints in 149 ha). This must mean either that the alluvium was already present during this period but flints were not being discarded onto it, or more likely that much of the alluvium has formed subsequent to the Neolithic/Early Bronze Age. If the latter is correct,

and this is confirmed in some localities by the presence of Late Bronze Age sherds in these deposits (Bradley *et al.* 1980, 286), then the use of these areas remains unknown, the obvious alternatives being that they were lowlying, wet, and unsuitable for use, or that sites have been sealed beneath the floodplain deposits. There is an indication of this in one field at Ufton Nervet (3740) where the freshness of the few flints found suggested that they had only recently been ploughed up from the alluvium.

An attempt may be made to consider the distributions and densities of the flints as representing patterns of landuse but there are limitations. The flints may have been discarded over hundreds of years but the picture they present tends to be two dimensional, giving no insight into possible sequences and episodes of use. As yet, there is a lack of environmental data to which the evidence might relate. In addition, the flints may have been discarded through a variety of activities. The identification of settlement sites remains difficult. This may largely be owing to the low intensity of the field-walking and perhaps the nature of the raw material, but it may also reflect the nature of the settlements. At present, the character and economic base of these sites are obscure.

Burnt, Unworked Flint

Burnt, unworked flint was not collected systematically but noticeably higher densities were observed in four fields (Table 4). Two of these were concentrations, while the other two were more general scatters. In itself this material is undatable. In only one case were other finds found in the same field in any numbers: at Cold Ash (3761), 18 medieval sherds came from the same field as a general scatter of burnt flints. The medieval finds may represent clearance of the woodland, but it seems very unlikely that this would have been achieved by the wasteful method of burning; and would this have been sufficiently intensive to have burnt the flints?

The general lack of finds associated with these examples suggests either that they reflect a very short-lived activity, or that they belong to a period when finds of pot or flint might not be expected, for example, later Bronze Age or Saxon. Richards (1978, 15–16) suggests that a date range from the Middle Bronze Age to at least the Late Iron Age can be expected for scatters of burnt flints on the Berkshire Downs, and that they are unlikely to represent permanent settlements. The concentrations,

Table 4 1976–77 Survey: concentration of burnt, unworked flint

PRN 3557 SU 56986342	Brimpton. General scatter over much of the field. Plateau gravel. Level, gently sloping ground with a small stream running along the south-east side of the field named Burnt House Ground on the Tithe Apportionment. Other finds include 3 flint flakes and 2 medieval sherds.
PRN 3572 SU 56686527	Brimpton. Concentration. River gravel. Other finds — 2 flint flakes and 2 medieval sherds.
PRN 3573 SU 5651634	Brimpton. Concentration. Plateau gravel/Bagshot Beds. Immediately adjoining a small stream in a small gully. Other finds — 1 flint flake.
PRN 3761 SU 51536936	Cold Ash. General scatter. Bagshot Beds. Above a small gully. Other finds — 3 flint flakes and 18 medieval sherds.

18

at least, may represent the cooking sites, burnt mounds, or *fulacht fiadh* discussed by Bradley (1978, 83). These have a wide geographical range and can date from the Early Bronze Age to the post-medieval periods. They are usually next to a supply of water, but this is the case for only two of the sites listed. For a full discussion of burnt mounds, see Buckley 1990.

Pottery

Whereas the earlier prehistoric periods are represented almost entirely by finds of flints, the later prehistoric and historic finds are limited almost entirely to pottery. This has consequences for the amount of material that is recovered, pottery being less durable than flint. It also restricts the comparisons that can be made between the earlier and later periods as the range of activities leading to the discard of flints is likely to be wider than those which have generated the scatters of pot. If pot is not recovered from an area this need not mean that the area was not in use at that time, but merely that pot was not being discarded onto the fields or that it has not survived ploughing and weathering processes.

Prehistoric
The prehistoric wares recovered are mostly coarse, flint-gritted, to a greater or lesser extent, and liable to disintegrate when exposed to weathering in the topsoil. Several sherds were found that had been, or were being, split apart by the frost, and large sherds were very rare. Quantities were small and a site represented by only a few sherds may easily have been missed. Furthermore, the few coarse body sherds are rarely diagnostic and so are difficult to date within the prehistoric framework, or even, in some cases, to distinguish from similar Romano-British and medieval coarse wares.

Only three find spots of possible Neolithic pot were noticed (Mf. 4), one sherd only in each case (Appendix 5). One of these sherds was on plateau gravel in a field which produced no flints at all (3545). The other two were both on the floodplain terrace; neither was associated with above average numbers of flints (3745 and 3746).

No recognisable Early Bronze Age material was found, probably because of the nature of the fabrics

which would not necessarily survive in the ploughsoil. Of the remaining prehistoric pottery, one relative concentration may be of Deverel-Rimbury type (3562). Two other find spots are probably of later Bronze Age date (3539 and 3577; Mf. 5, Appendix 5). Other later Bronze Age pottery may be present but it has been included with the remaining prehistoric pottery which is broadly assigned to the Late Bronze Age/Iron Age; the small quantities generally prevent greater precision than this. Material of this late prehistoric date was found in 33 fields (Mf. 6). Nineteen of the find spots were represented by fewer than four sherds; the rest ranged from four to 20. The find spots of four or more sherds, and some of less than this, are described in Appendix 5.1, but it is important to remember that with the generally small quantities of prehistoric pot being found, even a single sherd may be of significance.

Romano-British
This constitutes a large proportion of the pottery recovered because the wares were manufactured in large quantities and in hard fabrics that have survived centuries of ploughing. Consequently, it is possible to be more confident in denoting the location of a site. Romano-British material was found in 61 of the 242 fields walked (Mf. 7). In most cases, only a few sherds scattered over the field are presumably the result of manuring. But there are 14 concentrations that are more likely to represent settlement sites (*see* Appendix 5.2), although with some of the smaller scatters, the nature of the site must remain unclear.

Saxon/medieval
For the medieval period, as for the Romano-British, sites are relatively easily identified by the large quantities of surface material. During fieldwalking, 806 sherds of medieval pottery were found in 92 of the fields walked, mostly only as a few sherds (Mf. 8). Some concentrations (five or six) are very marked and may represent settlement sites but others (another six or seven), though more marked than the light scatter that is found over many of the fields, are of less obvious significance. These have been included in Appendix 5.3 for comparison. Only a handful of find spots included Saxo-Norman pottery and invariably only a sherd or two. No earlier Saxon pottery was found. The low number of sherds and

Table 5 1976–77 Survey: summary of Iron Age pottery from fieldwalking

Geology	Total sherds	Total find spots	Sherds/ha	Sites	Sites/km^2
River gravel	37	8	0.12	3	1.00
Alluvium	45	5	0.30	3	2.01
London Clay	37	8	0.12	2	0.63
Bagshot Beds	17	5	0.16	4 (3.5)	3.30
Plateau gravel	9	4	0.02	2 (1.5)	0.38
Reading Beds	1	1	0.02	–	–
Chalk	–	–	–	–	–

Where sites overlap two geologies the number of sites per kilometre square has been calculated by giving a score or a half to each geology and the adjusted number of occurrences is shown bracketed in the sites column.

Table 6 1976–77 Survey: summary of Romano-British pottery from fieldwalking

Geology	Total sherds	Total find spots	Sherds/ha	Sites	Sherds from sites	Sites/km^2
River gravel	139	14	0.46	2	103	0.66
Alluvium	225	10	1.51	4	215	2.68
London Clay	118	19	0.37	4 (3.5)	87	1.10
Bagshot Beds	80	11	0.75	3 (2)	56	1.89
Plateau gravel	40	9	0.10	2 (1.5)	22	0.38
Reading Beds	52	3	1.02	1	48	1.89
Chalk	–	–	–	–	–	–

the low level of intensity of the survey, limits the reliance that can be placed on the analysis of these results. The fieldwalking evidence will be further influenced because many settlements may have continued in use from the medieval period to the present day, so that the density and distribution of sites suggested by fieldwalking is unlikely to be a true reflection on the pattern of settlement.

Discussion

Two of the three find spots of probable later Bronze Age date were on river gravels: the rim sherd of a bowl came from the edge of the floodplain terrace on an island of gravel surrounded by alluvium at Aldermaston (3539); a sherd with stabbed decoration was found on the floodplain just below the floodplain terrace at Brimpton (3577). If these finds indicate the presence nearby of settlements, in both cases the use of the floodplain could have been one aspect in their siting and economy. The third find spot, at Brimpton (3562), was on the side of a small spur of Bagshot Beds on a hill slope above the Enborne. In an area where the gravel terrace is of restricted size this site, on the spring line junction of the London Clay and Bagshot Beds, is well placed to use a variety of potential soil types and environments. The site is somewhat similar in location to several Iron Age and Romano-British sites; there may well be more and, indeed, it is perhaps likely that the pattern seen later was already established or being established in the later Bronze Age.

It is useful to consider the Iron Age and Romano-British pottery distributions together to avoid putting undue weight on the Iron Age evidence. Firstly, the finds are few and the significance of each find spot uncertain: a single sherd might indicate a settlement site but the widespread scatter of a handful of sherds makes it difficult to pinpoint any site. Secondly, because of the lack of diagnostic sherds and the similarities in fabric, it is not always possible to distinguish between the coarser fabrics of the Romano-British assemblages and those of the Late Iron Age. For convenience, the Iron Age label has been used for those sherds which could not be dated more precisely than Late Bronze Age/Iron Age. Tables 5 and 6 summarise the results of the field-walking. Find spots refer to fields in which sherds have been found. Sites refer to find spots which are thought to represent settlement sites. This can be done with far more confidence for the Romano-British than for the Iron Age sites.

The distribution of Iron Age and Romano-British material is broadly similar, both in type of location and distribution, and in specific location. Twenty-four of 30 Iron Age find spots have Romano-British material in the same field. Twelve Romano-British sites also have possible Iron Age sherds, although some of this may be coarse wares of the same date. There are at least seven or eight examples of co-location of Iron Age and Romano-British sites, although this need not demonstrate continuity of occupation. Only five Iron Age sites do not appear to have been used in the Romano-British period; only one of these has Romano-British material at all. One of these is on river gravel and four are on the valley side (two on London Clay, two on Bagshot Beds).

There are two main locations for the sites, on the floodplain and floodplain terrace of the valley floor, and on the valley side (London Clay, Bagshot Beds, plateau gravel) (Table 7). The two areas seem to have been equally in use in both the Iron Age and the Romano-British period. The overall frequency of sites in the area walked was approximately one per km^2 which is comparable with the figure produced for the Upper Thames (Miles 1982, 63).

It is useful to compare the character of Romano-British sites on the valley floor and valley side. Table 7 shows the estimated size of each of these sites in square metres. The figures are very approximate but nevertheless they do indicate that the sites on the valley side tend to be smaller than those on the valley floor. The smaller settlements can scarcely be more than single farmsteads or small hamlets. The nature of the settlements represented by the more extensive concentrations is difficult to determine from the present data but, at face value, the evidence might mark these out as settlements of more than one farmstead. Although larger, these sites do not appear to be anything more than simple farming settlements; no building materials, tiles, or tesserae were found on any of the sites. Their size is perhaps a reflection of local topography, with dissected hill slopes of spurs and gullies encouraging a dispersed pattern of single farms on the valley side, perhaps in a fairly wooded environment, while the broader spaces of the valley floor resulted in a

Table 7 1976-77 Survey: size of Romano-British sites on valley side and valley floor

	Area in m^2							
	0–500	500–1000	1000–1500	1500–2000	2000–2500	2500–3000	3000	3000 +
Alluvium	–	–	–	–	–	–	2	2 (700+10000)
River gravel	–	1	–	–	–	–	–	1 (16000)
Valley side	1	–	–	2	2	2	–	–

Total number of sites = 13

greater degree of nucleation. It is, however, only a matter of degree; the numerous Romano-British sites situated at the junction of the Kennet and Enborne suggest that the pattern is of dispersed rather than fully nucleated settlement. The scatter of cropmark enclosures also suggests this.

The actual density of settlement is difficult to assess. Although figures have been given in Tables 5 and 6 for the number of sites per km2, this is not meant to imply contemporaneity. Indeed, the four Romano-British sites on the floodplain, at the junction of the Kennet and the Enborne, are apparently in two pairs, each containing one early and one late site (Brimpton, 3576 and 3577; Woolhampton, 3749; Aldermaston, 3533). This seems to imply a slight shift in settlement location.

Most of the medieval find spots consist of no more than a few sherds, frequently only two or three, and presumably reflect manuring patterns. This can be a useful indication of areas of medieval landuse. For example, a scatter of sherds in a narrow strip of fields running up the valley side at Aldermaston suggests a medieval origin for the house known as 'The Hornets', now demolished (3521 and 3523, SU 584046). This strip of fields is flanked by woods.

In six or seven cases, concentrations are sufficiently marked to suggest that they represent a settlement site. A further five find spots are rather vague concentrations and can only be regarded as possible sites (*see* Appendix 5.3). Alternatively, these could be manuring scatters that are for some reason denser than normal. The distribution of pottery of this date is presented in Table 8. In total, seven sites were found on the valley floor and four on the valley side. As with the Romano-British scatters, none are particularly extensive (Table 9) but,

unlike the Romano-British material, the size of the medieval scatters does not seem to bear any relation to their position on valley side or valley floor. Presumably these sites represent single farmsteads or small hamlets.

Some of the sites relate to present or post-medieval features, suggesting medieval origins. For example, a small concentration beside a former stream at Brimpton was quite probably the site of a mill rather than a farming settlement (3450). At least five sites are close to roads or trackways: one small site at Brimpton (3594), for example, is next to a hollow-way called Water Lane. Two concentrations of material (3617) were found at Enborne, indirectly called Jacob's Green, on an 18th century estate map, but not now extant. A scatter alongside the road at Padworth (3649/50), associated with a raised area of darker soil, may suggest an orderly arrangement of tofts and crofts, a village even, but the quantities of pot are small. These are probably garden plots rather than house plots. A concentration on alluvium at Thatcham (3699) adjoins an existing farm (Bank's Farm); here there may have been slight shrinkage or movement of settlement, or the scatter might even be midden material from the site of the present farm.

In considering the densities of pottery from the different soil types, the low densities from the plateau gravels are very noticeable (Table 8). In the 399 hectares walked, only 31 sherds were found. This suggests that cultivation on much of the plateau gravels was very limited and accords with the late documentary evidence of heath in these areas. On the other hand, the densities on the Bagshot Beds and London Clay are higher than the figure for the river gravels. There can be little doubt

Table 8 1976-77 Survey: summary of medieval pottery distribution from fieldwalking

Geology	Total sherds	Sherds/ha	No. of find spots	No. of sites	Sherds from sites
River gravel	164	0.55	19	2–3	71–84
Alluvium	235	1.58	9	1–4	102–214
London Clay	285	0.90	39	2–3	142–155
Bagshot Beds	88	0.83	17	2–3	39–55
Plateau gravel	31	0.07	20	–	–
Reading beds	3	–	–	–	–
Chalk	0	–	–	–	–

Table 9 1976–77 Survey: size of medieval 'sites' (probable and possible) on the valley side and valley floor

	Area in m^2							
	0–500	500–1000	1000–1500	1500–2000	2000–2500	2500–3000	3000	3000 +
Alluvium	–	–	1	1	–	–	–	2 (15.000+ 20,000)
River gravel	* 1+1	–	–	1	–	–	–	
Valley side	–	1	1	–	–	–	–	*2+1 (*3500+5400 *10,000)

* = probable sites

that the river gravels were used extensively as open fields.

Tables 10 and 11 summarise a comparison between Romano-British and medieval find spots. Whilst it may be simplistic to suggest that direct comparison can be made between different timespans and perhaps different processes of sherd discard, nevertheless, there are questions that should be considered. Are the medieval find spots in broadly similar areas to the earlier find spots, reflecting a similar pattern of landuse? What types of location have evidence for use in the Romano-British but not in the medieval period, and conversely, what areas seem to be in use in the medieval period which have not produced evidence of Romano-British activity?

Of the 92 fields with medieval pot, 40 (43%) also had Romano-British pot. Areas in use in the Romano-British period, as suggested by find spots of pot, were generally also in use in the medieval period (Table 10, columns 1–3). This is particularly the case on the alluvium, London Clay, and river gravels and, to a lesser extent, on the Bagshot Beds, but on the plateau gravels there are larger areas where there were Romano-British but not medieval sherds. There was an increase in the number of medieval find spots on all geologies except the alluvium, where there was a decrease. The greatest percentage increase was on the plateau gravel and, to a slightly lesser extent, on London Clay. With these increases there should be a greater likelihood that fields producing Romano-British pot on the plateau gravels or London Clay will also produce medieval pot, but as already stated, it is on plateau gravels that the

coincidence of Romano-British and medieval find spots is lowest. The alluvium and river gravels have the lowest percentages of find spots, producing medieval but not Romano-British pot and these also have the lowest percentage changes in the frequency of find spots between the two periods. The densities of sherds per hectare on the different geologies are broadly similar for the Romano-British and medieval periods. The main difference is the higher density of sherds on London Clay in the medieval period.

Some interpretation may be suggested for these results. On the plateau gravels we have seen that there is a large increase in the number of find spots but the densities of sherds per hectare are still very low and, compared to the other geologies, the medieval find spots are often in different locations to the Romano-British find spots. This suggests a low intensity and some discontinuity of use, perhaps reflecting short-term, occasional, or outfield cultivation, perhaps on soils that tend to impoverishment rather than improvement with continued use.

On the London Clay there are indications of greater intensification of use. Firstly, the densities of sherds are higher compared to other geologies for the medieval period than the Romano-British period (Tables 6 and 8). And then, whilst 79% of Romano-British find spots on London Clay also produce medieval sherds, suggesting continuity in the use of particular areas, or at least a reuse of these areas, there is also a high percentage increase in the number of find spots, suggesting extension or colonisation into new areas. Much of this could have been as forest clearance.

Table 10 1976–77 Survey: comparison of Romano-British and medieval pottery find spots

Geology	Romano-British	Romano-British and medieval		Medieval	Medieval without Romano-British finds	
Plateau gravel	9	4	44%	20	15	75%
Bagshot Beds	12	8	67%	17	8	47%
London Clay	19	15	79%	39	23	59%
River gravel	14	10	71%	19	8	42%
Alluvium	10	8	80%	9	2	22%

The results from the river gravels suggest the use of similar areas in both periods. On the alluvium, the decrease in the number of medieval compared to Romano-British find spots is slight, but it contrasts with the increase in find spots for other geologies. The Romano-British and medieval find spots tend to be in the same area, which is frequently on the very edge of the floodplain, perhaps in some cases on flood loam covering river gravels. The relative density of sherds is also high, as for the Romano-British period, but the implication this has for explaining the medieval landuse is unclear. For the Romano-British period, there are several clear concentrations suggesting settlement sites on the floodplain but few other sherds to indicate that the floodplain was used for anything other than grazing or meadows. The medieval situation is rather different. There is only one clear concentration and, although there are three other possible sites, none of these needs be more than a manuring scatter (except perhaps at Thatcham, 3688, where the finds, though few, include relatively large fresh sherds). Manuring is suggested by a scatter of sherds in fields on the floodplain surrounding the site at Banks Farm, Thatcham (3699). With adequate drainage, parts of the floodplain may have been used for cultivation as well as grazing or meadow. The manuring, implied by the scatters of pot on the floodplain may, however, have been equally to improve grassland as to grow cereals. Sites like Banks Farm and perhaps Chamberhouse Farm, Thatcham (SU 520656), may nevertheless reflect a more intensive use or colonisation of parts of the floodplain in the medieval period. This would have depended upon the provision of a system of drainage.

This suggested intensification in the use of the floodplain contrasts with the apparent decrease in the number of medieval as opposed to Romano-British find spots, but this may be because, for most of the floodplain, common rights applied to its use as meadows, rights which would have been zealously guarded. In this system, the floodplain would be just one component in a more broadly based use of the valley and so specialised settlements, as seen in the Iron Age or Romano-British period, are unusual.

Fieldwalking on cropmark sites
Fifteen areas of cropmarks were walked (Appendix 4). Only in three or four cases was there a close correlation between the cropmarks and the surface collection. Three enclosures and one area of linear features were associated with Iron Age or Romano-British material (3746, Wasing; 3531, Aldermaston; 3582, Thatcham; 3721, Ufton Nervet). Two Iron Age sherds were found 60 m from a fourth enclosure, although there were no finds from the enclosure itself (3639, Mortimer). Two other groups of small rectangular enclosures were walked without result (3525, Aldermaston; 3736, Ufton Nervet). Four ring-ditches were walked but probably at too low a level of intensity for meaningful results, although it was noticeable that a concentration of flints seemed to

Table 11 1976–77 Survey: percentage change in number of pottery find spots — Romano-British to medieval

Geology	Romano-British	Medieval	% increase
Plateau gravel	9	20	122
Bagshot Beds	12	17	42
London Clay	19	39	105
River gravel	14	19	35
Alluvium	10	9	10

fade away in the vicinity of the ring-ditch at SU 471692 (3514, Donnington).

Discussion

Appraisal of Fieldwalking Methods and Results

The system of fieldwalking used in the 1976–77 survey was found to have its advantages and disadvantages. The method was certainly suited to this particular survey, being convenient for a single walker and allowing large areas to be covered in the limited time available. Numerous 'sites' were identified and a broad idea gained of the overall densities and range of finds throughout the area. This survey can be regarded as a first trawl of the area, testing its potential.

The main disadvantages of the survey method hinge on problems caused by the low level of intensity of the walking. Firstly, there is a likelihood that sites will be missed. For example, a small concentration of Romano-British sherds from the cropmark enclosure at Wasing (3646) was missed in the normal course of fieldwalking and only identified when the cropmark site was walked separately. Dense concentrations of material 50 m wide are very likely to be found. However, of the 14 concentrations of Romano-British sherds, six were less than 50 m wide. Most of these smaller concentrations were in the order of 40 m across and the likelihood of discovery is still high, but for every discovery of a concentration of sherds only 10 m^2, as at Burghfield (3601), there is a probability of another four sites which have been missed. The problem is greater for sites represented by low densities of prehistoric sherds.

The survey method is perhaps not sensitive enough to deal with sparse scatters of material, and in particular the flints. At this level it has proved very difficult to interpret the low densities of material that have been produced. The lack of clear concentrations (except on the chalk) is surprising and may imply either that concentrations of material tend to be very small and therefore easy to miss, or that the significant changes in densities are subtle and not very susceptible to low intensity fieldwalking. If these problems are to be tackled, further fieldwalking here should be carried out more intensively by a gridded collection system and by teams rather than individuals.

It is worth emphasising that it is dangerous to use the results of fieldwalking as negative evidence. For a variety of reasons many sites cannot be found by this method alone. For example, no surface material was found to complement the cropmark evidence of two groups of enclosures. More striking still, fieldwalking at SU 606681 (Beenham, 3555) produced six flints and one medieval sherd immediately next to an area which had just been found on excavation to contain a later Bronze Age settlement and a Roman hypocaust (Bradley *et al* 1980; Cowell *et al.* 1978)

When the results of the 1976–77 survey were first written up, several recommendations were made (Appendix 6). Many of these have been taken up by the subsequent survey and others have been superseded by more recent planning legislation and are discussed in the final section of this volume.

4. Surveys 1982–87

Extent and Aims of the Surveys

Between 1976 and 1979, the gravel pits in the county, mostly in the Kennet Valley, were visited regularly by S.J. Lobb for the Berkshire Archaeological Unit and, where possible, archaeological features recorded. However, the scale of mineral extraction and the rate of discovery of archaeological sites, meant that this process was very haphazard and inadequate for the investigation and recording of sites. The *Minerals Local Plan* was under discussion and it was clear that gravel extraction would continue to expose and destroy archaeological sites at a steady rate. The 1976–77 survey had provided the impetus for further archaeological work in the Kennet Valley, emphasising the need for a long term and forward thinking strategy and had established a theoretical and methodological framework. The 1982–87 survey was funded by the Department of the Environment/English Heritage with additional grants from Berkshire County Council in the later years. The results of the fieldwalking have now been accessed into the County Sites and Monuments Record (SMR).

In 1983, with English Heritage support, the County Council appointed an archaeological officer to develop and maintain the SMR and provide archaeological advice on planning matters and local government issues. The *Minerals Local Plan* for Berkshire was adopted as a Statutory Local Plan in 1984 at a time when the structure plans for Berkshire were coming under scrutiny and were to be reviewed; the *Review of Berkshire Structure Plans, Draft Replacement Structure Plan* was completed in 1985, submitted to the Secretary of State for the Environment in January 1986, and finally published in 1989. These changes in policy provided further stimulus to the survey.

Broadly, the aims of the survey were to assess the changes and development of settlement patterns and landuse, as well as the economy and environment of the Lower Kennet Valley. This was intended as a review of the state of knowledge and an assessment of the archaeological potential of the different topographical zones in the valley. While these broad aims have remained unchanged, the emphasis of the project changed subtly over the years in response to the reorganisation of the archaeological establishment in the county and the emergence of planning policies towards archaeology in the face of increased development proposals.

Initially, the aims of the project were particularly directed at the prehistoric periods. However, as proposals for the protection and recording of the archaeological resource in the county were being formulated, it became clear that this approach was both illogical and erroneous. The archaeological potential and importance of the Kennet Valley clearly did not end with the Roman occupation of the area and a broader based, multi-period landscape study was seen to be more relevant and expedient in the changing political climate.

Strategy

Field Survey

Survey was concentrated in two areas within the Lower Kennet Valley: a transect across the valley between Thatcham and Aldermaston (Fig. 2) and the Burghfield area. Small areas were also examined around two specific archaeological sites and the results of these surveys have been published with the associated excavation reports: at Riseley Farm, Swallowfield (Lobb and Morris 1991–93), in the neighbouring Blackwater Valley; and Crofton, Great Bedwyn, in the valley of the River Dunn, a tributary of the Upper Kennet, where a small research excavation was carried out across the ditch of a possible Neolithic causewayed enclosure in 1984 (Lobb 1994).

The Transect

Between 1984 and 1987, a broad approach was adopted to assess more general trends and settlement patterns in the Lower Kennet Valley. A transect across all topographical zones of the valley, 8 km wide between the 52 and 60 easting lines of the National Grid, was selected for survey (Fig. 6). The transect was at right angles to the main axis of the river which runs through the middle of the area, and contained the range of geology and topography which occurs in the Lower Kennet Valley. It was felt, therefore, that the sample provided by the transect was representative of the general area. The survey area contained large tracts of gravel with existing and proposed extraction quarries and included many of the fields which were walked by Rose. The re-examination of some of these fields would provide the opportunity to examine in detail some of the scatters identified which were suggested as possible sites, and to compare the different methods and results of the two surveys.

Further fieldwalking, commissioned by Berkshire County Council, was carried out by Wessex Archaeology in 1988–89 and the results from those fields within the transect have been included in this report. The results from the other fields outside the transect are reported in the next chapter of this volume.

The Burghfield Area

This area was under considerable threat from gravel extraction and increasingly from redevelopment due to the expansion of Reading. Since the war, large areas have been destroyed by gravel extraction, and by 1982 it was clear that further applications would be made to exploit the remaining gravel reserves in the area. Some

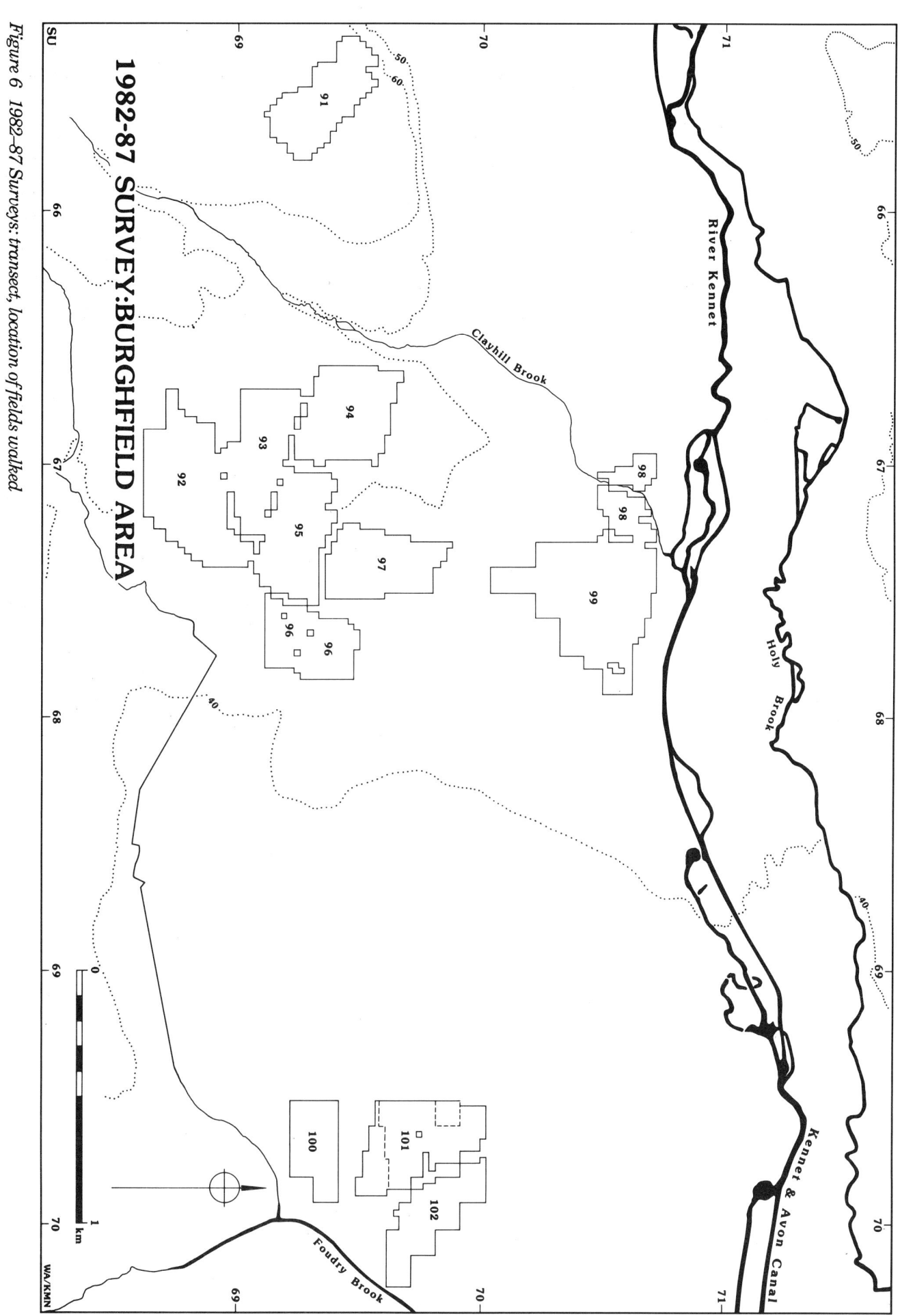

Figure 6 1982-87 Surveys: transect, location of fields walked

Table 12 1982–87 Surveys: summary of excavations and watching briefs

Name/parish	Code	Date	NGR	Type	Archaeology	Reference
Pingewood, Burghfield	W15	1982	699694	exc.	BA ring-ditch + RB field system	Lobb and Mills 1994
Riseley Farm, Swallowfield	W33	1982	735636	exc.	Meso. flint scatter, BA ring-ditch, IA enclosure, LIA/RB enclosure	Lobb and Morris 1994
Shortheath Lane, Sulhamstead	W104	1985	643676	exc.	BA cremation cemetery	Butterworth and Lobb 1992
Field Farm, Burghfield	W70	1982	4672703	w/brief/exc.	LN occupation, BA ring-ditches + cremation cemetery	
	W109	1985–87	676704	exc. and w/brief		
	W267	1989	674706	exc.	Saxon inhumation cemetery	Butterworth and Lobb 1992
Meales Farm, Sulhamstead	W115	1986–87	639685	w/brief + exc.	RB ditches and cremation + med. occupation	Lobb et al. 1991
Anslows Cottages, Burghfield	W100	1985–86	693710	eval. + exc.	LBA waterfront + occupation + RB and Saxon timber structures in river channel	Butterworth and Lobb 1992

archaeological finds and sites were recorded by salvage operations and several excavations and watching briefs, carried out in the area in the gravel pits, had provided a large body of information; unfortunately large areas were also destroyed without any archaeological investigation and record (Fig. 5). In 1982 and 1983, the arable fields in and around the gravel pits were examined. A small amount of time was also spent on watching briefs. This allowed the possibility of examining on- and off-site distributions, thereby providing an immediate context for the known sites and an assessment of the archaeological potential of those areas under threat.

Excavation

Several excavations and watching briefs were carried out during the course of the survey work and the reports of the results have been published separately; details are summarised in Table 12. With the exception of Anslows Cottages (W100), they were all carried out as part of the Kennet Valley Survey and were funded by the Department of the Environment and English Heritage. Anslows Cottages was evaluated and excavated in advance of gravel extraction and was funded by English Heritage, the gravel company, and the district and local authorities. In addition, from 1985, with the implementation of Berkshire County Council's new policy towards archaeology, a number of evaluations have been carried out within the survey area; these are described and discussed in more detail below (Chapter

7). These excavations and evaluations have clearly provided the opportunity to examine detailed aspects of the settlement and landuse patterns, as well as the evidence for the environment and landscape change; this information is incorporated in the general discussion of the development of the landscape (Chapter 8) where relevant.

Methods

Fieldwalking

Extensive survey
The method of extensive surface survey remained constant throughout the four seasons of fieldwork in order to maintain consistency and to facilitate comparison within the project. Collection method followed the system adopted by other survey projects carried out by Wessex Archaeology, based on the method devised by Woodward (1978). The use of a common system was intended to allow broad comparability between projects in the region. Using the National Grid as the framework for the survey, the hectare formed the common collection unit; within the hectare the number and spacing of collection units varied between the projects (Richards 1985).

Previous work had suggested that densities of surface finds in the Kennet Valley Survey project area were likely to be low by comparison with other geographical zones. Furthermore, because of the potentially small areas of certain types of anthropogenic activity, especially in the prehistoric periods, it was decided to adopt a 25 m grid within the hectare, resulting in 16 collection units per hectare, each 25 m long and spaced 25 m apart. Assuming a visibility span of 2–2.5 m in each transect, this provides a sample of 8–10% of the field surface. Using a standard recording sheet, the variables recorded for each hectare include soil type, lighting, weather, state of field surface and crop growth (weathering and visibility of finds), and collector's name for each unit. Local topographic features, earthworks, and soilmarks were sketched on the hectare record where relevant and general observations noted on a summary sheet for each field. Fields were given arbitrary names, generally related to nearby settlement or mapped features, and numbered. For ease of reference, field numbers have been used throughout the text, tables, and figures where finds distributions or sites have been mentioned. Details of various field attributes can be found in the archive.

All artefactual material of all periods was collected. Although the post-medieval period did not fall directly within the scope of the project, pottery and tile dating to this period were collected for comparative reasons and because the density of material might indicate intensity of agriculture in more recent times; furthermore, because of the difficulties of distinguishing in the field Roman and medieval tile and some pottery types from the post-medieval material, it was safer and more efficient to collect them. Iron objects and slag were generally collected and/or recorded but discarded. Burnt flint was collected because of its common association with prehistoric, and possibly Romano-British, settlement. Animal bone was not collected, although particular concentrations would have been mapped. Catalogues of all finds recovered can be found in Appendix 8.

Selection of fields to be surveyed was made largely on a subjective basis according to availability at the time of fieldwork, and preference was given to blocks of adjoining fields. The selection process was, however, tempered by the need to examine a representative sample of each of the defined topographical zones. There was no selection in favour of areas with previously recorded archaeological information and such information, where it existed, did not influence or alter the method adopted. In the Burghfield area, most of the remaining fields in and around the gravel pits and known archaeological sites were examined, expanding southwards off the river gravels onto the higher ground of the valley side. A very small area of plateau gravels above this area was examined. Because of the predominant agricultural practice in the area, fieldwalking was mostly carried out in the autumn.

In the transect, 754 ha and 158 ha in the Burghfield area were examined.

Detailed survey
More intensive surface collection was carried out in only two areas at Pingewood in the Burghfield area. This included 12 ha to the south and two small areas to the north of the motorway. The latter were examined as part of the evaluation of the archaeological potential of the Reading Business Park site at Smallmead Farm. This area, under threat from redevelopment, lies at the edge of an extensive cropmark complex which had largely been destroyed by gravel extraction without much archaeological observation. A 10 m grid was laid out to correspond to apparent key areas of the cropmark features; the surface of the 10 m squares was totally examined and finds retrieved. The area between and adjacent to these total collection areas was collected in the standard way on a 25 m grid.

Phosphate Survey

In conjunction with surface finds collection, soil samples were taken on a 25 m grid, corresponding to the collection units, from a sample of fields for analysis of phosphate levels. At Manor Ash Moats (8), additional samples were taken at 5 m intervals from two transects across the monument; at Pingewood (101) samples were taken on a 10 m grid in areas where total collection was carried out. This survey was included in order to test the usefulness of this type of analysis as a prospection method, using a broad grid in conjunction with surface collection as part of an extensive survey.

Soil samples for testing the level of phosphate were collected from most of the fields walked and those from 28 of the fields walked were processed. Generally, samples were taken at 25 m intervals on the grid used for the fieldwalking. In some instances, more detailed sampling was undertaken, for example, over the earthworks at Manor Ash Moats, where samples were collected at 5 m intervals from two transects crossing the centre of the earthwork. In areas of total collection at Pingewood, each collection unit was sampled, that is each 10 m square. The samples from 28 of the fields walked were processed.

The method used was devised by R. Entwistle (1984) and is based on the widely used molybdenum blue reaction which produces a blue colour that is proportional in intensity to the phosphate concentration and records available phosphate.

Woodland Survey

Within the transect, a small number of woodland areas were searched for earthworks (Fig. 2). Because of the restrictions in time, the effort was concentrated on the more extensive areas of woodland and those close to extensively fieldwalked areas. Where possible, the ground was covered in regularly spaced transects up to 200 m apart making use of existing paths and tracks, but in many cases the thick undergrowth, topography, and boggy areas made systematic survey very difficult.

Finds Analysis

The finds from both the Burghfield area and the transect were examined using the same methods and, in the case of the pottery, a single fabric type series adopted. However, the finds distributions from each area will be discussed separately. All finds were examined by L. Mepham, with the exception of the worked flint which was examined and identified by P. Harding and the relevant sections relating to the methods and distributions are discussed by them. The stone fragments were identified by David Williams. Throughout the text, the term 'cluster' has been used to signify a higher density of material generally with definable boundaries; the term 'scatter' has been used to identify more general spreads of material with no obvious focus.

Worked flint

A total of 3077 pieces of worked flint was collected during the survey from both collection areas. All pieces of flint were examined and catalogued by 25 m run. Because of the low level of diagnostic retouched tools, a broad chronological framework was suggested on the basis of technological aspects. The diagnostic products of deliberate blade technology were recorded separately from those of flake technology. Blade production has been associated with Mesolithic activity in the Kennet valley (Wymer 1962) but is assumed here to pre-date the Late Neolithic, and has been loosely termed 'earlier prehistoric'. The decline of blade production and its replacement by a flake technology is taken to represent 'later prehistoric' activity. Chronological divisions cannot be defined more closely because of the absence of diagnostic retouched tools. Similarly, the possibility of intrusive pieces in any concentration cannot be discounted.

Blade technology is characterised by prepared blade/let cores, waste flakes with parallel negative blade scars, flakes and blade/lets with abraded butts, and crested blades. Cores were mostly of single and opposed platform types and made on nodules, although some were occasionally made on flakes. Platform abrasion is a technique used on prepared cores which removes overhang and strengthens the front of the core. Percussion can then take place close to the edge of the striking platform. Undiagnostic waste flakes from these industries cannot be separated from similar material produced by industries using unprepared cores. Blades which show no previous blade scars on the dorsal surface, or which are determined by a fortuitous guiding ridge, are also regarded as undiagnostic.

Burnt flint

All burnt flint collected during fieldwalking was discarded after quantification. Because of the large quantities recovered, the mean weight per 25 m collection unit was calculated for the whole of the area examined within the transect: 104 g with a standard deviation of 200 g; a separate figure was calculated for the collection units in the Burghfield area (including 25 m, 10 m, and total collection units): mean weight 103 g with a standard deviation of 249 g; excluding the finds from the more intensive fieldwalking; a mean weight of 131 g can be suggested for the 25 m collection units. The results were plotted in groups relating to the mean weight and standard deviation. This method aims towards some objectivity, eliminating biases in collection, and highlights particularly dense concentrations, but masks low density clusters within individual fields. Concentrations were defined on the basis of three or more runs in one hectare with a weight of more than the mean weight plus two standard deviations. All fields with a mean

weight greater than the mean for the two areas have been listed in Tables 15 and 20.

Pottery

A total of 3789 sherds (56,108 g) was collected during fieldwalking from both the Burghfield area and from the transect. The pottery was analysed using the standard Wessex Archaeology recording system, and was divided into broad fabric groups on the basis of dominant inclusion type (eg flint, grog etc.). These fabric groups were then subdivided into fabric types on the basis of macroscopic inclusions, using a hand lens (x8 magnification); 48 fabric types were identified, and these fell into six fabric groups: flint-tempered (Group F), grog-tempered (Group G), limestone-tempered (Group L), sandy fabrics (Group Q), fabrics with rock inclusions (Group R), and 'established wares' (Group E), eg samian, Surrey White Ware etc.

Diagnostic material was rare, and so dating the various fabric types was not always straightforward; generally, however, enough diagnostic pottery occurred within each fabric type to enable dating to a broad chronological period but not necessarily to a specific time span within that period. Only one fabric type (L800) is undated. Having said this, some problems were encountered in assigning individual sherds to particular fabric types. The difficulties of distinguishing, for example, prehistoric flint-tempered fabrics from early Roman Silchester Ware have been noted elsewhere (Cowell et al. 1978, 26). Other distinctions are equally ambiguous, particularly among the sandy fabrics, where it is sometimes difficult to divide Romano-British from medieval wares. Late Bronze Age and Iron Age sandy fabrics, in many cases, are also very similar and can rarely be assigned to a specific period in the absence of diagnostic vessel forms. The unstratified nature of a pottery assemblage derived purely from fieldwalking, means that no assumptions of date can be made based on associated pottery; indeed, it is very dangerous so to do. Many scatters of pottery contain material of widely differing periods. Post-depositional abrasion, particularly for the more friable prehistoric fabrics, also makes accurate identification more difficult. These limitations should be borne in mind when assessing the reliability of the pottery identifications.

The scarcity of diagnostic vessel forms amongst the survey material means that dating of the individual fabric types is thus heavily dependent upon comparisons with dated material from nearby sites. Comparative material is particularly rich for the Burghfield area. Several fabric type series exist for sites of Late Bronze Age, Middle–Late Iron Age, and Romano-British date at the eastern end of the Kennet Valley, eg Knight's Farm and Aldermaston (Bradley et al. 1980), Ufton Nervet (Manning 1974), Anslows Cottages, and Field Farm, Burghfield (Mepham 1992), though it should be remembered that not all these sequences are securely dated. Within the fields walked in the Burghfield area, excavations by Wessex Archaeology have taken place at Field Farm, part of the Knight's Farm complex (Butterworth and Lobb 1992), and the block of fields around Smallmead Farm (Dawson and

Lobb 1986); the pottery assemblages from these sites range from Late Neolithic to medieval and are particularly useful for comparison with the fieldwalked assemblage, though again it should be noted that none of the excavated groups is securely dated. Further west there are fewer comparative assemblages. To the south-west of Newbury, a Romano-British kiln has been excavated at Hamstead Marshall (Rashbrook 1983). The material from Silchester (Timby 1985) is useful for reference for material from both survey areas.

For the medieval material, use has been made of the reference collections from Newbury (Vince, in prep; Hawkes forthcoming) and Reading (Underwood forthcoming), and, to a lesser extent, Oxford (Haldon 1977; Mellor 1980). As the project area falls between Newbury and Reading, the distribution of the various fabric and vessel types may have implications for trading and market influences. Fabric series also exist for rural sites in the area, eg Meales Farm, Sulhamstead (Mepham 1991).

The pottery from the 1976–77 survey which was found within the later survey areas, was reassessed and classified according to broad fabric group, ie dominant inclusion type, although it has not been fully incorporated into the fabric series for the 1984–87 assemblage. This has enabled comparisons of date to be made between the two assemblages.

The post-medieval pottery was not examined in the same detail as the earlier pottery. It was merely divided into three groups of earthenwares on the basis of fabric colour; and two groups of stoneware, on the basis of fineness of fabric, plus two stonewares of known source. Vessel forms were not noted. This group formed the bulk of the fieldwalked assemblage.

The occurrence of sherds in each 25 m collection unit has been plotted by period and is listed in the archive. Much of the pottery occurs in small quantities, most often as single sherds in a fairly large area, or as low density scatters dispersed over a large area. The number of sherds collected is insufficient for any valid statistical analysis and observations on the distributions are based on subjective judgement. While it is recognised that even single sherds of pottery may be significant in such a sparse distribution, a number of apparently nucleated groups can be suggested on the basis of close proximity of sherds or larger numbers occurring together.

Brick and tile
The majority of the brick and tile collected during fieldwalking was discarded after quantification. Exceptions were pieces which could be positively identified as Romano-British, ie fragments of *tegula*, flue tile etc; it proved virtually impossible to distinguish between Romano-British and post-medieval brick and tile on the basis of fabric alone, although some fragments were tentatively identified as Romano-British on the basis of similarity of fabric with diagnostic pieces from the same field.

One tile fabric (Fabric A) appears to form a distinct group which could be consistently recognised amongst the tile collected. All examples of this fabric were retained. Tile of this type occurs throughout the areas walked, but was found in particularly large quantities

on a medieval moated site (Manor Ash Moats, SU 54506525), and on this basis, has been tentatively dated to the medieval period, although the pottery from the site might suggest a later date (*see* below). The fabric is moderately soft and comprises an iron-rich clay matrix, firing pink–orange to dark salmon pink, often with an unoxidised grey core. Inclusions consist of sparse, rounded quartz grains up to 1 mm in size, sparse irregular grog fragments up to 2 mm in size, and occasional sub-angular flint fragments. The tiles are generally *c*. 15 mm in thickness; surfaces are irregular, and are frequently scratched, though it is unknown whether this was a deliberate surface treatment or post-depositional abrasion. No complete examples were recovered, though some fragments of peg tiles were noted.

The remaining tile is assumed to be of post-medieval or modern date, although it is recognised that fabrics of earlier material might exist. Recognisable forms, eg peg tiles, ridge tiles, were noted, but no record was made of the range of fabric types present.

The large quantities of tile recovered enabled plotting by mean weight and standard deviations. For the transect, the mean weight of tile per 25 m collection unit is 84 g with a standard deviation of 155 g, while the Burghfield area produced a mean weight of 176 g per collection unit (including 25 m, 10 m, and total collection units); in the latter area a figure of 151 g would be more representative of the 25 m collection units. All tile fragments collected are plotted in Figures Mf. 15 and 18. The identifiable Romano-British tiles and Fabric A distributions are plotted in Figure Mf. 18. Clusters were defined on the basis of three or more collection units in a hectare, with a mean weight greater than the mean for the area, plus four standard deviations and are listed in Table 23.

Results

Woodland Survey

Twelve areas of woodland were inspected (Fig. 2). Old quarry pits were identified in several woods, as well as many banks and ditches which are probably old woodland boundaries; none was felt to be of any great antiquity. Details of these earthworks can be found in the archive. Three of them may be of archaeological significance. A short stretch of a shallow ditch on Crookham Common (SU 533645) was observed running parallel to the previously recorded Bury's Banks, about 175 m to the east. At SU 571674, in Rowlands Copse, near Woolhampton, the modern parish boundary kinks around a deliberately constructed dam across the stream (now breached), possibly forming a pond of unknown function. To the north of this pond at Midgham Green (SU 567680), a possible rectangular enclosure with an external bank was recorded in the angle of the wood; this may reflect the change in road layout and woodland boundary, as recorded on Rocque's map of 1761. Another observation of possible archaeological significance was the discovery of quantities of burnt flint in the upcast from animal burrows at SU 54666845 in Blacklands Copse.

The difficulties of thick undergrowth restricting visibility and impeding systematic survey, and the lack of experience of some of the fieldwalkers in this type of work, make it impossible to calculate what proportion of sites may have been discovered or missed by this method. This problem is emphasised by the fact that the survey team failed to find one of the low mounds, previously identified by P.G. Rose (PRN3881, Appendix 3) in Wasing Wood which has not been disturbed since the time of the 1976–77 survey.

Phosphate Analysis, by M.R. Trott and S.J. Lobb

Samples from 19 of the fields within the transect and five fields in the Burghfield area were tested for soil phosphate levels. A summary of the results is presented in Table 13 and details can be found in the archive. Phosphate levels generally ranged from less than 100 Pppm (it was difficult to measure exactly using the comparator disc available) to 450 Pppm; in hectare 695698, which was subjected to total collection, and where samples were taken on a 10 m grid, there were some samples as high as 600 Pppm. The mean value for each field was calculated and ranged from 59 at Green Farm and Church Cottages (94 and 95), in the Burghfield area, to 284 at Harts Hill (13) in the transect (Table 13).

All the fields with the higher mean values (200 Pppm and above) also contained archaeological sites or significant finds clusters, except for Field Farm 1, Burghfield (97), which nonetheless is adjacent to a known archaeological site at Amners Farm. Conversely, it is true that many of the fields with low phosphate levels also produced significant surface finds distributions. Some of the lowest recorded levels came from fields where there were no significant finds distributions (Webbs Lane, 70 and 74) in the transect. The lowest mean value was recorded at Green Farm/Church Cottages (94/95) in the Burghfield area, where only transects across the centre of the fields were collected and processed, and the information is not therefore directly comparable with the low density finds scatters in this area. However, small, localised areas of higher phosphate levels are recorded which correspond to increased levels of burnt flint and Romano-British pottery; as the distribution of finds recorded at Green Farm is outside the area sampled, the significance of the low phosphorous level cannot be assessed.

In some cases, broadly enhanced values appear to be directly related to the changes in the soil within the field. At Field Farm (97) and Amners Farm (96) in the Burghfield area, there is a notable fall off in the values off the gravel area onto the clays. However, this could equally be a result of archaeological activity which has been identified at this site. There is a similar change in the phosphate values linked to soil type at Able Bridge/Boot Farm in the transect (23/27), this time increasing off the gravels up the slope onto the Bagshot Beds, London Clay, and the plateau gravel; here too, the distribution matches an increased finds density. In general, there is no pattern of lower or higher mean values relating to one particular soil type. In other areas topography may have influenced phosphate values, although, once again, correlation with archaeological information makes such an interpretation uncertain. At Ramsbury Hillfort (10), the phosphate levels from the area within the bank and ditch are broadly higher than the surrounding area; however, the lower levels outside the hillfort may be due to the steep gradient resulting in soil movement downslope.

Discussion

Although soil phosphate levels from the survey area are generally not very high, there is clearly some variability in the distribution. Using a 25 m sampling grid, it is most unlikely that anything other than broad trends and extensive activities will be observed. More intensive sampling on a 10 m grid, even though this is still fairly coarse, in hectare 695698 at Pingewood, Burghfield (101) which contains a cropmark enclosure, produced a more significant distribution pattern in relation to the finds distributions; however, it is also worth noting that the sampling at 25 m in the surrounding area, indicated a generally enhanced level in this area than elsewhere in the field. However, at Manor Ash Moats (8), in addition to the 25 m grid, samples were taken at 5 m intervals in two transects across the interior of the moated site; the resulting distribution shows no obvious pattern in relation to the earthwork. Clearly, the function and use of a site are important factors and interpretation of these characteristics is largely not discernible from surface finds distributions. A further difficulty in interpretation is implicit in the experimental error inherent in the method; reworking a small number of samples suggested an error of 60–70 Pppm. Given the low overall levels in the survey, this error margin could represent a significant variation in any field.

In conclusion, the phosphate survey, even using the broad grid as was adopted in the survey, has provided useful comparative data to the finds distributions, in some cases possibly suggesting a functional dimension which might not otherwise be indicated. However, this information can only be of a very general nature. Although the method is relatively speedy, the collection of samples and processing does add significantly to the fieldwork time and, with the problems of interpretation, the usefulness of phosphate sampling using the strategy adopted in the survey as a first stage prospection method is questionable.

Finds Analyses (the Transect)

Flint, *by P.A. Harding*
Of the 9540 25 m collection units in this area, 1897 (18%) produced 2534 pieces of flint. Most units in which artefacts were present produced one object (79%) and only 0.7% exceeded five pieces. The average density per hectare was 3.8 pieces (although this includes partially collected hectares) ranging from 55 pieces at Wasing Lower Farm to one, although a more accurate figure of 4.25 per hectare might be calculated, based on the 25 m collection units multiplied by 16.

The identification of concentrations by cluster analysis has not been attempted because most of the collection

Table 13 1982–87 Surveys: phosphate survey, summary of results

Field No.	Field name	No.	Mean Pppm	Min.	Max.	S.D.	Geol.	Archaeology	Comment
8	Manor Ash Moats	139	204	100	450	77	RG/LC	Moat. Tile concentration	No significant patterning.
10	Ramsbury Hillfort	155	155	100	350	50	PG	Hillfort	Higher values within earthworks but probably due to topography
11	Harts Hill Farm	93	191	100	400	64	LC/BB	Med/pot-med pot scatter	No obvious correlation with finds distributions
12	Harts Hill 1	413	173	100	400	73	LC/BB/PG	RB burials recorded at top of slope. Low density flint scatter near base of slope	Generally higher values at top of slope adj. to BA and RB site and RB burials. No obvious correlation with flint scatter
13	Harts Hill 2	100	284	100	400	77	PG	Burnt flint and flint cluster S. part of field. Excavation revealed BA and RB features	General even spread of high values (only S. part of field sampled)
15	Colthrop 1	116	175	100	350	64	LC	RB and med. pot scatter. Small low density burnt flint scatter	No significant patterning (only part of field sampled)
16	Colthrop 2	123	241	100	400	76	LC	See Colthrop 1 (adj. field)	Generally even distribution of high values down slope, becoming lower towards E. edge of field
17	Colthrop Manor	95	223	100	400	74	LC/BB	Flint scatter in E. part of field	Only part of field sampled. Generally even spread of high values at W. edge of field becoming lower towards flint scatter
23	Able Bridge	120	140	100	300	53	RG/LC	Flint and burnt flint cluster increasing in density up slope.	Only part of field sampled. General increase in values up slope
27	Boot Farm	203	219	100	350	71	PG/BB LC	As above	As above
33	Wasing Lwr Farm	834	203	100	900	74	All/RG	Cropmarks. Earlier and later prehistoric and RB finds clusters and general scatter across field	Earlier prehistoric flints seem to correlate to low P. values. Some higher values fall within later prehistoric flint scatter. Highest values partly corresponding to RB pot.
50	Kiff Green	101	200	<100	400	73	BB/LC	RB pot scatter and burnt flint concentration in S. part of field	Only part of field sampled. Even distribution of moderate values. No particular correlation with finds distributions

Table 13 continued

Field No.	Field name	No.	Mean Pppm	Min.	Max.	S.D.	Geol.	Archaeology	Comment
61	Woodcock	131	151	<100	400	66	PG/BB	Med. and post-med. pot scatter, flint cluster and burnt flint concentration	Only part of field sampled. Even distribution. No correlation with finds
63	Rookery Copse	81	178	100	450	60	LC	Flint and burnt flint clusters. Prehistoric and med. pot scatters	No correlation with finds. Small area of higher values partly corresponding with finds distributions
64	Cable Factory	61	143	<100	250	50	RG	Adj. to 63 RB scatter	No significant distribution
65	Hall Place Farm	21	130	<100	200	40	LC	Burnt flint concentration	Inadequate sample
67	Beenham Grange Farm	89	165	100	350	62	LC	Flint cluster and post-med. tile concentration	No correlation with finds. Small area of high values at edge of field adj. to wood
70	Webbs Lane 2	38	129	<100	250	47	LC	No significant distributions	No significant distributions
74	Webbs Lane 6	68	136	<100	200	45	LC	Flint scatter	No significant distribution
94/95	Green Farm/Church Cottages	168	59	<100	150	26	LC/RG	Low density prehist. and med. finds scatters. Small burnt flint concentration	Fairly even distribution
96	Amners Farm	148	237	<100	550	110	RG	Cropmarks. Low density flint scatter. Prehist. and RB sherds. Burnt flint concentration in NE part of field.	Flint
97	Field Farm 1	184	215	<100	350	99	RG/LC	Low density flint scatter	Higher values correspond to areas of RG in the field
99	Field Farm 3	331	280	100	450	84	RG	Cropmarks. BA sites. RB encl. Flint cluster and burnt flint concentration	Fairly even distribution over whole field. Highest values tend to be at edge of field and over old boundary
101	Pingewood 2	670	215	<100	625	81	RG	Cropmarks. Flint and burnt flint clusters. RB, med. and post-med. pot clusters	Phosphate values increase towards N of field in area of med./post-med. pot clusters and cropmark encl. Within total collection ha (695698) significant distribution in relation to finds correlation

areas are isolated from each other. Observations are therefore made on the basis of visual assessment of the distribution plans. The definition of concentrations in some areas is made difficult by the generally low overall density. Clusters defined by adjacent collection units of higher densities of finds are the most easily recognised. Although, scatters of both nucleated and diffuse character with lower densities may also be significant and may indicate areas of activity more clearly than isolated occurrences of higher density. Because of the problems of dating the material, identification of clusters is made more difficult where the flint appears to be of more than one period. The clusters which have been defined are listed in Table 14.

Figure Mf. 10 shows the total distribution of all flake material from the survey, and details are listed in the archive. These indicate that flint is present throughout the transect, although clusters are most prominent in the Enborne valley, especially at Boot Farm (27) on the plateau gravels, and at Wasing Lower Farm (33) on the river gravels and alluvium. North of the Kennet, a large concentration was found at Rookery Copse/Cable Factory (63/64), while smaller clusters are also apparent on the valley gravels. The alluvium shows contrasting lower densities. Equally, less material was found on the valley sides, although large areas of London Clay were unavailable for examination. The marked decrease in flint west of the Enborne at Arundells Copse (20) may be due to the presence of the heavier soils of London Clay. North of the Kennet, a scatter, or perhaps a series, of small clusters extending from Woodcock to Ferrises and Croft Cottages, suggests that tributary streams, fed from the spring line, may have attracted prehistoric settlement. Flint knapping debris on the higher plateau gravels is most marked at Boot Farm (27) to the south of the Enborne, with nucleated groups up to 100 m across north of the river, at Harts Hill (13) and Colthrop Manor (17).

Earlier prehistoric

The distribution of material and techniques associated with prepared blade/let core production (including flake material with abraded butts) was plotted in an attempt to isolate areas of earlier occupation (Mf. 9). The resulting plot shows a distribution which is generally complementary to the flake material. Precise dating can rarely be confirmed by diagnostic retouched tools. Material is present throughout the area, although most was concentrated along the rivers on the valley gravel.

The clusters of this period identified in the transect are listed in Table 14. Parts of two diffuse groups, approximately 250 m north–south by 300 m east–west, have been defined on the west bank of the Enborne, adjacent to the river. The first, at Arundells Copse (19), is composed mainly of flakes but also includes two end scrapers made on flakes. The other group, 1250 m to the north, at Lea Cottage (29), contains both flakes and blades with abraded butts, two end scrapers made on flakes, and a broken piercer. There is a general spread of material adjacent to the river in this area between the two clusters.

Two dense concentrations have been noted on the opposite bank of the Enborne at Wasing Lower Farm (33). One group (33a), extending in a band about 150 m wide, approximately 350 m along the edge of the river, includes 17 blade/let cores. Flakes and blades, some with abraded butts, three end scrapers made on flakes, and a tranchet axe comprise the remainder of the scatter. The second group (33b), 1250 m to the north–east, measures approximately 150 m in diameter and is on the edge of the valley gravel at the boundary with the alluvium. The assemblage of flakes, blades, and blade/let cores with abraded striking platforms, also includes a crested blade from core preparation.

Clusters along the Kennet are confined to a diffuse spread at Manor Ash Moats (7), approximately 500 m east–west by 150 m north–south (although the presence of later material makes definition difficult), characterised by flakes and blades with abraded butts. Most artefacts are concentrated in the south-east corner of the field, including the special finds which comprise two end scrapers made on flakes, and a possible fabricator.

Early exploitation of the spring line is suggested by a nucleated cluster, approximately 100 m in diameter towards the south end of Ferrises (60). Blades and tools are absent, the area being defined by four flakes with abraded butts and at least three others which may have been removed from prepared cores.

Activity on the Bagshot Beds and plateau gravels is generally sparse. But four pieces found together at Webbs Lane (72/73), including a side scraper made on a flake with an abraded butt, suggest that parts of the higher ground may have been occupied at an early date. A bladelet core, and two flakes with abraded butts from Ramsbury Hillfort (10), may also indicate some form of early occupation on the site.

Hammer mode, which may be chronologically significant, suggests that most material was removed with hard hammers; although where soft hammer characteristics were observed, they generally occurred among these earlier concentrations.

Later prehistoric

Flint from this period has been inferred from concentrations of flakes which lack specialised techniques of core preparation. The distribution of flake material indicates continuing occupation of the river valleys but suggests expansion on to the clay soils of the valley sides and the plateau gravels (Mf.10).

Details of the flint clusters identified are listed in Table 14. Clusters of material in the river valleys, where earlier prehistoric material has also been identified, are suggested at Manor Ash Moats (7), where there may be two *foci* of activity, and at Wasing Lower Farm (33). At Manor Ash Moats, the eastern cluster (7b) contained a fabricator and a knife, suggesting a later prehistoric date, while at Wasing Lower Farm (33c), a later date is suggested by the lack of blade material; the retouched flakes and scraper, however, provided no clue to date. An additional small cluster, on the edge of the river gravel terrace, was suggested at Fronds Farm (40) but contains no diagnostic material.

Also in the Enborne valley, the dense concentration at Boot Farm/Lane End (27/26), on the edge of the plateau gravels, in the south, contains no diagnostic flakes, cores or retouched tools to confirm date.

To the north of the Kennet, the largest group is found on the river gravel at Rookery Copse/Cable Factory

(63/64). There are insufficient diagnostic pieces for positive dating but a fragment from a semi-discoidal core, and a crested flake from a multi-platform flake core, confirms that this is a flake technology. The tools include a broken leaf arrowhead and four scrapers. In a similar location, at the base of the valley side on river gravel, a more diffuse scatter spreading over 600 m, was identified at Kennetholme Farm (86) and was associated with two knives, a scraper, an unclassified flake tool, and several retouched pieces.

Clusters in the north are restricted to small, undiagnostic nucleated groups, 100–150 m in diameter on the valley sides and edge of the plateau gravels. At Beenham Grange (67), one such cluster is associated with a piercer and a scraper.

Relevant tools have been described with their associated blade or flake cluster. There are, however, small concentrations of tools in the north of the area with no significant flake grouping (Mf. 12). Two piercers and three scrapers, with four miscellaneous pieces, were found in two small groups at opposite ends of Carbins Wood Lane (45 and 46). Three scrapers, a knife, a barbed and tanged arrowhead, and three retouched pieces were also found in a diffuse group at Webbs Lane (72–74). Flakes with abraded butts have already been described from Webbs Lane but no other significant clusters are apparent.

Deliberate retouched material is often difficult to identify. Most objects from the Kennet Valley Survey have heavily damaged edges which result from agriculture. 'Notches' are particularly common and have not been plotted.

One hundred and six tools and retouched pieces which have been catalogued are listed below. Most are associated with flake scatters but are individually undated.

Scrapers (32%) form the most recognisable group. The scrapers are all made on flakes retouched at the distal end by regular/irregular, direct, continuous, abrupt/semi-abrupt retouch into a convex scraping edge. They have a general distribution, of which 12 are associated with the blade/let clusters, although none are made on blades. Four were found with the early prehistoric material at Wasing Lower Farm (33, SU 533685) and are therefore possibly of Mesolithic date. Four scrapers from Rookery Copse (63, SU 592673) provide the best association with the flake industries.

The piercers, knives, and fabricators provide no additional chronological information. Two of the piercers occur in areas where earlier prehistoric material appears to predominate, while the other two appear to be associated with flake material. The knives are associated with flake clusters, such as at Rookery Copse (63) where a leaf shaped arrowhead was also found, and Kennetholme Farm (86–87, SU 548669), or occur in apparent isolation as at Able Bridge (in the Enborne valley).

The most diagnostic artefacts are described below. A Mesolithic tranchet axe from the early prehistoric cluster at Wasing Lower Farm (33, SU 572650), measures 80 mm long, 41 mm wide, and is 29 mm thick. It

has an oval cross-section and is slightly curved in profile. All cortex has been removed by bifacial hard hammer percussion. A single successful tranchet flake was removed to sharpen the blade.

A backed bladelet of probable Mesolithic date was found at Back Lane (28, SU 570648). The proximal end is missing but the left edge has been backed by continuous, abrupt, direct retouch, using an anvil to support the blank. The piece now measures 22 mm long by 11 mm wide and is 3 mm thick. A broken Neolithic leaf arrowhead from Rookery Copse (63, SU 590673) measures 24 mm long, 20 mm wide, and 5 mm thick. It has a plano-convex cross-section. The dorsal surface has covering retouch and similar modification has been used at both ends to straighten the profile.

A barbed and tanged arrowhead from the plateau gravel at Webbs Lane (72, SU 595696), is of Green's (1980, 117, fig 45) Sutton b type — small miscellaneous arrowheads with 'unshaped' barbs. The arrowhead measures 21 mm long by 21 mm wide, which is within the mean of this group of arrowheads (ibid, table V111.2), and is 4 mm thick. All traces of the blank have been removed by bifacial covering retouch. The tip is missing, probably broken by impact and may, therefore, have been discarded during use. The barbs are also missing but were probably not well formed. Rose found two similar arrowheads, which were also from the plateau gravels at Burghfield and Ufton Nervet, which he associated with hunting activity. Sutton b arrowheads are the most common form of barbed and tanged arrowheads (Green op. cit. 119). They are often found with inhumations or associated with Beakers, as at Earley, Reading, where 18 arrowheads of this type were found (Harding in prep.).

Discussion

The Kennet Valley Survey has shown that evidence of prehistoric activity, as demonstrated by flint knapping waste and tools, is apparent throughout the area. The low average density (3.8 per hectare) is consistent with previous results in the Kennet Valley (Rose this volume), despite the fact that raw material is plentiful. Rose noted that flint densities were consistently higher on chalk than on other geological types in the Kennet valley. Direct comparisons between the two surveys are difficult to make, owing to variations in the collection methods and the narrower range of geological types examined by the Kennet Valley Survey. However, Rose's Table 2 shows that, where comparisons are possible, river gravels have consistently produced more material in both surveys than the clays and plateau gravels. This is confirmed in the results of the present survey.

Rose also notes that densities should be related to individual geological types within fields rather than to the predominant geology. The effects of localised changes in geology can be seen clearly at Wasing Lower Farm (33), where alluvium covers the north end of the field and flint densities drop dramatically. Two pieces from the alluvium were in excellent condition, which may indicate that material is being uncovered by modern ploughing. Similar effects of geology can be seen at

Table 14 1982–87 Surveys, transect: flint clusters

Field No.	Field name	NGR (SU)	Amt.	Area (ha)	Density per ha	Geol.	Topography	% Blades	Tools	Cores
Earlier prehistoric										
7	Manor Ash Moats	551653	82	7.5	10.9	RG	terrace edge	7.6	4	10
19	Arundells Copse I	558636	28	7.5	3.7	RG	E. slope valley side	11.7	2	5
29	Lea Cottage	565647	81	7.5	10.8	RG	terrace	12.2	3	6
33	Wasing Lower Farm a	572650	202	6	33.6	RG	floodplain	11.5	8	29
33	b	582656	65	2.25	28.8	RG	floodplain	18.7	—	8
60	Ferrises	580679	17	1	17.0	BB	flat valley side	—	—	1

NB. includes later material see clusters no. below

Field No.	Field name	NGR (SU)	Amt.	Area (ha)	Density per ha	Geol.	Topography	% Blades	Tools	Cores
Later prehistoric										
13	Harts Hill	533685	50	2.25	22.2	PG	flat plateau edge	6.0	2	7
17	Colthrop Manor	541676	23	1	23.0	LC	S/SE slope just above break in slope	—	—	—
86/87	Kennetholme Farm	548669	56	17.3	3.2	RG/LC	terrace	3.5	5	7
7	Manor Ash Moats a	549653	31	3.75	8.3	RG	terrace	6.45	1	1
	b	553653	49	5	9.8	RG	terrace	2	4	4
26/27	Boot Farm/Lane End	567636	183	24	7.6	PG	flat plateau edge	1.1	4	8
46	Carbins Wood Lane 2	560685	12	0.5	24.0	PG	flat	—	4	1
45	Carbins Wood Lane 1	563685	21	3	7.0	PG	flat	7.6	4	2
33	Wasing Lower Farm	577655	120	27.5	4.4	RG	floodplain	>1	7	8

NB. includes earlier material — see cluster no. 1 above

NB. the focus of the site may cover a smaller area (figures below)

| 63/64 | Rookery Copse/ | 576655 | 90 | 12.5 | 7.2 | PG/ | flat | >1 | 5 | 5 |
| | Cable Factory | 592673 | 180 | 13 | 13.8 | LC/RG | edge of terrace | 0.6 | 0 | 9 |

Table 14 continued

Field No.	Field name	NGR (SU)	Amt.	Area (ha)	Density per ha	Geol.	Topography	% Blades	Tools	Cores
40	Fronds Farm	594666	25	3.75	6.7	RG	terrace	–	1	4
71–74	Webbs Lane 3–6	595696	58	17.3	3.3	LC	se/nw slope	6	8	2
67	Beenham Grange	597681	24	2	12.0	LC	terrace	–	3	–
Other small clusters (later prehistoric)										
60	Ferrises	580679	20	2.25	8.9	BB	none given on original table	5	–	1
51	Croft Cottages	574683	23	3.75	6.1	LC		4.3	–	4
50	Kiff Green	570684	16	2	8	LC		–	–	–
12	Hartshill Farm 1	533682	52	13.5	3.85	BB/LC		5.76	1	–

Arundells Copse 1 (19–20, SU 58636), where a band of valley gravel adjacent to the Enborne overlies London Clay.

The division of material into industries associated with blade production has provided a basic chronological framework which has confirmed that Mesolithic activity was more prevalent adjacent to the rivers. The quantities of flint are generally insufficient to provide detailed technological information about individual concentrations. Most tools have been found with waste material or in isolation, but small unassociated concentrations have been noted from the north of the transect (Mf. 12).

Flint knapping produces large quantities of durable waste. The raw material from the area is unsuitable for large-scale industrial production and most of the waste is probably derived from domestic knapping. Material on sites adjacent to rivers can be dispersed by flood (Harding *et al.* 1987), while fine grained sediments may allow vertical movement (Barton and Bergman 1982) which means that artefacts are not apparent on the surface. However, some of the densest concentrations in the survey area have been identified adjacent to rivers.

The presence of isolated material is more difficult to explain. It suggests that limited activity occurred in most areas at some stage, but it demonstrates neither contemporaneous nor large-scale occupation. It is also possible that some of this material could have been spread or introduced by agriculture, particularly where variations in the condition or patination occur. The general spread suggests that some activity had occurred in most areas by the Bronze Age.

Other Finds, by Lorraine Mepham

Burnt flint

Burnt flint was recovered from every field walked within the transect (Mf. 13) but the distribution is by no means even, and 22 fields or groups of fields produced a mean weight per 25 m collection unit greater than the mean weight for the whole transect (Table 15). These range in size from 0.5–10 hectares, but most appear to be discrete clusters of two hectares or less (many less than one hectare). They occur on all geologies and all topographical zones, although there is a clear preference for locations on the valley side and plateau edge, on the spring line or adjacent to streams. Some of the clusters on the valley bottom are either on the floodplain or the edge of the gravel terrace above the floodplain but up to 500 m distance from the river.

Clusters and scatters of lower densities may also be of significance but are not discussed here; for instance, at Harts Hill (12, SU 533685), a small cluster of burnt flint was identified corresponding to a later prehistoric flint scatter and prehistoric pot occurrence. Burnt flint distributions of low densities were seen to have significant patterning in relation to concentrations of particular types of finds and, not surprisingly, the density of burnt flint relating to finds concentrations varies from period to period. Another factor which may have influenced burnt flint density is collector bias. It is noticeable that all 11 fields walked by one team (1986) produced higher densities of burnt flint than surrounding fields on similar geology and topography, and eight of the 18 clusters identified fall within these fields. The same phenomenon has also been noted for post-medieval tile. On the other hand, relatively high densities of worked flint have been recorded in these areas, possibly relating to activity along tributary streams fed from the spring line; the concentrations of burnt flint may have a similar explanation.

Burnt flint is, of course, intrinsically undatable, but some of the clusters can be correlated with concentrations of other finds. Although surface association cannot be taken necessarily to imply contemporaneity, some tentative suggestions regarding the interpretation of these clusters can be made on the basis of these correlations. It should be noted first that no types of finds are consistently associated with higher densities of burnt flint.

Fifteen of the 25 clusters identified correspond to clusters of worked flint, although in most cases the two are immediately adjacent rather than exactly coincident and a further five have a scattering of later prehistoric flint in the same area. Five of these (7, 29, 33 a and b, and 60) are in the same area as earlier prehistoric flint clusters. At Harts Hill (13), closer examination of the distribution shows that the burnt flint is concentrated around the edges of the later prehistoric flint scatter, although subsequent excavation indicated a widespread distribution of Bronze Age features (Miles and Collard 1986). Five of these clusters (33, 40a and b, 50b and 63) are also associated with sherds of prehistoric (Late Bronze Age) pottery. Three Romano-British pot clusters correspond to burnt flint clusters (7, 33, and 50) and scattered sherds are present on five other burnt flint clusters, but in all cases sherds of prehistoric pottery are also present; at four of the clusters concentrations of medieval pot were also identified. Six clusters are unassociated with any other concentrations of finds, although in four cases worked flint is also present in small quantities and only two (49 and 85a) are unassociated with any other finds. In only one case (52) does a burnt flint cluster correspond with concentrations of medieval and post-medieval material and here the distributions are quite different.

The evidence would seem to suggest a predominantly prehistoric association for most of the dense burnt flint clusters identified. In general terms, the distribution of burnt flint is comparable with that of the worked flint; there are generally higher densities in areas with a high density worked flint and a similar fall off in both types of material has been noted on the London Clay of the valley sides (*see* flint report). Sherds of Late Bronze Age pottery are frequently, though not always, associated with the clusters of burnt flint.

Discussion

Interpretation of the burnt flint clusters is problematic. Not all are necessarily of the same date; associations with material of various dates from Mesolithic to Romano-British have been noted above. The possibility exists that some may represent the remains of burnt mounds which occur in all parts of the country (Hedges 1974; Barfield and Hodder 1989); this interpretation has been tentatively suggested for some of the burnt flint

Table 15 1982–88 Surveys, transect: burnt flint concentrations

Field No.	Field name	NGR (SU)	Area (ha)	Geology	Mean wt (g) 25 m	S.D. (g)	Distance from water (m)	Comment/Archaeology
7	Manor Ash Moats	54886538	1	RG	141	137	100–200	Two small scatters corresponding to flint clusters; RB material; post-medieval tile.
12	Harts Hill 1	5326800	2	LC	52	100	100	1 sherd prehistoric pot; flint scatter
13	Harts 13/14 Harts Hill 2	53256853	2.5	PG	171	283	150	Flint cluster, LBA site
25	Brimpton Common	56506315	3	PG	108	167	200	No corresponding clusters. Flint scatter
26	Boot Farm	56806355	5	PG	428	414	350	Flint cluster
27	Lane End	57036355	2	PG	348	396	100	Possibly part of a cluster in field 26
29	Lea Cottage	56206470	0.5	LC	183	388	400	Flint clusters in same field but different distribution
33	Wasing Lower Farm a	57256505	1	RG	125	152	50	On edge of flint cluster and RB cluster
33	" b	58306570	10	All.	125	152	100	General scatter of RB and prehistoric pot. Edge of flint cluster to south
40	Fronds Farm a	59306645	0.5	All.	234	287	200	Flint cluster, prehistoric, and medieval pot clusters
	NB. possibly two separate clusters " b							
42	Bazetts Plantation	55156835	1.5	BB	178	235	100	Flint scatter
49	Copyhold Farm	57406880	3	BB	204	232	100	Tile cluster in same field but different distribution
50	Kiff Green a	56906835	3	BB	344	377	50	Post-medieval pot cluster, flint, and RB pot scatter
	" b							
	NB. possibly all one site							
51	Croft Cottages	57056810	1	LC	344	377	25	Prehistoric flint scatter and pot occurrence
52	Abbey	57256845	2.5	BB	147	193	25	RB and medieval pot occurrences. Flint and p-med. clusters to south
52	Abbey	57606835	1	BB	162	223	200	Medieval and post-medieval material in same field but different distribution
60	Ferrises	57856795	0.5	BB	160	121	100	Flint cluster, medieval and post-medieval clusters
61	Woodcock	58356725	1.5	PG	233	194	250	Flint cluster and post-medieval pot cluster

Table 15 continued

Field No.	Field name	NGR (SU)	Area (ha)	Geol.	Mean wt 25 m (g)	S.D. (g)	Distance water (m)	Comment/Archaeology
63	Rookery Copse/Cable Factory	59006730	6	LC	374	215	200	Flint cluster; prehistoric pot cluster and medieval pot scatter
65	Hall Place Farm	59306755	2	LC	505	316	100?	Flint scatter; RB pot occurrence and post-medieval material
67	Beenham Grange	59656810	5	RG	140	130	100	Flint scatter
85	Park Farm 3a	52206880	1.5	CC	115	186	50	Flint scatter
	b	52506870	1	LC	115	186	25	No finds
86	Kennetholme Farm	54606695	1.5	RG	119	112	200	Flint cluster

Note: 'Area' represents the area of the main burnt flint concentration while the mean weight and standard deviation refers to the whole field

concentrations identified by fieldwalking in east Berkshire (Ford 1987, 42). A concentration of burnt flint adjacent to a river channel has been excavated to the east of the transect at Anslows Cottages (Butterworth and Lobb 1992), and some of the small, discrete clusters in a similar topographical position within the transect, eg Manor Ash Moats (7), might represent similar features. The larger clusters on the more marginal soils of the plateaux may have had a different function. Two of these clusters produced particularly high densities of burnt flint (more than 10 kg per hectare): at Boot Farm (26/27) and Kiff Green (50).

The association with Romano-British finds is more ambiguous. Two possible associations of burnt flint with Romano-British material have been noted above, but in both cases prehistoric material is also present. In a few cases, Romano-British sherds can be seen to coincide with very small-scale 'peaks', often consisting of only one run, eg at Harts Hill Farm (11), Harts Hill 1 (12) and Colthrop 1 (15), but the association is not consistent; most Romano-British sherds are associated with no corresponding increase in burnt flint density.

Pottery

A total of 2549 sherds (39,850 g) was collected in the area of the transect across the Kennet Valley. Of the 48 fabric types identified for the Kennet Valley Survey assemblage, 44 were present in this area, ranging in date from Late Bronze Age to post-medieval. All percentages are by weight of the total assemblage from the transect.

Prehistoric
A total of 28 sherds (0.49%) was collected from the survey area; five prehistoric fabrics were identified, two flint-tempered (F1, F2), and three sandy fabrics (Q21–23). The two flint-tempered fabrics can be dated to the later Bronze Age on the basis of comparison with excavated material from, for example, Knight's Farm (Bradley et al. 1980, 266). The dating of the sandy fabrics is more problematic. All three fabrics could be Late Bronze Age, as similar material has been found locally in contexts of this date, eg Field Farm, Burghfield (Mepham 1992 (b), Fabrics Q41, Q43); however, very similar fabrics have also been found in Middle–Late Iron Age vessel forms at Thames Valley Park near Reading (Mepham 1992 (d), Fabric B7). No diagnostic vessel forms were recovered.

The small number of prehistoric sherds recovered makes it impossible to draw any statistically valid conclusions from such a small sample. However, some apparent trends can be noted. Most of the find spots occurred as single sherds, although two small clusters are evident (Mf. 14; Table 16). The majority of the pottery occurred on the river gravels and alluvium, most notably near the confluence of the Kennet and the Enborne. To the north of the Kennet, small quantities of pottery are scattered across the London Clay (five sherds), and a single sherd was found on the Bagshot Beds.

The most discernible clustering is at Wasing Lower Farm (33) on the alluvium immediately to the south of the River Enborne, where 10 sherds fall within an area

of just under 10 hectares. Of this total, all except one sherd was of the Late Bronze Age flint-tempered fabrics. At Fronds Farm (40), 1.3 km to the east, a scatter of five sherds, in both flint-tempered and sandy fabrics, was found in an area of about 8 ha, corresponding to a low density flint scatter. On the opposite bank of the Kennet at Cable Factory (64), three sherds in a sandy fabric were recovered.

Romano-British
Twenty-three Romano-British fabric types were identified (156 sherds, 3.47%) Only five derived from a known source (samian, Oxford white and oxidised wares, Silchester Ware); the remainder comprised one flint-tempered fabric (F110), 10 sandy fabrics (Q120–122, Q124, Q125, Q127–131), and seven grog-tempered fabrics (G140–146). Fabrics Q122 and Q128 may be products of the Alice Holt kilns; Fabric Q127 may include Black Burnished Ware and/or local imitations of this fabric.

Finewares are represented only by samian (E100) and the two Oxford fabrics (E170, E171, Q126); the latter show no evidence of colour-coating, although post-depositional abrasion may have removed all trace of this. The remainder of the pottery consists entirely of coarse domestic wares and, as such, very little of it can be closely dated. There were no decorated sherds amongst either the fine or coarse wares.

Few diagnostic vessel forms were recovered, the most common rim form being undatable everted rims. Where vessel forms could be more closely dated, it appears that some fabric types cover a wide date range, eg Q121, Q127, both of which included both early and late vessel forms. Five of the seven grog-tempered fabrics are paralleled at Thames Valley Park, where they occur in 1st/early 2nd century vessel forms (Mepham in prep. (d), Fabrics C2, C4, C8, C9, C13). The sandy fabrics cover a wider range of variation within each fabric type, each type is thus more likely to include pottery from more than one source and covering a wide date range.

The distribution of Romano-British pottery is similar to that of the prehistoric material (Mf. 15; Table 16). Again there is a concentration on the gravels and alluvium (see Table 17), with low density scatters along the Rivers Kennet and Enborne; more nucleated clusters can be suggested at Mill Field (32) and Wasing Lower Farm (33), both on the floodplain terraces of the rivers. More dispersed scatters were identified at Manor Ash Moats (7) and Wasing Lower Farm (33). Increased use of the London Clay in this period is suggested by several isolated clusters identified to the north of the river. The cluster at Kiff Green (50) is particularly dense: 20 sherds in an area of less than one hectare. Little evidence was found for activity on the Bagshot Beds or plateau gravels.

Medieval
Nine medieval fabric types were identified (156 sherds, 3.33%). These comprise seven sandy fabrics (Q400–405, E450), one flint-tempered fabric (F410), and one fabric with chalky limestone inclusions (L430). Only one fabric derived from a known source (E450): a Surrey/Hampshire border white ware. The limestone-tempered fabric (L430) and sandy fabric (Q403), with voids probably

Table 16 1982–88 Survey: transect, pottery clusters and scatters

Field No.	Field name	NGR (SU)	No. sherds	Area (ha)	Topography	Geology	Type
Prehistoric							
33	Wasing Lower Farm	583657	10	6.75	floodplain terrace	G	scatter
40	Fronds Farm	594665	5	8.5	floodplain	All.	scatter
Romano-British							
7	Manor Ash Moats	550653	14	9	terrace edge	G.	scatter
15	Colthrop	537673	5	0.25	above break in slope	LC	cluster
32	Millfield	566659	26	2	floodplain terrace	G	cluster
33	Wasing Lower Farm a	574651	9	1	terrace edge	G/A	cluster
(five sherds to the east of this scatter may indicate that it is more extensive)							
	b	583658	9	4	floodplain	A	scatter
	c	582656	12	35	terrace edge	G/A	scatter
41	Basingstoke Road	598665	9	21	floodplain	A	scatter
50	Kiff Green	570682	20	1	plateau edge	BB/LC	cluster
66	Oakwood Farm	589682	4	0.375	valley side	LC	cluster
88	Kennetholme Farm	553675	6	0.75	valley side	LC	cluster
Medieval							
11/82	Hartshill Farm	527683	14	2.8	plateau	LC/BB	cluster
15/16	Colthrop	537673	20	0.25	valley side	LC	cluster
31	Brimpton Manor Farm	557656	4	1	floodplain	A	cluster
32	Mill Field	567659	6	2	floodplain	A	cluster
38/40	Fronds Farm/	596664	27	26	floodplain	A/G	scatter
41	Basingstoke Road						
52	Abbey	575684	10	2.25	valley side	LC/BB	scatter
60	Ferrises	579680	5	1.5	valley side	BB/PG	scatter
61	Woodcock	580675	5	1.75	valley side	PG	cluster
72/73	Webbs Lane	593694	11	4	plateau	LC	scatter

Table 16 continued

Field No.	Field name	NGR (SU)	No. sherds	Area (ha)	Topography	Geology	Type
Post-medieval							
10	Ramsbury Hillfort	523695	18	0.5	plateau	BB	cluster
11/82	Hartshill Farm	527684	44	3	plateau	LC/BB	cluster
19	Arundells Copse	554638	23	2	valley side	LC	cluster
33	Wasing Lwr Farm	583654	180	20	terrace	G	scatter
35–37	Breaches Gully	584646	120	5	valley side	G/LC/BB	cluster
38	Aldermaston Bridge	594662	21	1.5	floodplain	A	cluster
41	Basingstoke Road	598665	86	8	floodplain	A/G	cluster
50	Kiff Green	569684	120	8	valley side	BB	cluster
52	Abbey	575683	66	5	valley side	LC/BB	cluster
55	Fodderhouse Copse	583689	61	2	valley side	LC	cluster
59	Allotment Gdns	584691	29	1	valley side	LC	cluster
60	Ferrises	583672	46	2	valley side	BB	cluster
61	Woodcock	585672	86	4	valley side	PG	cluster
62	Woolhampton Park	571668	48	3	valley side	PG	cluster
		586669	32	1	valley side	LC	cluster

Table 17 1982–87 Surveys: transect—location and density of pottery by period. Numbers of sherds are given, with density of sherds per hectare in brackets

	Area (ha)	Prehistoric		Romano-British		Medieval		Post-medieval	
Alluvium	71.8	16	(0.22)	49	(0.68)	32	(0.45)	171	(2.38)
Gravel	177.8	6	(0.03)	46	(0.26)	25	(0.14)	424	(2.38)
London Clay	298.6	5	(0.02)	43	(0.14)	75	(0.25)	967	(3.24)
Bagshot Beds	90.6	1	(0.01)	14	(0.15)	9	(0.10)	414	(4.57)
Plateau gravel	114.9	0		4	(0.03)	19	(0.17)	253	(2.20)
Total	753.7	28		156		160		2229	

resulting from the leaching of limestone inclusions, fall within a group of fabrics identified from the late 12th century in Newbury, and for which a source in the Mildenhall area has been postulated (Vince forthcoming, Group B fabrics). Flint-tempered fabrics, such as F410 and Q405, are found in Newbury from a slightly earlier date, 11th–12th century (*ibid.*, Group A fabrics); whilst sandy fabrics occur from the late 12th century in both Oxford and Newbury (*ibid.*, Group C fabrics). All the fabric types, except L430, are paralleled locally in the assemblages from Meales Farm, Sulhamstead (Lobb *et al.* 1990 (c), Fabrics 20, 21, 23, 24, 26) and/or Pingewood (Mills 198, Fabrics 9a, 9b, 9c, 11, 12, 13). On both sites, vessel forms indicated a late 12th–14th century date.

Diagnostic rim and handle forms recovered indicate that, as might be expected, the finer sandy fabrics (Q400–402) were used for jug/pitcher forms, whilst coarser fabrics (eg Q403, F410) were used for cooking pots, although cooking pots are also occasionally found in sandy fabrics. This functional differentiation between fabrics is emphasised by the occurrence of glaze and decoration.

Glaze is not common and occurs only on the sandy Fabrics E450, Q400, Q401; it is generally mottled green or greeny–yellow in colour, but occasionally translucent glaze occurs on Fabrics Q400 and Q401, which appears orange–red. Decoration is likewise rare: two body sherds in Fabric Q401, and one rim sherd in Fabric F410, have incised decoration, and there are two handles, in Fabrics Q400 and Q401, with stabbed decoration. Fingertipped rims and bases are absent, though this is a common technique in the area (cf. Vince in prep.); 14.3% by weight of the medieval assemblage is glazed and/or decorated.

Apart from the range of inclusion types, there appear to be few similarities between the Survey assemblage and the medieval collections from either Newbury or Reading, though there would seem to be closer affinities with the former group: all three major fabric groups identified at Newbury (flint-tempered, limestone-tempered and sandy fabrics) are present in the survey area. Glaze and decoration, as would be expected, is far more frequent in the urban assemblages from Newbury and Reading, and vessel forms amongst the latter group show a higher frequency of fine jug/pitcher types, in contrast to the dominance of coarse cooking pot types in the Kennet Valley.

The medieval material from the transect shows a considerable shift away from the areas where Romano-British material is found in the greatest concentration (Mf. 16; Table 16). Although there is still a moderate amount of medieval pottery on the gravels and alluvium (*see* Table 17), the density is less than in the Romano-British period and, at the same time, there is an increase in the amount of material on the valley sides (0.22 sherds per hectare), especially to the north of the Kennet.

Only one small, high density scatter was recorded, at Colthrop Manor (15/16). This included sandy, flint-tempered, and limestone-tempered fabrics. The cluster falls just above a break of slope on the valley side north of the river. A low density scatter was identified on the floodplain at Fronds Farm/Basingstoke Road (40), near the confluence of the two rivers. A number of small groups can be seen on the clays of the valley side to the north of the Kennet.

There are no obvious chronological trends in the distribution. Both the earlier flint-tempered wares and the later fine sandy wares are found throughout the area walked and do not occupy mutually exclusive areas. There are no apparent concentrations of fine glazed and/or decorated sherds.

Post-medieval

The post-medieval material comprises the bulk of the pottery assemblage from the transect (2229 sherds, 92.71%). No detailed fabric analysis of this material was undertaken; the pottery was divided into three groups of earthenwares and five groups of stonewares. For the purpose of this analysis, all earthenwares have been considered as 'post-medieval', despite the fact that some earthenwares were being produced at the end of the medieval period.

The earthenwares were defined on the basis of fabric colour: all red earthenwares (Q600), probably including products of more than one kiln; pinkish earthenwares (E640); and white to pinky–buff earthenwares (E630), most of which probably originate from the Surrey/ Hampshire border. The red earthenwares in particular cover a wide range of coarseness of inclusions. All three groups include both glazed and unglazed wares, and there are examples of slip-decorated vessels in the red and pink wares.

Two stonewares had a positively identifiable source: Westerwald Stoneware, with its distinctive blue-glazed decoration (E670), and Basalt Ware (E671), a hard, black stoneware produced in England from the late 18th century. The remaining stonewares were divided into those which were incompletely fused, ie individual grains still visible to the naked eye (Q601), and those which were completely fused, ie grains no longer visible (Q602). The former group is generally salt-glazed in shades of mottled brown and includes all the identified sherds of bellarmine jugs. The fabric is either grey or creamy–buff in colour. The latter group has grey or creamy–white fabrics and glaze is either in shades of brown on the grey wares (though rarely salt-glazed), or colourless on the whitewares.

No analysis of vessel form was undertaken for the post-medieval material and no closer dating within the period has been attempted.

The amount of post-medieval pottery recovered is much greater than the other periods and the distribution is consequently far wider and denser (Mf. 17; Table 16). All fields, except one, produced pottery of this period. There is an increase in density of pottery over preceding periods on all geologies (see Table 17). The river gravels show a relative decrease in popularity, while the Bagshot Beds shows a corresponding increase producing the greatest density. Continuing the trend noted in the medieval period, the greatest density of pottery now falls on the valley sides (3.55 sherds per hectare).

The pottery is not evenly distributed over the survey area, and several areas of denser concentration can be discerned. South of the River Kennet, there are denser clusters at Wasing Lower Farm (33), Breaches Gully (36), and Basingstoke Road (41). North of the Kennet, there are scatters at Hartshill Farm (11), Woodcock (61), Kiff Green (50), Abbey (52), Ferrises (60), and Fodderhouse Copse (55). These scatters occur on all geologies and several overlap more than one geology, eg at Breaches Gully, the scatter overlaps gravel, London Clay, and Bagshot Beds. They are also found at various topographical locations: on the floodplain immediately adjacent to the river (Basingstoke Road), on plateau edge (Harts Hill Farm, Kiff Green), and on the valley slopes in between (Woodcock).

Other smaller scatters can also be observed, for example at Woolhampton Park (62), Ramsbury Hillfort (10), and Kennetholme Farm (86). These smaller scatters generally occur on the edges of fields and may represent dumps of material as hard core in a gateway or demolished buildings.

Discussion
Although the quantities of pottery dating from periods prior to the post-medieval are small (344 sherds altogether, compared with 2229 post-medieval sherds), some trends through time are apparent and some review of the various factors affecting the distribution of the pottery should be made.

In the prehistoric period, the greatest density of pottery derives from the alluvium, followed by the river gravels (see Table 17), though the figures are based on totals of 16 and 6 sherds respectively; greater densities of pottery might have been expected, particularly on the gravels. One of the major factors affecting the survival and recovery of prehistoric pottery must be the extremely friable nature of many prehistoric fabrics. Similarly, low densities of prehistoric pottery have been encountered by other surveys (Shennan et al. 1985, 75; Ford 1987, 44; Gaffney and Tingle 1989, 88).

Distribution is denser in the Romano-British period on all topographic zones. Quantities are again small, but again, similar densities have been recovered by other surveys (Shennan 1985; Ford 1987, 44). The greatest density again occurs on the valley floor (see Table 17). Some differentiation in terms of type of settlement and agricultural activity might be expected between the different topographic zones, as in east Berkshire, where the influence of base geology was found to be reflected in the types and quantities of Romano-British field-walking finds (Ford 1987, 93). No such differentiation could be observed amongst the pottery from fieldwalking. Fine wares occur on all soil types and the evidence is insufficient to indicate any chronological trends in the distribution, as have been suggested, for example, on the Berkshire Downs (Gaffney and Tingle 1989, 241); both early and late material occur in the same locations and in similar quantities.

It is possible that the majority of Romano-British pottery recovered by the survey derives from agricultural practice, being spread over the fields with manure, rather than from occupation activity, an interpretation which would explain the low density, dispersed nature of the Romano-British pottery distribution. Manuring practices in this period have been recognised, for example, in east Berkshire and the Berkshire Downs (Ford 1987, 95; Gaffney and Tingle 1989, 210).

The fieldwalking evidence for the medieval period shows a shift from the valley floor to the valley sides, with a decrease in pottery density on the former to 0.30 sherds per hectare. As for the Romano-British period, the distribution on the valley sides concentrates on the south-facing slopes along the Kennet Valley. Known medieval settlements are generally more common on the valley sides than on the river gravels, for example, Brimpton and Wasing, where they would have been more centrally placed within the strip parishes which extended from the plateau to the River Kennet. The continuity of use of such settlements will, of course, affect the distribution pattern of fieldwalking finds, since the nucleus of medieval settlement will not be available for walking. As for the Romano-British period, manuring practices are assumed to account for the presence of the majority of medieval sherds recovered.

It may be the case that pottery alone is a poor guide to the extent of settlement and other activity during the medieval period. Despite the apparent expansion of settlement on to the valley sides during this period, the quantities of pottery recovered are only very slightly higher than for the Romano-British period (four sherds more) and previous fieldwork (1977–78) recorded a drop in quantity from the Romano-British to the medieval period (113 sherds less). Excavation at Meales Farm, Sulhamstead, although the site should not necessarily be regarded as typical of medieval sites in the transect, produced only a very poor pottery assemblage, despite the fact that a medieval manor is presumed to exist in the immediate vicinity (Lobb et al. 1991); and at Manor

Ash Moats, fieldwalking over a medieval moated site produced large quantities of tile but only one sherd of medieval pottery.

The same factors will limit the recovery of post-medieval pottery; the extent of present day settlement, and the distribution of pottery recovered during field-walking, will reflect an essentially rural pattern of activity. The relatively large amounts of post-medieval pottery recovered, compared with earlier periods, might enable a more detailed examination of trends in distribution and any intensification of agriculture within the transect.

If we assume that the bulk of the pottery has reached the fields through manuring, it could be suggested that the areas with the densest distribution of pottery represent areas taken into cultivation at a relatively early date in the post-medieval period, or perhaps earlier in the medieval period. It can be noted that, in several cases, post-medieval clusters coincide with dispersed, low density scatters of medieval pottery, for which an interpretation as manuring scatters could be suggested, eg Basingstoke Road (41), Abbey (52) and Harts Hill Farm (11/82), although this is by no means invariably the case. Also, it is noticeable that in most cases the post-medieval clusters fall within the boundaries of fields marked on the Ordnance Survey (OS) map (1975 edition); this is particularly marked where adjacent fields have been walked and produced relatively little pottery, eg Wasing Lower Farm and Abbey. Thirteen of the 17 clusters identified fall on the valley sides, emphasising the increased use of this topographic zone during the medieval period.

Tile

Romano-British
Within the transect, 47 pieces of Romano-British tile were collected from nine fields (Mf. 15, Table 18). This total includes six fragments of flue tiles, 11 possible *tegulae*, and one possible *imbrex*. Most of these occur with clusters or scatters of Romano-British pottery but in three cases they occur as isolated finds.

The tile is found largely on the valley floor, to the south of the River Kennet, and in the Enborne Valley; a few pieces were also found on the valley side on the clays and sands in the Enborne Valley. One fairly extensive scatter was identified on both gravels and alluvium at Wasing Lower Farm (33), where 34 fragments were collected over an area of approximately 50 ha. A small concentration of 18 pieces, including three possible *tegulae* within this scatter, coincided with a small concentration of Romano-British pottery (centred SU 57376512), c. 100 m from the course of the Roman Road from *Calleva Atrebatum* (Silchester) to *Corinium* (Cirencester). Fieldwalking, in 1977–78, recovered a relatively dense scatter of Romano-British pottery converging on SU 579655, to the north-east, possibly associated with a cropmark complex (Gates 1975, map 1).

To the north of the Kennet on the London Clay, a small, dispersed scatter of six fragments of tile, includ-ing two flue tiles and one *tegula,* were collected from Colthrop Manor (15/16) from around a small, dense scatter of Romano-British pottery (centred SU 53706731). This small scatter lies just above a break of slope on the London Clay of the valley side.

It should be noted, of course, that these fragments of tile have not necessarily been recovered from their original locations; building material from Romano-British buildings was frequently reused in later periods. For example, bricks and hypocaust tiles were said to have been built into the church at Brimpton (Peake 1931, 100). Possible sources of the material can be found at Aldermaston Wharf, to the north of the River Kennet, just outside the transect area (Cowell *et al.* 1978), and at Silchester (SU 640625) on the plateau gravels to the south. While Romano-British tile does occur in association with pottery of the same period, in most cases, the density of finds is rarely high enough to indicate settlement activity, although evidence from Wasing Lower Farm might suggest some activity associated with a cropmark complex, and the small concentration at Colthrop, might represent an isolated building. In eight of the nine fields, medieval pottery also occurs, perhaps suggesting that some, at least, of the Romano-British material reached the fields as part of manuring practices in later periods.

Tile of Fabric A is widespread over the area of the transect (Mf. 18); however, the distribution is by no means even, and several distinct concentrations can be observed. Comparatively little material was found on the plateau overlooking the valley, although there are a few small concentrations on the Bagshot Beds around the edge of the plateau gravels to the north of the River Kennet. The distribution on the London Clay of the valley sides is slightly denser, though the fields with the highest concentrations of tile tend to be near the bottom of the valley sides, near the interface with the gravels of the valley floor. One scatter of exceptionally high density was recorded at Manor Ash Moats (8), where a large amount of tile was collected within a medieval moated site (SU 54506525). The distribution showed a sharp fall off in density beyond the mound in the centre of the moat, although a relatively high density of tile was recorded in the field immediately to the east (7). On the valley floor, there are relatively high densities of Fabric A in fields on the river gravels along the Kennet and Enborne rivers, and also on the alluvium at the eastern end of the transect.

The clusters of tile of Fabric A rarely appear to coincide with clusters of medieval pottery, although it must be remembered that the distribution of medieval pottery within the transect is sparse in comparison with that of the tile and few clusters were recorded. Where clusters of medieval pottery do occur, for example at Colthrop (15/16) and Aldermaston Bridge/Basingstoke Road (40/41), tile of Fabric A also occurs in the same fields, though not necessarily in any great density; the highest densities of tile do not coincide with the highest densities of pottery. This is particularly noticeable in the case of Manor Ash Moats (8), where only one sherd of medieval pottery was recovered from the field containing the moated site, and one further sherd from the

Table 18 1982–87 Surveys, transect: Romano-British tile occurrences

Field No	Field name	NGR	Geol.	No. frags	Description / comment
15	Colthrop	53806710	LC	6	includes 2 flue tiles and 1 *tegula*. Dispersed
27	Boot Farm	56406398	LC	1	*tegula*
29	Lea Cottage	56406460	RG	1	flue tile
32	Mill Field	56656595	All.	1	flue tile
33	Wasing Lower Farm	57406510	RG	34	includes *tegula*, flue tiles and 1 imbrex. 2 clusters
37	Breaches Gully	58356425	BB	2	1 piece flue tile
40	Fronds Farm	59306655	All.	1	*tegula*
41	Basingstoke Road	59656645	All.	1	*tegula*

field to the east (7). Both sherds fell outside the main concentrations of tile; equally only three sherds of post-medieval pottery were found in this area.

The possibility must be considered that not all tile identified as Fabric A is of medieval date. A few of the clusters of tile appear to coincide with high densities of post-medieval pottery and tile. This can be observed, for example at Manor Ash Moats (7), where the high density cluster of tile of Fabric A across the earthwork coincides with a similar cluster of other tile, generally assumed to be of post-medieval date. It is possible that some of the tile broadly classified as post-medieval may in fact be earlier in date and it is noticeable that at Manor Ash Moats, only three sherds of post-medieval pottery were recovered.

Post-medieval

Post-medieval tile is ubiquitous within the transect and was found in every field walked. Twenty-eight fields, or groups of adjacent fields, contained densities of tile which were greater than the mean weight for the whole transect (Mf. 19), although only 16 of these contained high density clusters. A high density cluster was also defined in one field (26) which had an overall weight lower than the mean for the transect.

The denser clusters are found on all soil types, on valley floor, valley sides, and plateau overlooking the valley, though there appears to be a concentration on the south-facing slopes at the eastern end of the transect. Nine of the 15 scatters identified fall in this area, and this includes three of the five densest scatters. While topographical factors may account for this distribution, other variables should also be considered. All of the 11 fields walked by one particular team (1986) produced dense scatters of post-medieval tile and this included four of the five densest scatters recorded (*see* also burnt flint, above). It is noticeable that other fields walked on the south-facing slopes by other teams, even those adjacent to fields walked in 1986, have not produced similar densities of post-medieval tile.

Small, localised concentrations of post-medieval material, which apparently marked the sites of demol-

ished buildings or backfilled quarries, were generally noted in the field, but were not always collected. Most of the fields show a general higher density distribution with small concentrations. Several of the smaller nucleated concentrations correspond to the site of buildings now demolished, some of which are marked on Rocque's map of 1761; others mark the course of abandoned trackways and roads. At Manor Ash Moats (8), an exceptionally high density (mean weight 3129 g) of post-medieval tile was collected over the area of the mound in the centre of the moated site, coinciding with a similar scatter of tile of Fabric A (*see* above). The high density and localised nature of the scatter would indicate the site of a substantial building; this is confirmed by documentary evidence which suggests that there was a manor house within the moat in the 14th century which was probably demolished by the mid 16th century.

Most of the tile concentrations are matched by higher densities of post-medieval pottery but the converse is not always true. The distribution indicates clustering around farms and buildings which date back to at least the middle of the 18th century and most likely results from manuring the fields rather than settlement.

Non-local and worked stone

Fieldwalkers were encouraged to collect all fragments of stone deemed to be worked or not local to the region and a small number of fragments were recovered. Of the 19 pieces of worked stone collected, nine were whetstones (fragmentary and complete) made of sandstone; four were thought to be building materials of greensand, greenstone or limestone; three were quern fragments of lava stone and Pennant sandstone; the remaining pieces were of unknown function but showed signs of working. The unworked fragments include ironstone, limestone, and old red sandstone and probably mostly derive from road metalling or land fill. Most of the worked pieces are undiagnostic types and are intrinsically undated. Because of the small number of pieces their distribution shows no particular pattern. Associations with medieval and post-medieval pottery is common, but whetstones

Table 19 1982–87 Survey, Burghfield area: flint clusters

Field No	Field name	NGR	Quantity	Area (ha)	Density per ha	Geol.	Topog.	% Blades	Tools	Cores
Earlier prehistoric										
	Field Farm	670705	17	1	17	G	terrace	2	–	–
Later prehistoric										
19	Field Farm	674706	13	1	13	G	terrace	–	2	2
20	Pingewood (3.5)	695695	24	0.68	35.4	G	terrace	–	1	–

NB. This field was totally collected. For rough comparison the density has been divided by 10.

at Kiff Green (50), Burghfield Road (92), Mill Field (32) in the Kennet Valley, and at Wasing Lower Farm (33) in the Enborne valley are associated with higher densities of Romano-British pottery. Fragments of lava stone at Woodcock (61) and Fronds Farm (40) north of the Kennet, show similar broad associations but a fragment from Brimpton Manor Farm (31) came from an area with very few surface finds, although a cropmark enclosure has been identified.

The Burghfield Area

Flint, *by P.A. Harding*
Five hundred and forty-three pieces of worked flint were recovered from the 156 ha examined in the Burghfield area (Figs. Mf. 20–23), producing an approximate average of 3.5 pieces per hectare. The actual density recorded may be less than this because the collection at Pingewood and Smallmead included areas of total collection (Table 19). Flint artefacts were found in only 15% of the 2208 collection units; 81% of these contained only one piece while 15% contained two. There was a diffuse spread of material over the whole area, with a decrease in density in areas off the river gravels on the London Clay (about half the area collected was on the London Clay and produced 34% of the flint artefacts). Little significant clustering was evident but three small groups were identified, all on the river gravels.

Palaeolithic
One flake found at Green Farm (94) may be of palaeolithic date (Mf. 20). This flake has an ochreous staining and is made from light grey flint with cherty inclusions. It is in a sharp, slightly rolled condition. The edges are chipped and one edge is missing. The ridges between the flake facets have also been pitted by battering. The flake measures 122 x 114 x 32 mm. It has a maximum width midway along its length and terminates in a hinge fracture at the distal end. The flake scars on the dorsal surface indicate that it was removed from a prepared core. Flakes, some of which terminate in hinge fractures, were removed from both edges to prepare a domed surface but it is uncertain whether this included flaking from the distal end. All cortex has been removed. The butt shows that the flaking angle was prepared by faceting before the flake was detached by hard hammer percussion. The axis of percussion is parallel to the long axis of the flake. Flakes of this type are typical of those

classified by Bordes as sub-circular Levallois flakes (1961, 31, pl. 3, 1 and 2).

Earlier prehistoric
Only a small amount of blade material was present (Mf. 20). The five blade cores, three of which came from the London Clay at the edge of the river gravel, were apparently unassociated with any particular clusters (Mf. 21). A distinctive cluster of 17 pieces was identified within hectare SU 670705, at the edge of the river gravel and alluvium at Field Farm (98). This group was in superb condition, with a light brown staining and included: three blades; a crested flake, which was probably removed from a multi-platform core during rejuvenation, and a flake with a faceted butt from a core with opposed platforms. Tools include: a small broken core tool and an end scraper which give no clue to the date of the cluster (Mf. 22).

Later prehistoric
Most of the flint from this area indicates a flake industry. A small cluster was defined within hectare SU 674706 at Field Farm (99), where a slightly higher density of flint was identified, including several retouched pieces and cores, but the group lacks any clear definition. The 13 pieces in this group were undiagnostic and include a broken, bifacially worked tool and a scraper.

A small concentration of flint was identified in the total collection at Pingewood (101b). The flint contains no diagnostic material, although the use of platform abrasion on two flakes suggests that some of the flint in the area may be of earlier prehistoric date.

Of the few tools found (Mf. 22), only one is diagnostic. This is a fragment of a ground flint axe found at SU 67437008, Field Farm (99) close to a discoidal tool with bifacial working of unknown form, but apparently not associated with any clustering of other flints. A fabricator made on a blade had been found in this area during previous fieldwalking. The relatively large number of tools and retouched pieces, particularly at Field Farm and on the clays to the south, are noteworthy and may attach some significance to this area. The cores show a similar distribution to the tools (Mf. 21) and suggest a broad distribution of activity on the river gravels and along the edges of the terrace on the clays.

Discussion
If the identification of the flake from Green Farm (94) as a Levallois flake is correct, and there is no reason to

Table 20 1982–87 Surveys: Burghfield area, burnt flint concentrations

Field No.	Field name	NGR centred	Area (ha)	Geol.	Mean wt/(g) 25 m	S.D.	Distance water m	Comment Archaeology
94	Green Farm	6670690	1	LC	129	219	250	RB + med. pot clusters in same field but different location
96	Amners Farm	67706925	2.2	RG	161	242	100	Corresponds with cropmark enclosures
98	Field Farm II	67107058	1.9	RG	228	397	20	Corresponds to early prehist. flint cluster
99	Field Farm 3	67557060	8.25	RG	228	397	50–100	Possibly two foci corresponding with cropmark enclosures (RB + post-med.); flint cluster + prehist. pot occurrence. Post-med tile clusters
101/	Pingewood (25 m)	69606970	3.9	RG	130	148	25	Small clusters along edge of old river channel
102	Smallmead	70106980	0.25	RG	164	268	25	As above

doubt it, the derivation of the object may be of some interest, although as a surface find its significance remains uncertain. The find came from the London Clay, above the level of the river gravel terrace, and at the base of the slope of the valley side below the gravel terrace marked on the Drift Geology map as plateau gravels. The sequence of terraces is not as clearly defined as those of the Thames Valley further east. The plateau gravels around Burghfield are generally thought to be Late Anglian (470,000 BP) Silchester Gravels (Gibbard 1985). Flakes of Levallois technique are found from the Lynch Hill Gravels (250,000 BP) but are unknown before this date. In this area there is no clearly defined terrace between the river gravels of Devensian age (Cheetham 1975) and the plateau gravels. However, Wymer (Wessex Archaeology 1993) argues against confining all valley gravels to a Devensian age, suggesting that earlier gravels may also be represented.

At present this flake must be regarded as a surface find which may have moved downslope through solifluction from the surface of the plateau gravels, or be a product of a remnant gravel terrace in the vicinity.

The two earlier flint clusters were found on the floodplain terrace at the edge of the floodplain, not far from the Clayhill Brook, although the few blade cores found on the London Clay suggests some expansion off the gravel terrace. The distribution of the flake material, including the cores and tools, indicates continued exploitation of the floodplain terrace, with some expansion onto the edge of the heavier soils of the London Clay.

Other Finds, by Lorraine Mepham

Burnt flint
Burnt flint was ubiquitous throughout the areas examined. Six clusters were noted in the Burghfield area, all on the river gravels (Mf. 23, Table 20). These range in size from 0.5–8 ha, although the largest may be separated into two clusters of 3 and 5 hectares. At Field Farm (99), a large high density scatter was recovered along the edge of the river gravel terrace centred on SU 675706. Cropmark enclosures, one possibly of Iron Age date, the other probably post-medieval (Richards in Butterworth and Lobb 1992), have been recorded in this area; a low density flint cluster was also identified in the western part of the burnt flint concentration. A smaller cluster, covering about 1 ha, was noted on the edge of the alluvium, 100 m to the west of this (98) in an area where a flint cluster of earlier prehistoric date was identified. At Amners Farm (96), the cluster covers an area of about two hectares and corresponds almost exactly with cropmark features (Gates 1975, map 11). One of these, at Smallmead (102), was dated by subsequent excavation to the Late Bronze Age period (Dawson and Lobb 1986) and is situated, together with the other clusters in the adjacent area (101), next to an old water course; further excavation at this site has identified extensive later Bronze Age settlement.

In contrast, the excavated cropmark site at Field Farm (99) produced very low densities of burnt flint, although a large, high density scatter was recovered to the north-west within the same field.

Table 21 1982–87 Surveys: Burghfield area, pottery clusters and scatters

Field No.	Field name	NGR	No. sherds (ha)	Area	Topog.	Geol.	Type
Prehistoric							
99	Field Farm	67437055	3	>1	terrace	RG	cluster (Collared Urn)
100	Pingewood	69806930	15	1	terrace	RG	scatter
(includes 1 sherd of Collared Urn)							
101	Pingewood	69756950	4	2	terrace	RG	scatter
102	Smallmead	70006995	25	10	terrace	RG	scatter
Romano-British							
94	Green Farm	66636945	12	0.5	valley side	LC	cluster
100	Pingewood	69836932	26	1	terrace	RG	cluster
101	Pingewood	69806955	12	2	terrace	RG	scatter
102	Smallmead	69806980	7	2	terrace	RG	scatter
Medieval							
92	Burghfield Rd	66706870	12	3	valley side	LC	scatter
94	Green Farm	66606940	14	4	valley side	LC	scatter
101	Pingewood	69546985	50	1	terrace	RG	cluster
101	Pingewood	69806955	12	3	terrace	RG	scatter
Post-medieval							
92	Burghfield Rd	68256875	71	4.5	valley side	LC	scatter
101	Pingewood	69656985	35	3.5	terrace	RG	scatter
101	Pingewood	69556985	274	1	terrace	RG	cluster

Pottery

A total of 1240 sherds (16,258 g) was collected in the Burghfield area from the 2208 25 m collection units, 15 from 10 m collection units, and 6 from total collection units. Thirty-five of the 48 fabric types identified for the Kennet Valley assemblage as a whole were present, ranging in date from Early–Middle Bronze Age to post-medieval.

Prehistoric

All the prehistoric pottery collected was identified as Bronze Age and can be paralleled in the Late Bronze Age assemblages from Aldermaston and Knight's Farm (Bradley *et al.* 1980) in the Kennet Valley. One sherd from Field Farm (99) is comparable to a Collared Urn fabric in the excavated assemblage from the same field (Mepham in Butterworth and Lobb 1992).

The distribution of prehistoric pottery is very sparse and consists mainly of single sherds scattered widely over the area walked (Mf. 24, Table 21), although only three of the 56 sherds collected were from fields on the London Clay. Only one apparent cluster was recorded where 44 sherds are dispersed over an area of approximately 35 ha around Smallmead Farm (102) and Pingewood (100/101), with no apparent concentration within this area. All the pottery from this cluster was of Late Bronze Age date, apart from one possible sherd of Collared Urn, and consist almost entirely of sherds in flint-tempered fabrics (F1, F2). Subsequent excavation in this area has revealed evidence of Late Bronze Age activity (Dawson and Lobb 1986; Moore and Jennings 1992).

In contrast, the area around Field Farm and Knights Farm, where excavation has indicated fairly extensive occupation on the river gravels in the Bronze Age (Butterworth and Lobb 1992; Bradley *et al.* 1980), produced only five sherds (18 g) of Bronze Age date, none from areas where prehistoric features have been excavated.

Romano-British

The Romano-British pottery comprises 14 fabric types, of which only three can be ascribed to known sources, although at least one of the sandy wares (Q122) might have originated from the Alice Holt kilns (cf. Lyne and Jefferies 1979, Fabrics B/C). Two of the sandy fabrics (Q122, Q123) are paralleled in the excavated assemblage from Pingewood (Mills 1991–3, Fabrics 2a/2b, and 2c respectively), though they do not occur at the latter site in any diagnostic forms. For example, Fabric Q122

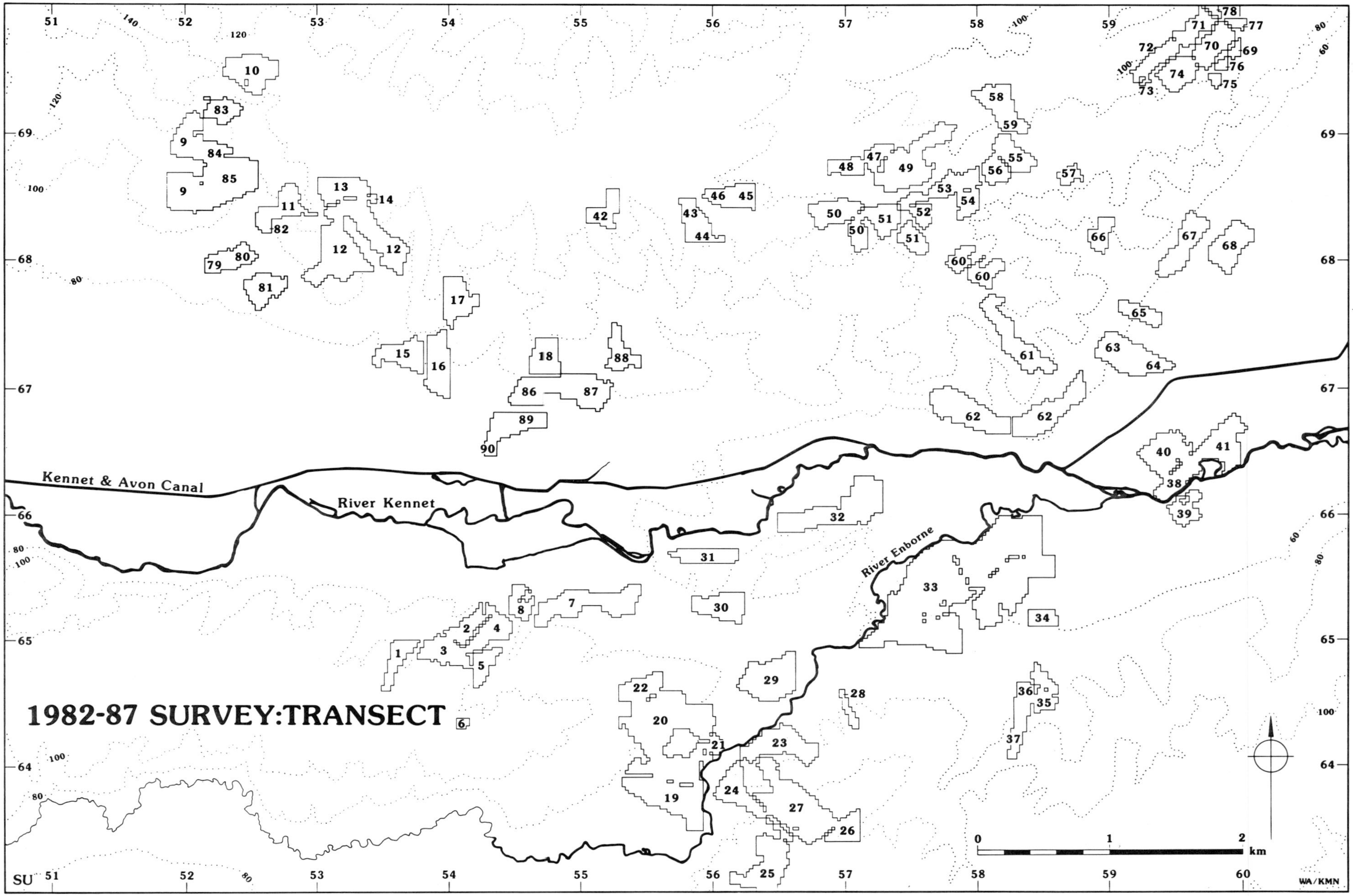

Figure 7 1982–87 Surveys: Burghfield area — location of fields walked

Table 22 Burghfield area: pottery by geology through time

	Area (ha)	Prehistoric	Romano-British	Medieval	Post-medieval
Gravel	78.1	36 (0.46)	15 (0.19)	15 (0.19)	202 (2.59)
London Clay	67.0	3 (0.04)	20 (0.30)	40 (0.60)	349 (5.21)
Total	145.1	39	35	55	551

occurs in flanged bowl forms, datable to the 3rd–4th century AD, as does Fabric Q124. A fabric very similar to Q125 was found in 1st century AD vessel forms at Anslows Cottages (Mepham in Butterworth and Lobb 1992, Fabric S7). All three of the grog-tempered fabrics are paralleled at Pingewood (Hawkes 1986; Mills in Lobb and Mills 1991–93, Fabrics 7, 6a, 5 respectively), and two (G140, G141) also at Thames Valley Park (Mepham in Barnes *et al.* forthcoming. (d), Fabrics C4, C9 respectively) where they are found in mid to late 1st century AD vessel forms. Grog-tempered fabrics are also known at Silchester in 1st century AD contexts (Timby 1985).

The distribution of Romano-British pottery is again very sparse (Mf. 25, Table 22). Only two clusters can be discerned. The first covers a very small area at Green Farm (94), where 13 sherds (104 g) were recovered from an area of less than one hectare. All the sherds are in coarse sandy, unoxidised fabrics of unknown source; the only diagnostic sherd being the rim of a flanged bowl, a type common in 3rd–4th century AD contexts.

The second cluster occurs again around Smallmead Farm (102) and Pingewood (100 and 101), in the same general area as the scatter of prehistoric pottery (*see* above). A total of 54 sherds (990 g) was collected from an area of about 25 ha, with an apparent concentration towards the south (centred SU 698694) where the crop-marks indicate ditched enclosures and a trackway, subsequently dated by excavation to the early Romano-British period (Lobb and Mills 1991); the distribution may be biased by the different methods of collection employed in this area. The majority of the pottery consists of sherds in coarse, unoxidised, sandy fabrics, but there are also sherds of 1st–2nd century grog and flint-tempered fabrics, the latter including Silchester Ware. Fine wares are represented by a few sherds of samian and Oxford Ware. The assemblage thus seems to include both early and late Romano-British material. Subsequent excavation in this area produced evidence of early Romano-British activity in the area immediately to the north of the main cluster of pottery (Dawson and Lobb 1986); again, the pottery shows no tendency to concentrate in areas where Romano-British features were excavated.

Medieval

Only one of the nine medieval fabric types (E450) has a positively identifiable source, being characteristic of Surrey/Hampshire border wares. One fabric, tempered with inclusions of schist (R420), is probably a continental import. With one exception (Q400), all the sandy fabrics are paralleled locally in the assemblages from Meales Farm, Sulhamstead, and Pingewood,

although only one (Q401) is paralleled directly at Reading. On the whole, the Burghfield assemblage shows little similarity with the medieval assemblage from Reading; the fabrics are generally coarser and there are fewer glazed and decorated sherds. The assemblage appears to have closer affinities with pottery from further west in the county, in particular Newbury. Evidence for glaze and/or decoration was found on 14.4% (by weight) of the medieval material. Glaze is confined to the sandy fabrics E450 and Q401; the latter fabric also includes the only decorated sherds: one body sherd with incised decoration, one finger-tipped rim, and two body sherds with white slip decoration.

Medieval pottery was recovered from all but one of the fields walked, although the distribution is generally dispersed (Mf. 26; Table 21). One very dense scatter was recovered during total collection at Pingewood (101), apparently from a small rectangular enclosure visible on the aerial photographs where 50 sherds were collected from an area of just less than one hectare, showing a definite concentration towards the centre of the area. Roque's map (1761) shows a building and associated plot in this area. Both wide spaced walking and total collection showed a fall off in density outside this area, although a dispersed scatter of 12 sherds was identified across the southern end of the field. This cluster included both flint-tempered and fine sandy fabrics, some sherds of the latter from glazed vessels, as well as one sherd of a possible import (Fabric R420), and the only examples of Surrey Ware from the Burghfield area. No closely datable vessel forms were recovered, but the fabric types present suggest a 12th–14th century date.

Elsewhere, the distribution of pottery is fairly dispersed and low density over the whole area (0.38 sherds per hectare). One small, dispersed cluster occurred at Green Farm (94), centred on the same area as a scatter of Romano-British pottery (*see* above). To the south, another small, low density scatter was observed, in a field immediately to the north of the village of Burghfield (92).

Post-medieval

The post-medieval material comprised the bulk of the assemblage. The group was divided into earthenwares and stonewares, the former group being divided broadly into red earthenwares (Q600), pink/buff earthenwares (E640), and white earthenwares, probably originating from the Surrey/Hampshire border (E630). The red earthenwares in particular vary quite considerably in coarseness of inclusions and include both glazed and unglazed wares. The glaze varies from olive green through orange–red to dark purplish–brown and is usually found on the internal surface. Some examples

Table 23 1982–87 Surveys: Burghfield area, Romano-British tile occurrences

Field No.	Field Name	NGR	Geol.	No. frags	Description
92	Burghfield Rd	67006800	LC	8	2 possible *imbrices* and 2 *tegulae*
93	Burghfield Rd	66996916	LC	2	
100	Pingewood	69676947	RG	2	box flue tile and *imbrex*

were decorated with trailed white slip which was then glazed.

The pink/buff earthenwares also include both glazed and unglazed wares; the glaze is often olive-green in colour, though orange–red glazes also occur. The white earthenwares are invariably glazed, usually with either mid to light green or greeny–yellow glaze, though there are a few examples of darker brown–green glazes. One example was decorated with trailed red slip and glazed.

Stonewares were divided into fabrics which were incompletely fused, ie grains still visible to the naked eye (Q601), and fabrics which were completely fused (Q602). The former group is invariably salt-glazed, with mottled glaze in varying shades of brown, and includes at least one sherd probably deriving from a bellarmine jar. Fabrics are buff or buff/grey in colour. The latter group, with buff/white or grey fabrics, include slightly later bottle/jar types. In addition, a few sherds of Westerwald Stoneware were identified (E670).

The distribution of post-medieval pottery (Mf. 27, Table 22) shows a marked increase in density over the preceding periods (79.77 sherds per hectare). Over much of the area, the pottery is distributed relatively evenly, though there are some blank areas. The density of material shows a marked decrease towards the north of the area covered and there are large blank areas in the fields immediately to the south of the Kennet, around Field Farm (99). To the west, the distribution around Smallmead Farm (102) is also sparse.

A high density cluster was identified by total collection at Pingewood (101) and possibly extending to the east, corresponding to a smaller medieval concentration, probably on the site of a building shown on the 18th century map. Small, nucleated clusters can be suggested to the south of this field. In the fields north of Burghfield village, the distribution is more evenly spread with no real clustering, although one apparent concentration can be observed immediately to the north of the village (92), corresponding to old field boundaries marked on the OS map.

Discussion

Only three of the 56 prehistoric sherds collected were from fields on the London Clay, although one other sherd was found right on the edge of the gravel terrace, and could have been subject to down slope movement off the London Clay of the valley side. This dominance of the river gravels is not surprising, given the wealth of archaeological evidence for later Bronze Age activity in this area; in fact, an even greater density of pottery on the gravels might have been expected (*see* Table 22). One fairly dispersed scatter was picked up over the area

around Smallmead Farm (102), where subsequent excavation has revealed evidence for later Bronze Age settlement (Dawson and Lobb 1986; Moore and Jennings 1992), though no obvious clustering was apparent over areas where Late Bronze Age features were excavated. At Pingewood (100), just to the south, the scatter of prehistoric pottery came from the area surrounding a cropmark ring-ditch and linear features; subsequent excavation confirmed a prehistoric date for the ring-ditch and suggested Romano-British activity at the site (Lobb and Mills 1994). However, in the area around Field Farm (99), where excavation has also produced evidence for extensive prehistoric activity (Bradley *et al.* 1980; Bradley and Richards 1980; Lobb 1985; Butterworth and Lobb 1992), prehistoric pottery was notably lacking from the surface material.

A number of factors may be responsible for the lack of pottery, including subsequent agricultural practices, the friable nature of prehistoric pottery, and non-recognition during collection. The relative abundance of pottery around Smallmead Farm (102) may be partly due to disturbance of this area during the post-medieval period; part of the area was used as a sewage works in the 19th century and subsequently landscaped. Patches of the underlying subsoil, brought up by recent ploughing, were observed during collection. Augering showed that the topsoil in this area was not more than 0.3 m deep. In the fields around Field Farm, immediately to the south of the River Kennet, the depth of overburden above the gravel may be much greater, and the relative paucity of post-medieval pottery in this area might indicate less activity in this period likely to disturb earlier material.

In the Romano-British period there is a slight increase in the amount of material on the London Clay of the valley side and this tendency is continued in the medieval period. To a large extent, material from both periods is found in the same general areas. Both of the clusters identified in the Romano-British period coincide with clusters of medieval material, although this is unlikely to indicate continuity between the two periods, merely that the same types of location were being used in both periods. The Romano-British cluster at Smallmead Farm (102) is found to the south-east of the main concentration of medieval material.

No evidence was recovered to support the possible location of Sheffield at Trash Green (91); the field immediately to the north produced only three medieval sherds.

Although the total quantity of post-medieval pottery is fairly evenly divided between the river gravels and the London Clay, the distribution appears generally denser and is more evenly dispersed on the clay of the valley side. If the distribution pattern of post-medieval pottery can be related to the intensity of agriculture during this period, the areas of higher density distribution might indicate areas which have been under cultivation for longer than areas with a lower density of pottery. In the fields to the north of Burghfield village, higher concentrations of post-medieval pottery coincide with apparent concentrations of medieval pottery, suggesting that these areas have been under cultivation, at least since the medieval period, and at least one of these concentrations can be seen to fit quite neatly within field boundaries marked on the OS map.

Tile

Romano-British

Twelve pieces of Romano-British tile were recovered from the Burghfield area (Mf. 25; Table 23). Ten of these occurred in fields on the London Clay of the valley side to the north of Burghfield village (92). They were dispersed over an area of approximately 25 ha, with no apparent concentrations, and unassociated with any scatters of pottery of the same period; in fact, only two sherds were recovered from the same area. The remaining two pieces were recovered from the valley floor (100) and occurred in the same field as a small scatter of Romano-British pottery, although only one piece of tile was found in the same area as the pot scatter.

Fabric A (not plotted) was only positively identified after some of the fields in this area had been examined. Three fields, walked prior to the 1984 season, are thus artificially blank areas in the distribution. Tile of Fabric A is concentrated in fields to the north of Burghfield village, with highest densities immediately adjacent to the village (92). Elsewhere distribution is sparse; relatively low quantities were recorded at Trash Green (91), despite the possible presence of the deserted village of Sheffield in an adjacent field. On the valley floor, tile of Fabric A is noticeably absent, with only one small, low density scatter around Smallmead Farm, though it should be noted that two of the fields walked prior to 1984 fall in this area. This factor might explain the lack of tile in the field to the west of Smallmead Farm where a high density scatter of medieval pottery was recorded.

Evidence for coincidence of medieval pottery and tile of Fabric A is somewhat ambiguous. Medieval pottery is found in the same fields as tile of Fabric A to the north of Burghfield, though again, the highest densities of tile do not necessarily coincide with the highest densities of pottery.

Post-medieval

Post-medieval tile is similarly widespread in the Burghfield area, occurring in every field walked, though again, the distribution is not evenly dispersed (Mf. 28). Densities are highest in the fields on the London Clay of the valley side, especially immediately adjacent to Burghfield village (92); all but one of the fields on this geology have mean weights greater than the mean per 25 m collection unit for this area. Two small clusters were identified near the edges of fields (94 and 95) on the London Clay. Only one other field (96) at the junction of the valley side and the gravel terrace, has a particularly dense distribution, and this is immediately adjacent to Amner's Farm. The other fields on the valley floor all have a relatively low density of tile, although a small cluster is evident at Field Farm (98) where a cropmark enclosure has been dated by excavation to this period (Richards in Butterworth and Lobb 1992). On the gravels at Pingewood (101), a dense cluster within the totally-collected hectare corresponds to clusters of medieval and post-medieval pottery and burnt flint within a cropmark enclosure. The surrounding area also contained a higher density of tile. The distribution of post-medieval tile appears to correspond quite closely to that of post-medieval pottery; relative densities between fields are similar, and immediately to the north of Burghfield village, particularly dense concentrations were noted of both tile and pottery in the same area.

Non-local stone

The seven pieces of worked stone from this area include possible building materials of greensand and limestone, two quern fragments of sarsen and millstone grit, and two whetstones. The unworked pieces include limestone and sandstone fragments from similar locations to the above pieces. All pieces were found in areas where cropmarks have been recorded and where finds of all periods are generally found.

5. Kennet Valley Survey Middle, 1988–89

Extent and Aims of the Survey

With the experience of the earlier surveys a new project was proposed in the survey area. This was intended to be more problem orientated and to examine selected areas which were likely to come under threat in the near future. The *Structure Plan* was intended to cover a period up to March 1996 and the *Minerals Local Plan* up to 1991; both were soon to be reviewed. Areas examined included those which might be suitable for housing development and the area to the west of Newbury which is likely to come under pressure when the Newbury By-Pass has been constructed.

Strategy and Method

Fieldwalking was carried out in six main areas (Fig. 8); two of these (Dunston Park/Park Farm and Kennet-holme) fell within the area of the 1982–87 Transect and the results have been included in that section. The remaining four were on the periphery of the built up area of Newbury.

The methods adopted for surface collection and finds processing were the same as the 1982–87 surveys with the exception that no phosphate survey was carried out. In addition, a pilot auger survey was carried out in the Midgham area (W298, Fig. 8) to test the usefulness of this method in identifying archaeological potential on the floodplain, which is generally unavailable for field-walking.

The finds were all scanned by Julian Richards (flint) and Lorraine Mepham (other finds) and catalogued. A catalogue of all finds can be found in Appendix 9.

Finds Distributions

Flint

A total of 2434 pieces of worked flint was collected from 4341 collection units, although only 1547 (35.5%) produced flints; of these 62.5% produced one piece only. The overall average density was 7.8 artefacts per hectare. The distribution of all flint artefacts is illustrated in Figures Mf. 30 and 31.

The earliest artefact collected is a possible Palaeolithic Levallois type flake from Lower Henwick Farm 6 (137), which is on the valley side on Reading Beds and London Clay and is presumably not *in situ*. Very little blade material (29 pieces) and no diagnostically early tools were collected. The most notable density was 11 pieces with characteristics of blade production (11% of the collected material) at Lower Henwick Farm 1 (131), on the river gravel terrace to the north of the River Kennet, scattered over an area of about 5 ha.

Several clusters of flake material with associated tools were identified: in the Lambourn Valley around Donnington Castle (104–112) and in a dry valley off the Lambourn Valley at Shaw (126, 129 and 130), in the Kennet Valley at Enborne Gate to the south of the river (117–119), and at Lower Henwick Farm (131) to the north of the river. The clusters in the Lambourn Valley have much higher densities than elsewhere in the Middle Survey Area, possibly reflecting the proximity to the Upper Chalk and greater availability of large quantities of good quality flint.

The most notable cluster identified was at Donnington Castle 1 (104), on the river gravel above the floodplain of the Lambourn, where the predominantly

Table 24   1988–89 Survey: flint clusters

Field No.	Field name	NGR	Quantity	Area (ha)	Density per ha	Geol.	Topog.	% Blades	Tools	Cores
104	Donnington Castle 1	452689	198	13.1	15.1	RG	N. slope	2	14	12
106	" 3a	458685	80	4.7	17	RG	N. slope	1.25	4	6
107	" 4	455694	80	5.7	14	RG/C	S. slope	1.25	2	3
108	" 4a	452699	59	3.2	18.43	RG/C	hill top	5	2	–
109	" 5	456697	81	5.7	14.2	RB/PG	hill top	–	2	1
110	" 6	455698	129	6	21.5	RB/PG	hill top	–	–	2
112	" 8	465691	158	6.9	22.9	RB/C	hill top	–	–	6
117	Enborne Gate	451662	190	11.8	16.10	RG/RB	terrace	–	–	–
118	"	450660	42	2.6	16.15	RB	N. slope	–	3	–
126	Shaw 2	483690	72	5.9	12	C	E. slope	–	2	6
129	Mousefield Farm 1	485691	78	6	13	RB	W. slope	1.2	–	–
130	" 2	482687	140	6.5	21.54	C	W. slope	0.7	1	9

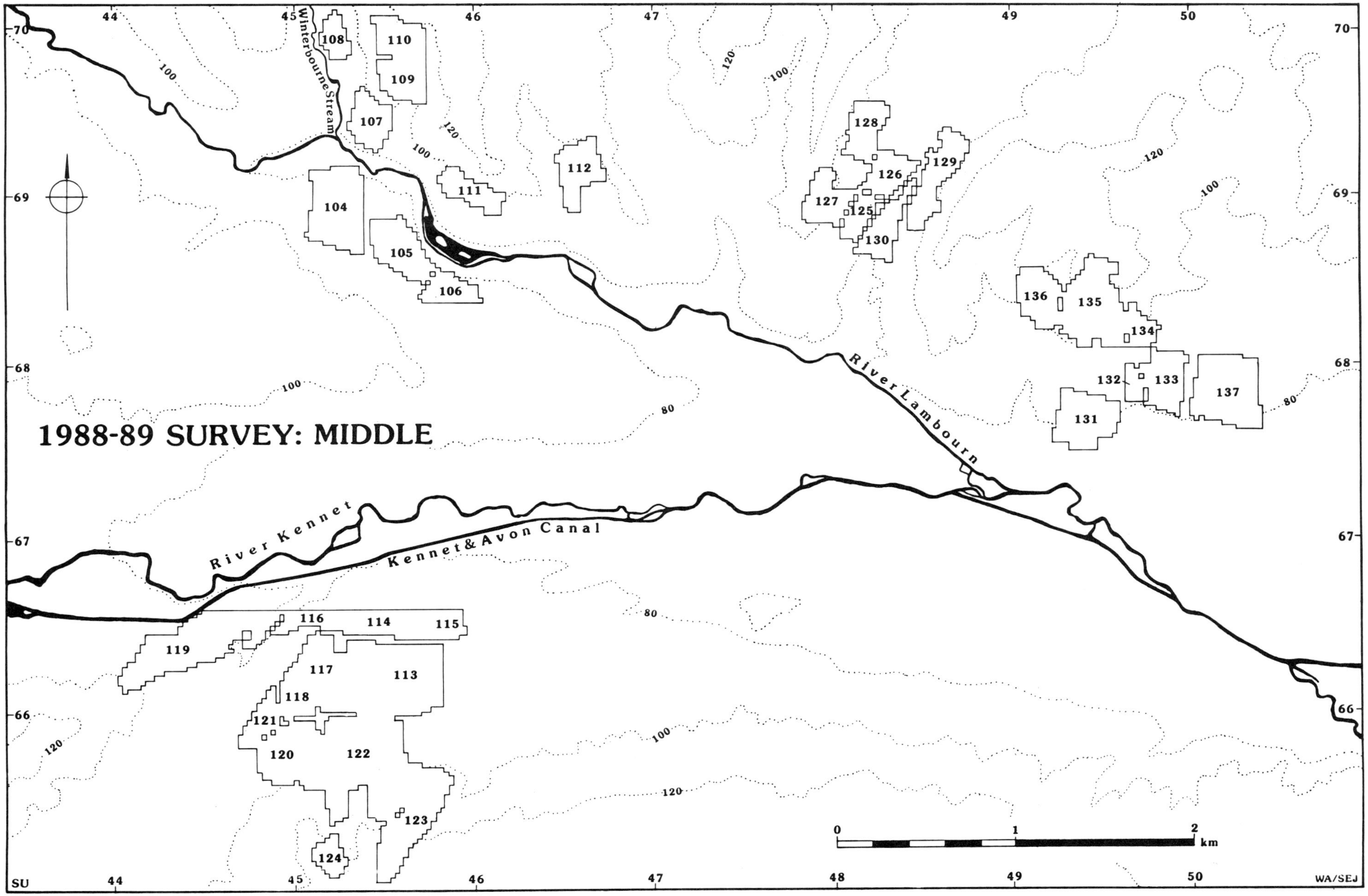

Figure 8 1988-89 Survey Middle: location of fields walked

flake assemblage was associated with a variety of tool types, including 10 scrapers, two piercers, a broken fabricator, and a reworked fragment of a ground flint axe. At Enborne Gate Farm (117/118), the flint tools appear to occur around the southern and eastern edges of the main concentration of flake material and include scrapers, a knife, and a transverse arrowhead. To the west, the cluster (119) contained two knives and a bifacially worked tool. Transverse arrowheads were also found in association with flint clusters at Shaw (126) and at Lower Henwick Farm (131). Several of the clusters did not contain any tools, although retouched material was generally present (Table 24). Core material was notably sparse, perhaps reflecting the more domestic nature of these sites.

Discussion

The distribution of the flint clusters from this survey generally reflects the preferred location for occupation in the earlier prehistoric periods on the river gravel terrace, although lower density expansion onto higher ground is suggested. The Lambourn Valley also appears to have been well settled, perhaps because of the proximity of the chalk and likely flint sources, although none of the clusters indicate flint production on an industrial scale.

Burnt Flint

Burnt flint was present in every field examined (Mf. 32). Eleven fields produced clusters of higher than average densities, although in three cases the clusters spread over adjoining fields (fields 109/110, 114/115, and 117/118/120) (Table 25). Five of the burnt flint clusters correspond to flint clusters and scatters, and one (117) also produced sherds of prehistoric pot; of these five clusters, two were in areas which also produced clusters of post-medieval material. Two of the burnt flint clusters corresponded to post-medieval material only and another cluster had a similar distribution to a medieval pottery scatter and post-medieval tile cluster. Two clusters were in fields which produced no other significant finds distributions. All of these clusters came from lower ground, at the base of slopes on the river gravels, or near the edge of the gravels on Reading Beds. The cluster at Lower Henwick Farm (134) is an exception as it was recorded on a small patch of remnant plateau gravel, 750 m from a water source; there were no other significant finds distributions in this field. The sites at Donnington (109, 110, 111) are all adjacent to, or up to, 100 m from a water source; similarly the cluster at Lower Henwick Farm (131) is 100 m from the river. All the others are much further from a water source. The areas of the scatters are within the range found in the

Table 25 1988–89 Survey: burnt flint concentrations

Field No.	Field name	NGR (centred)	Area (ha)	Geol.	Mean wt/(g) 25 m	Distance to water (m)	Comment
109	Donnington Castle	45606990	10.5	C	120	100	flint cluster
110	Donnington Castle	45656960	0.75	C	187.5	100	flint cluster
111	Donnington Castle a	46156895	0.63	RG	161		adjacent
	b	45856910	0.75				
114	Enborne Gate Farm	45906650	0.5	RG	138	500	medieval pot cluster, tile cluster
115	Enborne Gate Farm	45696600	2.25	RG	208.5	500	
117	Enborne Gate Farm			RG	228.5	400	flint cluster, prehistoric pot sherds, p-med. med. pot sherds tile cluster
118	Enborne Gate Farm	45106610	7	RB	251	400	flint cluster, tile cluster
119	Enborne Gate Farm	44306630	4.12	RG	117.5	200	RB pot, p-med. cluster
120	Enborne Gate Farm	45106590	2.8	RB	115	600	p-med. pot and tile cluster
131	Lower Henwick Farm	49406770	0.5	RG	99	100	flint scatter
134	Lower Henwick Farm	49756820	0.63	PG	143.5	750	

1982–87 survey, with most of them covering less than a hectare (Table 25).

Both correspond to higher than average densities of tile and are in fields adjacent to a farm and to a former track (shown on Rocque's map).

Pottery

Of the 1803 sherds (33,383 g) collected, five sherds are prehistoric, three sherds were Romano-British, 86 are medieval, and 1709 were post medieval. A small number of clusters was identified (Mf. 33–34; Table 26).

Prehistoric and Romano-British
The prehistoric pottery, probably of Late Bronze Age date, was found in fields 117, where a flint cluster was also identified, and 123. The Romano-British sherds came from fields 119 and 135.

Medieval
A cluster of 52 sherds of medieval pottery was recovered in field 114, covering an area of approximately six hectares. This partly corresponds to a cluster of ceramic building material and probably marks the site of a medieval building; a building is shown in this position on Rocque's map of 1761. In field 123, 10 sherds of medieval pottery were recovered from an area of two hectares on the clays of the valley side, but the significance of such a small number of sherds of this period from the field surface cannot be suggested from such a broad-based survey; this find spot is close to the old parish boundary between Enborne and Newbury. The remaining medieval sherds occur in small numbers in each field, mostly in the fields to the west of Newbury.

Post-medieval
Post-medieval pottery was found in every field walked. This was generally a fairly dispersed spread (Mf. 34) and presumably represents distribution by manuring on the fields. Clusters can be identified in fields 113 and 117.

Tile

The ceramic building material recovered comprised largely tile fragments assumed to be post-medieval in date, although some of it is almost certainly medieval. No Romano-British fragments were recognised. Fragments of Fabric A were identified but have not been plotted separately because of the small quantities; details can be found in the archive.

In common with the previous survey, post-medieval tile occurs in every field (Mf. 35). Twenty-three fields of the 34 fields examined contained densities which were greater than the mean weight calculated for the transect of the 1982–87 survey (Mf. 36); some of the clusters identified may be part of larger distributions, covering several fields, for instance fields 113, 114, and 115. The high overall density for this survey may be due to the position of many of the fields examined on the edge of built-up areas. The highest density clusters occur to the west of Newbury around Enborne Gate Farm (113, 114/115, 119, and 124) and at Shaw (128). In fields 114 and 115 the tile cluster corresponds to a cluster of medieval pottery and is on the site of an earlier building which is visible on Roque's map; this cluster, and that in 113, are around the edge of a farm and adjacent to a former trackway. A medieval association is also suggested by the medieval pottery cluster in field 123. The cluster in field 113 corresponds to one cluster of post-medieval pottery. The lower density tile cluster in field 117 also corresponds to a post-medieval pottery cluster. The cluster at Shaw, in field 128, is located interestingly adjacent to a wood named 'Brick Kiln Wood' on 18th century maps and may repay further investigation. The cluster in field 119, which covers an area of at least 7 ha, is adjacent to an old gravel quarry but is not noticeably

Table 26 1988–89 Survey: pottery clusters and scatters

Field No.	Field name	NGR	No. sherds	Area (ha)	Topography	Geol.	Type
Prehistoric							
117	Enborne Gate Farm	45106625	4	3.5	terrace	RG	scatter
Medieval							
114/5	Enborne Gate Farm	45606650	52	6.5	terrace	RG	scatter
123	Enborne Gate Farm	45706560	10	2	slope		scatter
Post-medieval							
113	Enborne Gate Farm	45756620	259	1	terrace	RG	cluster
117	Enborne Gate Fm	45206620	210	5	terrace	RG	scatter

Table 27 1988–89 Survey: post-medieval tile concentrations

Field No.	Field Name	NGR (SU)	Area (ha)	Clustering	Geol.	Mean wt(g) 25 m	Comment
111	Donnington C.	45906910	1	nucleated	RG	87	
112	Donnington C.	46606920	2.5	dispersed	RB/C	87	
113	Enborne Gate Farm	45706620	8	nucleated	RG/RB	181	adjacent to farm buildings and old track
114	Enborne Gate Farm	45606650	5	nucleated	RG	292	" "
115	Enborne Gate Farm	4856650	1.75	unknown	RG	287	" "
116	Enborne Gate Farm	45206655	1.75	nucleated	RG	126	adjacent to dismantled railway line
117	Enborne Gate Farm	45206625	2.75	dispersed	RG/RB	157	corresponds to post-med. and med. pot clusters
118	Enborne Gate Farm	45006605		dispersed	RB	171	
119	Enborne Gate Farm	44706625	7	nucleated	RG	222	adjacent to old quarry
120	Enborne Gate Farm	44906580	1	dispersed	RB	125	
121	Enborne Gate Farm	44806595	?	unknown	RB	132	
122	Enborne Gate Farm	45506560	4	dispersed	LC	91	
123	Enborne Gate Farm	45706560	1.5	dispersed	LC	96	
124	Enborne Gate Farm	45256520	?	unknown	LC	203	
125	Shaw	48106880	2	dispersed	C/RB	93	adjacent to wood named Brick Kiln Wood
126	Shaw	48356910	0.75	dispersed	RB	144	" "
127	Shaw	47906895	1	dispersed	RG	107	" "
128	Shaw	48106930	2	dispersed	RG/RB	222	" "
129	Mousefield Farm	48556910	3	dispersed	RB	155	adjacent to dismantled railway and old quarry
130	Mousefield Farm	48256795	2.75	dispersed	RB	140	" "
133	Lower Henwick Farm	49856790	2.25	dispersed	RB/PG	123	adjacent to farm buildings
135	Lower Henwick Farm	49456840	3.5	dispersed	LC	96	adjacent to Henwick Manor
137	Henwick Lane	50106750	2.75	dispersed	RB/PG	138	outskirts of Thatcham

close to the site of a building. The cluster in field 124 is difficult to interpret as it was found on the edge of the field and may simply represent dumping in a gateway. The other low density scatters in the area are all close to the scatter of houses near Skinners Green and may represent localised dumping of rubbish. The more dispersed scatters around Henwick and at Shaw may be more indicative of manuring on arable fields.

Pilot Auger Survey, by Michael J. Allen

A pilot auger survey was conducted at Midgham with the aim of investigating the potential in, and to develop a methodology for, structured auger survey as a tool for archaeological assessment of the floodplain in the Kennet Valley. Such a survey method was intended to identify and assess old river and stream channels and

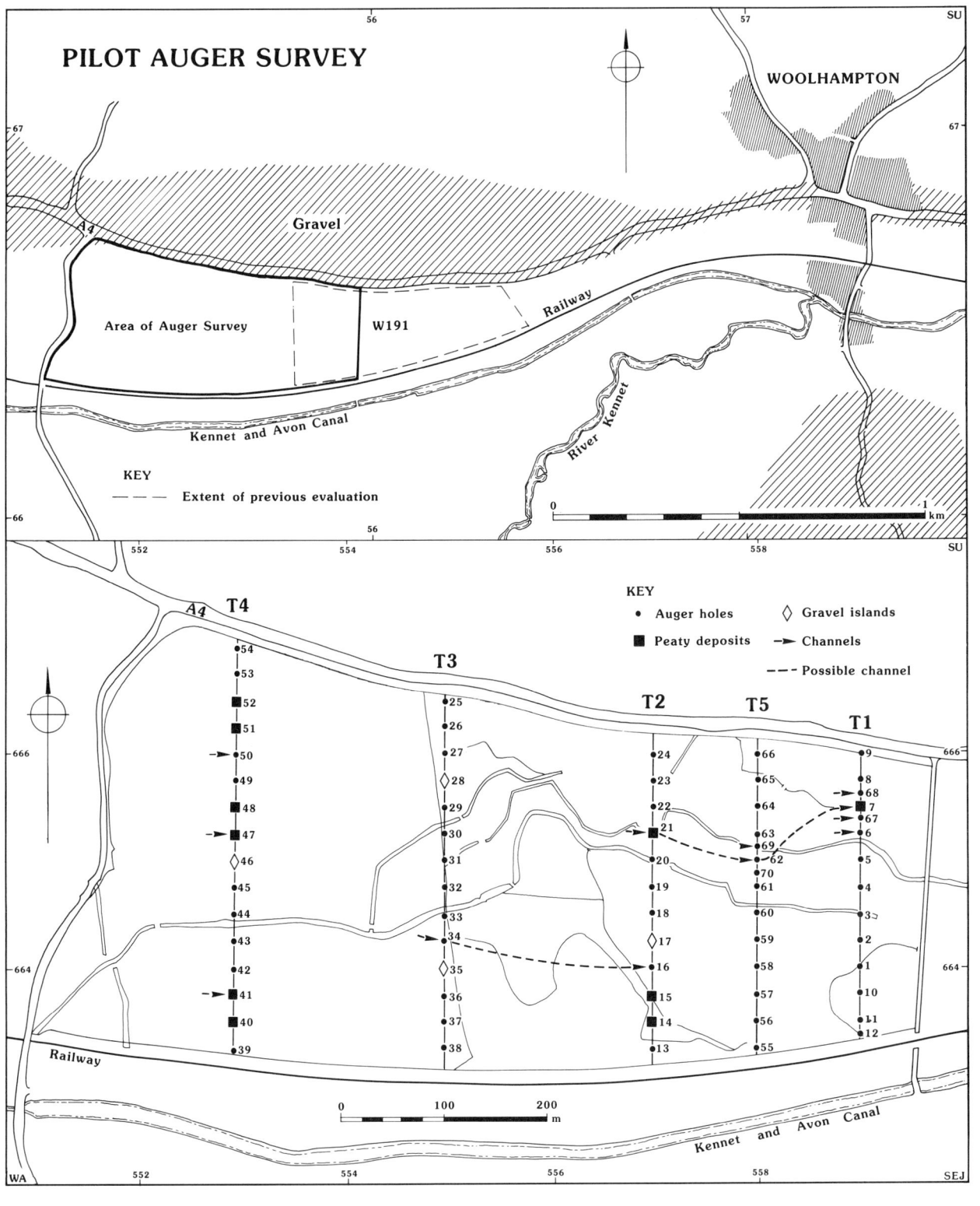

Figure 9   Location of pilot auger survey

alluvial deposits in order to reveal and isolate areas of relict 'islands' which might be expected to have high archaeological potential, specifically for the recovery of settlement activity.

In order to provide a reference for the results of this survey, an area was selected immediately adjacent to one previously evaluated by Wessex Archaeology (W191, Heaton and Lobb 1987, Appendix 10). The area investigated, originally by machine trenching and sub-

sequently by auger survey, lies between the Bath Road, which runs along the edge of the gravel terrace and the Kennet and Avon Canal, to the north of the present course of the river, and to the west of Woolhampton (Figure 9).

The survey area comprised approximately 27 ha on the floodplain of the Kennet, at an average distance of 500 m from the present river channel. The land is lowlying, approximately 3 m below the gravel terrace.

60

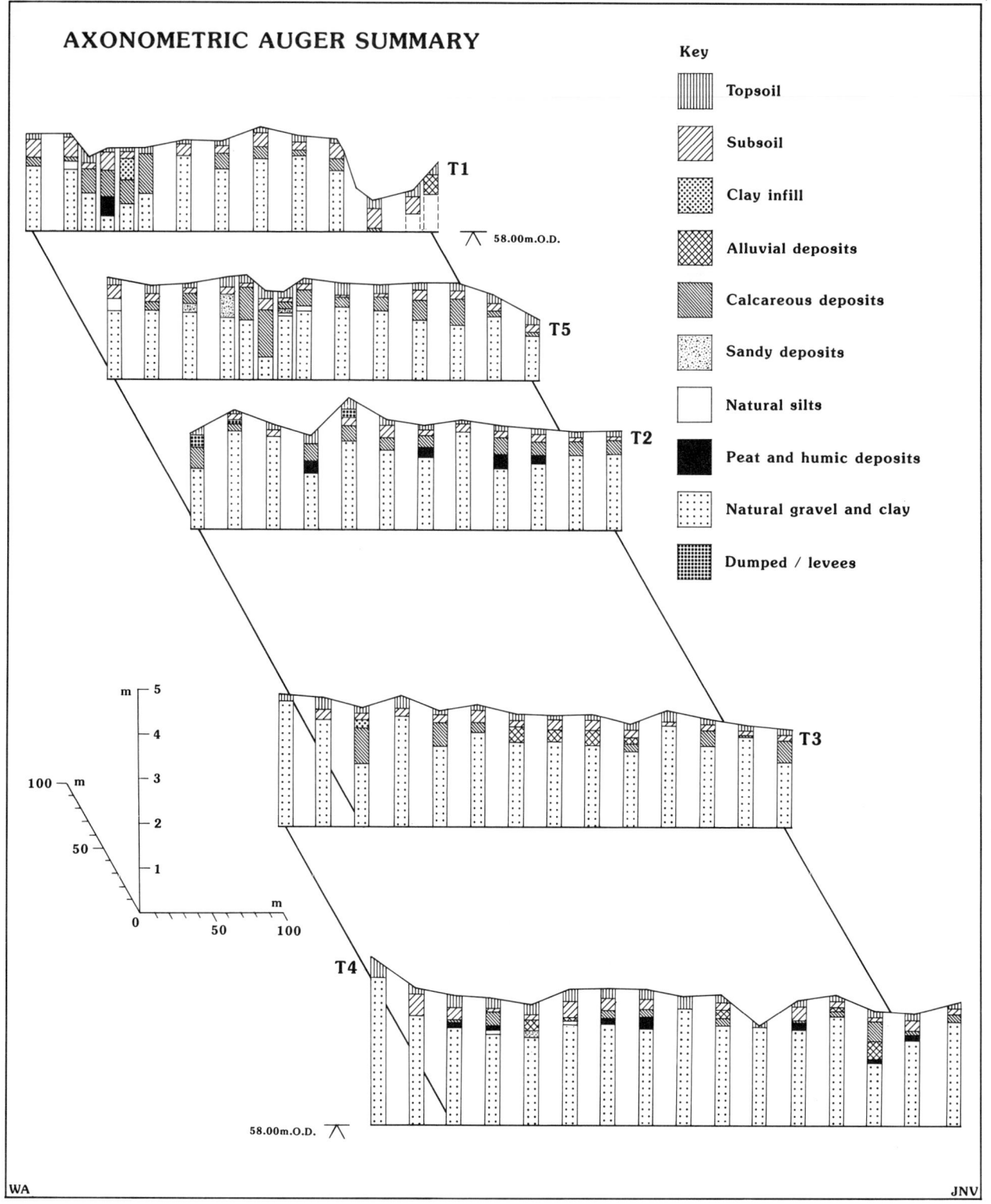

Figure 10   Axonometric auger survey

The surface of the fields undulated slightly and both field drains and the banks of a watermeadow system could be recognised as earthworks. Most of the area was rough pasture, although one field to the west of the area had recently been levelled and ploughed.

Methods
Five auger transects were investigated, all orientated on the National Grid. An auger record was obtained at

25 m intervals along each transect, although where clarification of results was required, the sample spacing was reduced to 12.5 m. The transects to the east of the plot (immediately adjacent to, and overlapping the previously evaluated area) were 100 m apart, and the western transects were 200 m apart. Hand augering was initially carried out using 1 inch (25 mm) diameter screw augers and dutch augers; where deposits exceeded a depth of 1 m, initial screw auger holes were

rebored using a larger, 100–150 mm dutch auger. A total of 70 auger holes in five transects was examined. In each case, soil colour, texture, and description were recorded for each visibly identifiable horizon. Each auger sequence was levelled to Ordnance Datum to provide a vertical correlation of recognised horizons.

Results

A series of palaeo-channels and gravel islands was identified; the augering was not intensive enough to define the extent of the islands but it is likely that they are restricted to less than 175 m diameter. Similarly, although channels were discovered in several places, the identification of individual channels over any distance, and consequently their mapping in plan, proved very difficult.

Augering revealed a number of identifiable horizons which enabled specific landscape interpretations to be made. Full details can be found in the archive and a summary is presented here and in Figure 9.

Fine sands and silts were observed overlying the clays and gravels in the lowerlying areas (probably in channels and depressions in the gravel), consistently associated with later episodes of fluvial sand or peat deposits (Fig. 10). Peat and humic peaty clays were predominantly in deeper auger profiles and probably represent wetter channel margins. In general, the sandy deposits, along with the peats, represent the earliest deposits on the site. Calcareous deposits, including tufa, tufaceous deposits, and calcareous muds, overlay the sands and peats adjacent to, or within channels. The upper levels of the channels were filled with clays and alluvial silts, indicating a reduction in both the volume and speed of water flow. The topsoil over the entire area was found to be fairly uniform, consisting of a brown silty loam, typically only 0.1–0.15 m thick. Moisture content varied according to location and was significantly drier in those areas under arable landuse. A more useful indicator of recent palaeo-environments was the subsoil,

which was predominantly more clay rich in areas previously much wetter than today, and which were possibly subject to occasional inundation.

In almost all cases (96% of auger holes), the natural, unsorted gravels were reached by augering, at depths varying from 0.20–1.75 m. In two cases (Auger Nos 53 and 54) immediately adjacent to the gravel terrace and clay slopes to the north, the natural gravel was overlain by clay deposits interpreted as being of colluvial origin which appear to have been deposited prior to any recognisable phase of anthropogenic activity.

Assessment of the methods

The methods described above have been demonstrated as capable of mapping more substantial palaeo-morphological features, although smaller features, such as minor channels, may not be so easily identified. Likewise, it may not be easy to distinguish between channels and isolated features unless closely spaced holes are augered.

Auger survey is minimally intrusive and labour intensive, although it does allow large areas to be examined relatively quickly, and may therefore be less cost effective than alternative methods of assessment. Machine excavated trenches have the advantage of revealing sections which may be more easily interpreted, but there are disadvantages, particularly within the topography of a floodplain. Extensive trenching is inevitably destructive and disruptive, particularly in wet areas, and excavations adequate for the examination of large features, such as major channels, may be unsafe in such conditions. Augering may be very usefully carried out as part of a multi-phase evaluation strategy to identify suitable areas for trenching, particularly in large, apparently featureless floodplain areas, or as an adjunct to field survey in order to identify quickly the depth of soils and therefore the significance of surface finds.

6. Synthesis

The three surveys were carried out using different approaches and methods and it is useful to compare and summarise the results of the surveys here. The 1982–87 survey transect across the valley re-examined 36 of the fields previously walked by Rose in 1976–77; the 1988–89 survey re-examined four fields. This allows some direct comparison, although the more general inferences drawn from the results of each survey are perhaps more relevant to the general aims of this report.

The use of the 25 m grid, adopted in the 1982–87 and the 1988–89 surveys, implemented recommendations for further work resulting from the earlier survey that a grid system should be adopted and that a larger sample should be examined; in the fields examined in the earlier survey, the collection units were generally spaced roughly 50 m apart, providing between 4% and 5% cover of the surface area, whereas the later survey examined 8%. In simplistic terms, it might be expected that the larger sample would produce proportionally more finds but this was not always the case. The gridded sample did provide more precise mapping of finds distributions, providing a broad context for landuse and settlement and making identification of higher density foci and possible boundaries more easy to interpret. In many cases, the later survey confirmed the potential significance of higher density clusters which had already been suggested by the earlier work and enhanced the distribution information; equally, new clusters were identified in areas previously walked. This highlights the potentially fickle nature of surface collections in this area and urges caution in estimating quantities and total populations. However, even if the method cannot be relied on to provide a total distribution pattern, the more general inferences concerning landuse need not be affected by these restrictions.

Flint provides the major evidence for the earlier prehistoric period. Examination of the quantities of flint collected within the transect and the 1988–89 survey suggests that flint is under-represented in the earlier survey, although with the consistency provided by a single collector, the same broad observations might be expected. The overall figures for the 1976–77 and 1982–87 surveys are broadly comparable. The 1976–77 survey suggested that scatters of densities greater than three per hectare might be significant, representing 'sites', although this figure incorporates material from the whole survey area, including the chalk where higher densities were identified (Rose this volume). Within the transect area where there is no chalk, the average density is more like 1.1 per hectare. For the 1982–87 survey, an average density of 4.25 per hectare (or 3.8 per hectare based on overall area) was calculated for the same area, although the interpretation of potentially significant clusters was not based solely on this factor; technological observations and variety of tool types and retouched pieces were considered equally important in the composition of the cluster assemblages, and identified clusters were not always of high density. For the Kennet Valley Middle Survey (1988–89), the overall average density of flint is 7.8 pieces per hectare. This is higher than in the two earlier surveys. The field team for this survey included more experienced fieldwalkers than had been used in the years of the the 1982–87 survey, which may partly account for this increased density, but it is also possible that the distribution reflects a true pattern. While interpretation at a more detailed and specific level is made easier by the gridded collection adopted by the later surveys, the same general conclusions appear to have been drawn concerning the broader landuse in the earlier prehistoric period.

Comparative material from excavated sites in the area is provided by a number of sites of Mesolithic date but there are no known sites of the Early Neolithic period. The material found from fieldwalking generally lacks diagnostic types to allow more positive dating to specific period or to characterise the nature of the activity. The results of all surveys showed a preferred location for the floodplain and terrace edges of the Kennet and Enborne, particularly the latter. Several of the find spots recognised in the earlier survey were reconfirmed by the later survey and new clusters were identified in areas previously walked, notably at Wasing Lower Farm (33a). In addition, the later survey confirmed the sometimes tentative identification of the earlier survey of flint of this period in areas off the floodplain and suggested that this activity was in fact more widespread; clusters and scatters of blade material were identified mostly on the edge of the plateau gravels, although some exploitation of the valley side is suggested.

In the later prehistoric period, the flint distribution again shows a preference for the floodplain terraces but there appears to have been greater expansion onto the clay soils of the valley side and onto the plateau gravels. The distribution pattern is consequently of a dispersed nature with clusters of small size occurring, sometimes associated with tools and/or cores.

The low density of cores of both periods suggests knapping at a local level according to immediate demand and need. At only one site, Wasing Lower Farm (33, 1982–87 survey), is there any indication of production on a more industrial scale. At this site, 37 cores, predominantly of blade production as well as core fragments and debitage, were found in an area of about 2.5 ha; a large number of blades and flakes (130) was also found in the same area but only nine retouched pieces and recognisable tools, including a tranchet axe. However, recent analysis of use-wear on a sample of the flint assemblage from a Mesolithic site at Thatcham, has suggested that many of the flakes and blades were used as tools (Grace in Healy *et al.* 1992), which may explain this apparent low density.

Very few tools were collected in the earlier surveys but are of a similar range to the later survey, with scrapers predominating; the axe fragment identified in the earlier survey is now thought to be a Y-shaped tool, a type generally assigned to the Late Neolithic period (Richards 1990). While the later surveys did not collect a large number of tools, the distribution of those that were found in the transect and in the Middle Survey area has some interesting implications (Mf. 12 and 31). The ratio of implements to debitage is generally not as high as might be expected from domestic assemblages (Holgate 1988, 50) but the clustering of tools of different type from some sites might suggest occupation areas of later prehistoric date (Holgate 1988, 68; Gardiner 1988). These core areas were identified on the floodplain terrace, often at the junction of the gravels and the heavier soils of the valley side, or in prominent positions on higher ground overlooking the valleys, adjacent to springs or streams.

Despite the excavated evidence for small-scale occupation in the Late Neolithic period from Field Farm (99) in the Burghfield area (Butterworth and Lobb, 1992), this is barely reflected in the surface flint distribution from the field, although a small cluster of flake material was identified (Harding this volume) among a more widespread scatter, and the number of retouched pieces and cores does draw some attention to the area. Only a few tools were identified, including a fragment of a ground flint axe. The excavated flint assemblage, although small in quantity, was of mixed date and the nature of the occupation very low key, so it is not surprising that the surface material does not appear significant. However, this example does emphasise the need for caution in interpreting the settlement pattern from surface scatters in this region.

Comparison with the distribution of blade material (Mf. 3 and 10) suggests that some areas, previously occupied in the earlier prehistoric period, continued to be exploited in the later Neolithic and Early Bronze Age periods, but the foci of occupation in each period appear to have moved largely. The sites at Manor Ash Moats (7, 1982–87 survey) and possibly Speen (3660, 1976–77 survey) may be exceptions to this. At Field Farm (99, 1982–87 survey), an earlier prehistoric cluster was found in the same area as a known Late Neolithic occupation site (Butterworth and Lobb 1992) and a small, later prehistoric cluster, although the nucleus of the settlement appears to have shifted.

With the decline in the use of worked flint in the later Bronze Age period (Bradley *et al.* 1980), the quantities produced, using the example of excavated sites in the area (*ibid*; Harding in Butterworth and Lobb 1992), are considerably less and the range of tool forms more limited. Many of the characteristics of flint assemblages from this period are based on technological aspects and are therefore unlikely to be easily recognised among surface scatters, especially where they are of a mixed nature.

Burnt flint was not collected in the 1976–77 survey, although the presence of higher densities was noted. In the later survey, it was systematically collected and the resulting plots (Mf. 13 and 32) indicate a widespread distribution. Burnt flint clusters, while essentially undated, occur in the same areas as finds clusters of all periods, although predominantly of prehistoric date. Many of the high density clusters identified cover a large area, such as at Boot Farm (26/27, 1982–87 survey), are clearly more extensive than the burnt mounds of Early and Middle Bronze Age date found elsewhere in the country (Barfield and Hodder 1987; 1989; Richards 1978; Buckley 1990). Whatever the source and function

represented by this material, it clearly represents an accumulation over a long period of time, indicating an established activity, presumably carried out by a settled population.

Like the Midlands sites, the burnt flint clusters are often unassociated with other types of finds and less typically, while they do occur fairly close to water sources, they are not necessarily found on the banks of streams, although we know that they do exist in these places, such as at Anslows Cottages in the Burghfield area (Butterworth and Lobb 1992). In the survey area, there appears to be a preferred location for the large clusters on the heavier, less fertile soils of the valley sides and plateau. The smaller clusters occur in all topographic zones, many of them on the alluvium or floodplain terrace, such as in the Burghfield Area, and may be more comparable with the burnt flint concentrations identified on the Berkshire Downs (Richards 1978, 15–16) and in east Berkshire (Ford 1987, 42), and with the burnt mounds of the Midlands and Orkney (Barfield and Hodder 1987a; Hedges 1975; Hodder 1990). The widespread occurrence and dispersed distribution pattern of most of this material suggest that some of it at least is the by-product of occupation, and excavations of prehistoric and Romano-British settlements in the area have indeed produced quantities of burnt flint. Whatever the interpretation of the function of these burnt flint concentrations, they clearly represent human activity, probably of later prehistoric date, and their widespread distribution, particularly the larger concentrations on the heavier soils, suggests some pressure on land resources resulting in expansion onto more marginal land.

Evidence for the later prehistoric, Romano-British, and medieval periods is largely dependent on the recovery of pottery which occurred in relatively low densities in the survey area; similar low densities from surface collections in neighbouring areas has already been noted (Mepham, this volume). It is interesting that the quantities recovered by Rose in the 1976–77 survey were far greater than that collected by the teams of people in the later surveys. Several fields with pottery from the earlier survey were re-examined in the later surveys and consistently less pottery was recovered. In one case, at Henwick Lane where the 1976–77 survey identified a Romano-British pottery cluster covering an area of 100 m^2 (PRN 3682), the 1988–89 survey failed to collect any Romano-British material at all (137). The earlier collection of surface finds may account for the lower quantities in these areas, although it might be expected that further ploughing in the intervening years would have brought more to the surface. However, the density of newly identified scatters is noticeably lower in the later survey. As field and weather conditions were very similar in the two periods of collection, this suggests that the recovery of pottery of all types during the later seasons was being affected by consistently low recognition by the various walkers. Some bias must be expected among teams of walkers of varying degrees of experience. Totals from the 1983–84 season show that, of the six individuals who walked regularly, one picked up more than twice as many sherds of prehistoric, Romano-British, and medieval pottery as any other walker. However, this individual also walked the greatest number of runs. For the 1984–85 season, nearly half the total of prehistoric, Romano-British and medieval pottery was collected by one individual; this is particularly noticeable at Smallmead Farm (102) in the Burghfield area, where this fieldwalker collected 26 of the 37 sherds recovered of medieval or earlier pottery.

A few sherds of Bronze Age pottery were recovered in both surveys but the fabric is fragile in the plough soil and therefore provides an incomplete and inconsistent pattern. The poor survival of prehistoric pottery in the plough soil has been noted elsewhere in the region (Shennan 1985; Ford 1987; Gaffney and Tingle 1989). The prehistoric pottery from the 1982–87 survey, which is thought to be entirely Late Bronze Age in date, can be interpreted as demonstrating a preference for lowlying locations but the evidence of the burnt flint seems to suggest a more widespread distribution. The prehistoric pottery from the earlier survey has largely been included with the Iron Age material because of problems of identification, although re-examination suggests that much of it is probably Late Bronze Age in date. The distribution in all surveys suggests a bias towards the valley floor but the few sherds found elsewhere seem to confirm the pattern suggested by the burnt flint, of expansion onto the higher ground, as well as continued occupation of the lowerlying areas. The quantity of pottery in the Burghfield area (Mf. 24), although less than might be expected in an area of proven extensive occupation in this period, does reflect the general settlement of the region on the valley gravels if not the specific sites. The burnt flint distribution in this area (Mf. 23) is perhaps more indicative of the specific locations. The few sherds off the gravels, again hint at some exploitation of the higher ground.

Evidence for the Iron Age from the fieldwalking is very limited. No pottery of this period was identified in the later surveys. However, this may be because of the problems of identification encountered in the earlier survey (Rose this volume). While at the beginning of the sequence some of the pottery may have been assigned to the Bronze Age and, at the end of the sequence, Late Iron Age sherds may not have been recognised among the coarse Romano-British pottery, no pottery distinctive of the Middle Iron Age period was recovered either. This may be a true reflection of the apparent lack of activity in this period (for a fuller discussion, see the final chapter of this volume) but equally it is clear that, at the beginning and end of the period, there is no distinctive change in the settlement pattern.

The Romano-British period is represented in the surface collections by pottery and tile, although the latter is certainly under represented in the distribution plots because of the difficulties of distinguishing fabrics of different periods; no tile was collected in the 1976–77 survey. Where fields were re-examined, the later survey has generally confirmed the significance of clusters previously identified, as well as identifying new ones, and the results from all surveys (Mf. 7, 15, 25, and 33) provide a complementary distribution plan.

Many of the sherds of pottery found in the surveys were small in size and abraded and may well have reached the fields through manuring; however, the presence of discrete, high density clusters suggests several settlement foci. These are distributed along the banks of the River Enborne and on the edge of the floodplain terrace south of the River Kennet; other clusters are reported off the edge of the floodplain terrace, on the heavier soils of the valley sides, or at the edge of the plateau gravels in prominent positions overlooking the valley. Contemporaneous tile was also found at two of the sites (15 and 33), possibly suggesting the proximity of more substantial buildings than the normal timber constructions known from sites in the area. In the Burghfield Area, a similar pattern was found, with the pottery clustering at the eastern edge of the area surveyed, suggesting settlement in the vicinity; this was subsequently confirmed by excavation (see above).

Using a simplistic model based on energy expenditure in relation to distance from settlement centre, as explored in the Maddle Farm Survey (Gaffney and Tingle 1989, 216), two settlement foci can be suggested within the survey area. The number of high density clusters in a small area near the confluence of the Enborne and Kennet Rivers, adjacent to the Roman Road, points to the location of a settlement focus to the south of the Kennet. The status of this area is perhaps further confirmed by the cluster of tile and the more dispersed spread in the surrounding area at Wasing Lower Farm (33), possibly indicating the centre of the economic territory, although the aerial photographs show very little to confirm this. The presence of the road is clearly an important factor in the situation of this site, allowing easy access to lands beyond the natural barrier provided by the River Enborne. To the north, however, the braided channel system of the River Kennet and its associated wetland may have acted as a territorial boundary. North of the river, the clusters of pottery are smaller in size, more dispersed, and away from the river gravels on more marginal agricultural land. A high density cluster occurs in the area adjacent to the known road side settlement at Thatcham (3682, Mf. 7) approximately 5 km to the west. The tile found at Colthrop Manor may represent a more substantial building but the low density pottery cluster associated with it perhaps indicates a more peripheral funciton. If these two sites do represent core areas then they would appear to be at the edges, rather than at the centre of their respective territories adjacent to the road.

The distribution pattern of the medieval pottery from the surveys is of a very dispersed nature suggesting extensive manuring. The low density of medieval pottery recovered from surface collection is a common phenomenon in the region (east Berkshire (Ford 1987); the Berkshire Downs (Gaffney and Tingle 1989), and is perhaps surprising considering the well known pressure on agricultural land in the early part of the period. However, this may be partly because many of the settlements of this period are buried beneath modern farms and villages which have continued to be used since medieval or earlier times. The medieval settlement pattern will be discussed more fully in the second half of this volume and it is pertinent here to discuss the significance of the distribution of surface finds.

The surveys produced slightly differing distribution patterns. More pottery was found in the 1976–77 survey, resulting in a generally dispersed distribution with a few clusters suggesting probable or possible sites, which may be no more than a single house. The 1982–87 survey in the transect produced very little pottery with no field yielding densities of more than 20 sherds; in the Burghfield Area, a large number of sherds (62) was collected during total collection in one hectare which contained a cropmark enclosure and probably represents the site of a building. The Middle Survey area produced only one significant cluster of pottery (114) at Enborne Gate. If Fabric A tile collected during the 1982–87 survey is assumed to be of medieval date, the resulting distribution pattern (Mf. 18) perhaps provides a more representative picture of landuse in this period.

The resulting distributions suggest continued widespread use of the floodplain and floodplain terrace for agriculture, with some expansion onto the heathland areas of the plateau gravels. The concentrations of finds perhaps indicate occasional isolated settlements (?farmsteads or single buildings) on the edge of the gravel terrace overlooking the floodplain, or occasionally on the floodplain, as at Banks Farm (3699, Mf. 8) and Woolhampton where a mill is suggested by the field name (3578, Mf. 8, 25 and 16).

Applying a simplistic and generalised regression analysis, the clustering of tile and, to a certain extent pottery, reflects several core areas. The influence of the villages of Aldermaston, Brimpton, and Woolhampton is perhaps reflected by the higher densities, assumed to be manuring scatters, on the open fields surrounding these settlements, and other smaller focal sites are suggested at Jacob's Green, Enborne, Banks Farm, and Manor Ash Moats, south of the river in Thatcham parish, and Colthrop Manor, and north of the river in the parishes of Thatcham and Padworth. The concentration of finds to the north of Woolhampton (51, 52, 60 and 61; Mf. 16) draws attention to this area which appears on the modern map as only a few isolated houses. However, Roque's map of 1761 shows a row of several houses alongside the road suggesting a sizeable hamlet and the pottery from this area perhaps indicates a medieval origin for the settlement. The siting of a settlement on the clay is atypical in the area and closer examination of Roque's map indicates that it is situated at the junction of the boundaries of the parishes of Beenham, Bucklebury, and Woolhampton. The Woolhampton boundary kinks away from the logical line in this area to include a piece of ground which protrudes into Bucklebury parish and it is possible that the location of this hamlet, and the use of the surrounding fields, may reflect some territorial tension in this area in the medieval period. Similar assertive behaviour may be indicated at Manor Ash Moats where clusters of Fabric A tile were on both sides of the parish boundary (7 and 8; Mf. 18), and at Wasing Lower Farm (33; Mf. 18) the parish boundary passes through the centre of the more dispersed cluster of Fabric A tile. The tile cluster at Fronds Farm (40 and 41; Mf. 18) is similarly situated at the edge of Aldermaston parish.

As with the medieval period, the pattern of post-medieval surface finds is necessarily limited as most of the settlements of the period are still standing. Far greater quantities of finds from this period were recovered and the distribution of both pottery and tile is widespread. The number of known settlements increased and correspondingly more land appears to have been taken into cultivation, with greater exploitation of the clay soils of the valley side and the marginal land at the edge of the plateau gravel than is evident in the medieval period. Tile of this period was found in every field walked and pottery in most, indicating continued cultivation of areas in all topographic zones. Apart from the higher densities of tile around settlements, the distribution is generally fairly evenly spread across the fields which suggests greater mobility and efficiency in muck spreading. In one or two areas where the distribution is more sparse, it is likely that they were only recently taken into cultivation. The pottery of this period is more irregular in occurrence and the greatest densities occur close to known hamlets and farmsteads, some of which appear to have been previously occupied in the medieval period, indicating some continuity of occupation; in other cases, where settlements are known to have continued in use and functioned in the same way, the post-medieval evidence is lacking.

7. Evaluations Within the Survey Area

For the purposes of this report and consistency the term 'evaluation' has been used throughout to describe the site investigations carried out as part of the planning process, to provide archaeological information, and to allow a full assessment of the implications of planning applications. As a result of policy EN26 in the *Berkshire Replacement Structure Plan* (Berkshire County Council 1989), 32 archaeological evaluations were carried out within the project area between 1985 and the end of 1989 (Fig. 11, Appendix 10). Seven of these were undertaken by other organisations and have been listed but not summarised in Appendix 10. Several evaluations were also carried out in Reading town centre but these have not been included in this assessment as they are discussed elsewhere (Hawkes and Fasham forthcoming). Since the end of 1989 further evaluations have been carried out in the survey area but have not been included in this discussion.

Many of the evaluations were on the floodplain or floodplain terrace, most often in areas where alluvium and peat occurs. A small number were on the valley side and the plateau gravels. In most cases, there was little or no known archaeological information within the evaluation sites but evidence from surrounding areas suggested the archaeological potential. As most of the evaluation sites (18) were on floodplain zones, which have traditionally been watermeadow or pasture areas, or on plateau gravels and clays which are largely uncultivated, they were generally not available for fieldwalking and indeed fieldwalking is of little use in areas of deep alluvial deposits. For similar reasons, these sites would not have been susceptible to the development of cropmarks. These investigations have, therefore, provided useful and haphazard opportunities to examine sites within the survey area which may not otherwise have been considered for archaeological investigation; they offer information which is complementary and supplementary to that gathered by surface collection and excavation.

The brief of most of the evaluations was decided by the County Archaeologist and was necessarily broad, especially for sites of archaeological potential where little or no evidence exists, the aims being to establish the presence or absence of archaeological deposits and, in the latter case, to identify their date, nature, extent, and state of preservation.

The areas of the sites to be evaluated varied between 1 and 80 hectares. Most of the proposed developments were for gravel extraction and the remainder were for housing and/or industrial development, including the large area of Reading Business Park. A small number were on the plateau gravels and one or two sites on the clays and sands of the valley sides. In most cases, there was little or no known archaeological information within the evaluation sites but evidence from surrounding areas suggested the archaeological potential.

The strategies, methodology, and practice of archaeological evaluations have been the subject of much discussion within the profession in recent years and it is not appropriate to present such a wide ranging analysis here.

What is presented here is a general discussion of the strategies and methods adopted and the results achieved by some of the evaluations carried out within the survey area. In general terms, the evaluations within the survey area were carried out by means of a combination of both manual and machine excavated test trenches. Areas sampled varied between less than 1% and 2% of the proposed development site, although it is now a general requirement that at least 2% is evaluated.

Strategies and methods adopted varied from site to site according to a number of constraints, such as the nature of the soils and the existing archaeological evidence. While the evaluation of specific archaeological features (such as cropmark features or finds scatters) may be problematic, especially where they are extensive, it is the 'blank' areas with no known archaeological evidence which present difficulties. A sampling strategy can be easily structured around specific features but 'blank' areas often provide no obvious direction. In some cases, topographical features may suggest a framework for a sampling strategy but often local topographical features may not be obvious on the ground or from the air.

In some cases, a systematic sampling strategy based on a grid system was adopted as an initial approach (eg Reading Business Park) with manual excavation of small (2 m²) trenches the primary method. In most cases, the grid used was based on the National Grid and was therefore not related to the boundaries or natural features of the site (eg Reading Business Park) and therefore provided a more objective sample. The strategy sometimes encompassed a second stage evaluation where machine trenches would be excavated to investigate either specific archaeological features already known, or those identified during the first stage of evaluation.

On other occasions, topographical features determined the strategy and position of trenches. Trenches were placed either systematically within transects, or on a grid basis; aligned on, or at right angles to the contours or natural features such as the river (eg Thames Valley Park); alternatively, trenches were sited subjectively, taking account of the topography in order to provide a sample of each defined zone which may be spatial (eg distance from the river) or topographical (eg across a terrace or a slope) as at Lower Farm, Greenham. In other cases, the strategies were based on expediency, especially in lowlying areas of the floodplain or the floodplain terrace where deposits are likely to be deep.

Where some archaeological information was available prior to the evaluation, the sampling strategy was more specific, sometimes providing a focus for wider sampling where extent was not apparent and needed defining. Trenches were excavated to examine specific

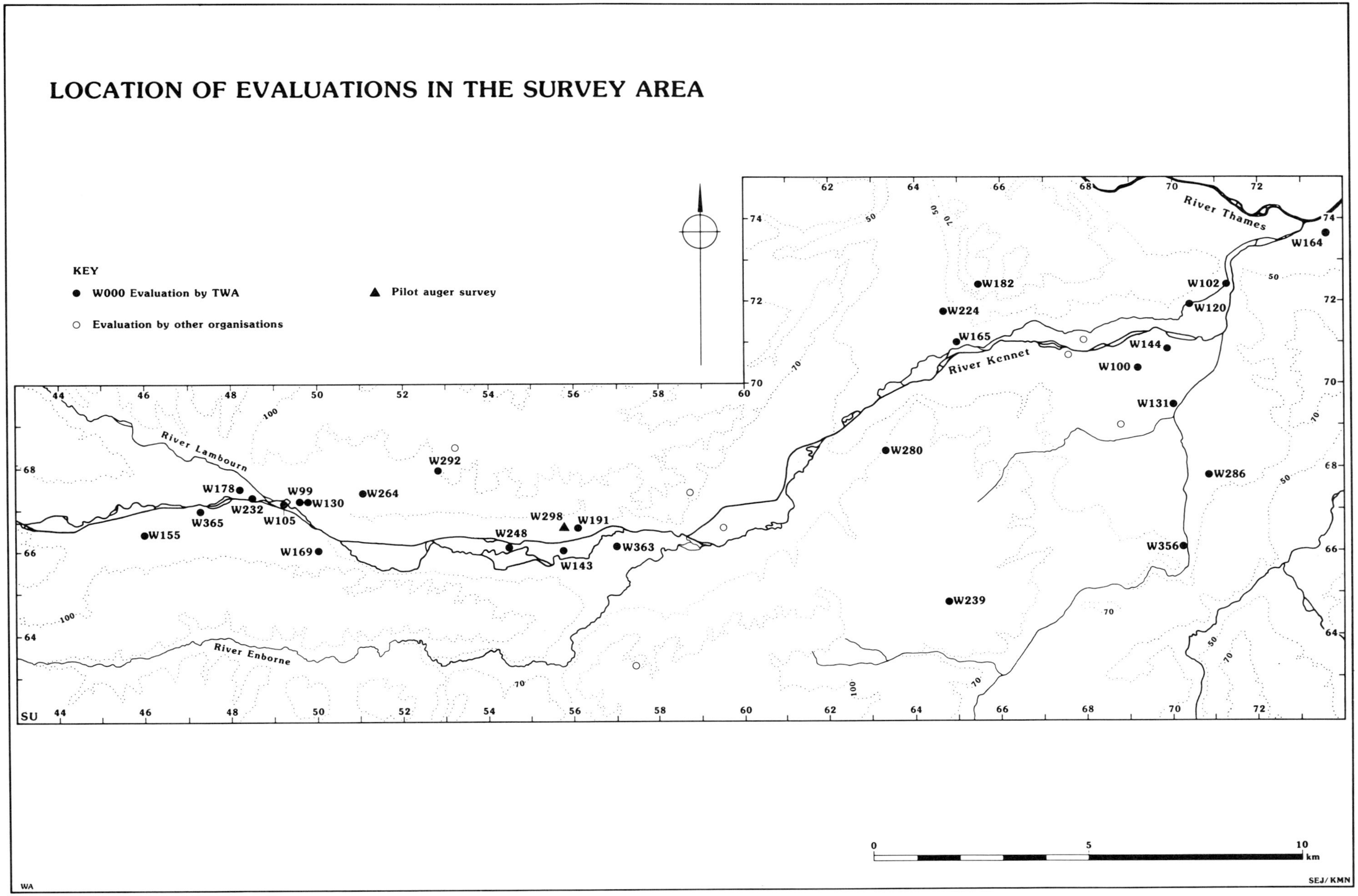

Figure 11 *Location of evaluations within the survey area*

features where confirmation of survival and indication of date were required.

The SMR provides a comprehensive guide to the existing archaeological evidence and provided both the initial impetus for evaluation and the basis for the project design. The information from aerial photographs in Berkshire has recently been updated and has been an important indicator of archaeological sites in certain localities. Environmental and topographic factors may also influence a project design. Where there is no known archaeological information available from either of the above sources, the environmental considerations might provide the initiative for the strategy. In areas where air photographs cannot be effective archaeological indicators, such as the valley floor which may be covered in deep alluvial deposits, they may show topographical features, such as submerged old river channels, which might influence the pattern of human behaviour. In the Kennet Valley, this is an important source of information and a trawl of available air photographs is often a useful first step.

Because of the time limits on determining planning applications and the need for the archaeological information, most evaluations were carried out at short notice and generally at times when land was no longer available for fieldwalking, either because the crop was too high, or because the land had not been ploughed and seeded, in anticipation of redevelopment.

Results

Only five of the evaluation sites had been totally or partially subjected to fieldwalking prior to the evaluation (W131, W280, W292, W363, and Hartshill Farm). In the case of Reading Business Park (W131), the fieldwalking identified significant clustering of finds of all periods which might be interpreted as sites (Fields 101 and 102, Burghfield Area, (Mf. 20–29) and this was vindicated by the results of the evaluation which identified extensive subsoil features of all dates (Dawson and Lobb 1986; Moore and Jennings 1992). At Hartshill Farm, Bucklebury, the fieldwalking identified a significant clustering of flint flake material and burnt flint (Field 13, transect, Mf. 10 and 13). While the flake material might suggest a site of Late Neolithic or Early Bronze Age date, the subsequent evaluation identified extensive Late Bronze Age features as well as a few pits of Romano-British date (Miles and Collard 1986). At Field Farm, Sulhamstead (W280), Dunston Park, Thatcham (W292), and Wasing Estate, Woolhampton (W363), the fieldwalking results were not considered to be of any significance, although a low level distribution of finds was recovered at Wasing Estate. The 1976–77 survey identified a significant cluster of medieval pottery in the evaluation area (Field no 3578, Mf. 8) which was not identified in subsequent fieldwalking in the transect. The evaluation at Field Farm, Sulhamstead exposed several ditches of a possible field system and a small enclosure, visible on the aerial photographs, but only two sherds of prehistoric pottery were recovered (Barnes and Lobb 1988). At Dunston Park, the evaluation of the area which was fieldwalked identified a Late Bronze Age site which was subsequently excavated, consisting of densely clustered pits

and post-holes (Barnes and Lobb 1989; Barnes 1990, Barnes et al. 1995) but again, the finds from the site were so sparse that it is perhaps not surprising that there was no significant surface pattern. The evaluation at Wasing Estate indicated a fairly wet floodplain environment and exposed a small number of undated features on higher gravel areas but provided no further enlightenment on the medieval pottery cluster (Farwell 1990).

Of the 32 evaluations in the project area, only five produced no direct archaeological information. In 12 cases the low density of finds, or the nature of the deposits, suggested that further excavation would not be necessary prior to redevelopment, although in some cases a watching brief was required. The level of information provided by the evaluations varied from site to site and this is perhaps the crux of the success of an evaluation strategy. It was generally possible to suggest presence or absence of archaeological deposits and their date with some degree of confidence. The assessment of the nature and extent of the deposits which is the type of information required for planning purposes in order to decide suitable curation or excavation strategies was more difficult.

In the context of the Kennet Valley Survey, most of the evaluations provided some archaeological or environmental information, even where no positive evidence was identified or where there were very few finds. The value of negative evidence is obvious. Several small evaluations have been carried out on the floodplain in a small area to the west of the Thatcham Mesolithic site (Lobb 1986b and 1987; Mepham 1986; Smith 1987). None produced evidence for Mesolithic occupation but, with the information already available from the SMR indicating the location of other find spots, and environmental work carried out in the region (Holyoak 1980), some idea of the contemporaneous environment is beginning to emerge. The soil profiles do provide some information relating to the position of the river, which may have influenced the selection of occupation sites, and subsequent changes in landuse and the environment which may have affected the survival of sites of this date. At Bellwood, Newbury, a single sherd of Romano-British pottery was found at the base of the peat and a few sherds of early medieval pottery and animal bone were found in a flood deposit sealing the peat (Lobb 1986). While none of these finds was *in situ,* they give some idea of the mobility of the river and the date of the development of the alluvial silts in this area. Similarly, the timber stake dating to the Saxon period, found at Theale, indicates a different landscape to the present day and suggests a date for the deposition of the alluvial deposits. Clearly, at both these sites, there was no sign of contemporaneous occupation but the finds have important implications for the interpretation of environmental and ecological change in the valley as a whole. More specifically, the evaluation at Mortimer suggested that Grims Bank was not a continuous earthwork in this location and that a stream on the same alignment probably provided a natural barrier serving the same purpose (Trott 1987).

Nine sites identified by evaluations were consequently designated as worthy either of preservation or further excavation (W100, W131, W143, W155, W164,

W169, W292, Hartshill Farm, Bucklebury, and Moores Farm, Pingewood). Large-scale excavations have been carried out at W100, W131, W164, W169, and W292; while a possible Late Bronze Age ironworking site within the Dunston Park evaluation area (W292), and a possible waterlogged Romano-British site at W169, Lower Farm, Greenham, is to be preserved by exclusion from the redevelopment area. The remaining sites have yet to be excavated pending redevelopment, or have been removed from immediate threat by planning refusal.

At W100, Anslow's Cottages, the evaluation identified a Late Bronze Age riverside site with waterlogged timber structure (Farwell and Lobb 1986). As this evaluation was carried out at a time when Berkshire's Planning policies were being formulated, it was not possible to preserve this site through the planning process; the subsequent excavations examined this site and also identified Romano-British and Saxon waterlogged structures within a former river channel (Butterworth and Lobb 1992). At Reading Business Park (W131), a series of Late Bronze Age sites in close proximity to each other was excavated, as well as a Romano-British site (Moore and Jennings 1992). At Thames Valley Park (W164), near the confluence of the Kennet and the Thames, large-scale excavations were carried out on the floodplain and on higher ground on the valley side. The evaluation had mistakenly identified a possible Early Neolithic ditch on the valley side and had confirmed a Late Iron Age/Early Romano-British date for a rectangular enclosure visible on aerial photographs (Barnes and Lobb 1987). The subsequent excavations reinterpreted the site as a Mesolithic flint working site and identified a possible Beaker burial as well as investigating the Late Iron Age and Romano-British enclosure. In addition, Mesolithic, later prehistoric, Romano-British, and medieval features were identified on higher gravel areas on the floodplain (Barnes *et al.* 1995). The evaluation at Lower Farm, Greenham (W169) had confirmed the presence of sometimes ephemeral features visible on aerial photographs, including a ring-ditch and a field system, and a lowlying Romano-British site. The ring-ditch was subsequently fully excavated (Heaton and Smith 1990) and the Romano-British site excluded from the planning per-

mission, while the field system is to be recorded by a watching brief. At Dunston Park, the evaluation identified two areas of Late Bronze Age/Early Iron Age activity (Barnes and Lobb 1989) on the edge of the gravel terrace at the base of the valley side. One of these areas was excluded from the proposed development, while the other was excavated in two seasons (comprising just over one hectare). The remains of several round-houses and associated timber structures and pits were recorded over most of the area investigated (Barnes *et al.* 1995).

Comment

Many of the evaluations described above were carried out during the formative stages of Berkshire's Planning policies. The results have certainly proved the need for evaluation work prior to planning determination and vindicated the tough line taken by the planning department. Furthermore, they provide some indication of the quantity of archaeological information which has been lost in earlier years of development. The evaluations have been successful in identifying the presence or absence of archaeological features within a development site, although it has not always been possible to suggest the extent of deposits identified. Interpretation of the results has also been difficult on occasion and in some cases the evaluations have not predicted the full range of deposits present. However, in many large-scale excavations there are often unforeseen features and deposits. Archaeologically, the evaluations have provided useful information for the project, although in some cases additional environmental evidence may have been interesting; however, this type of work is often beyond the scope of an initial evaluation. Detailed mapping, and limited analyses to characterise the soil types, perhaps combined with an auger survey as part of an evaluation strategy in areas on the floodplain, and possibly the river gravel terrace, might provide valuable information, both for the purposes of the evaluation and archaeologically. There are clearly some refinements and improvements in strategy and methodology to be made and this is likely to be an organic process as the results of more evaluations and follow-up investigations become known.

8. The Development of the Landscape

This section is not intended to be an exhaustive study of the evidence for each period, but reviews and summarises the evidence in the light of archaeological work conducted in the survey area (Fig. 11), offers basic models for occupation and landuse, and assesses the surviving potential. The traditional period labels have been used for convenience, although it is recognised that this artificial packaging may cut across continuing traditions and patterns. This is discussed more fully in the relevant sections and the chapter on the Late Neolithic–Early Bronze Age is a reflection of the problem.

Lower and Middle Palaeolithic

The area has been well covered by recent work. Chartres (1975; Cheetham, 1975) and Thomas (1961) examined the nature and sequence of the river gravel terraces into which the palaeoliths were mostly washed during the Pleistocene and the eastern part of the survey area has been reviewed by Gibbard (1982). A deep deposit of gravel at Woolhampton, believed to be at least partly of the Thatcham Terrace, has been studied in some detail, and although not associated with artefacts, did produce useful environmental evidence (Bryant *et al.* 1983). The archaeology has been summarised by Wymer (1968, 1988) and Roe (1978) and has beeen reviewed by Wymer in the Southern Rivers Project (Wessex Archaeology 1993).

In the Middle Thames, Hare (1947) recognised at least six terraces. Thomas attempted to correlate the Middle Thames sequence with that of the Kennet Valley but Chartres questioned the validity of such a correlation and gave the terraces local names, which were adopted by Cheetham. Both nomenclatures, and Gibbard's for the Reading area, are given in Table 27, which relates the gravels to their suggested ages (after Wymer 1968, 390–3). The gravels at the eastern end of the course of the Kennet, near its confluence with the Thames, have most recently been reassessed by Gibbard (1982 and 1985). Further west, the terraces are less easily recognised. The Hamstead Marshall Terrace, and other high level terraces, 45 m and higher above the

present floodplain of the Kennet, comprise most of the gravels mapped as plateau gravels and are otherwise known as the Silchester Gravels (Gibbard 1982; White 1902). Parts of this terrace have been related to the Black Park terrace of Late Anglian Age (Gibbard 1982). A small number of handaxes have been found at Hamstead Marshall, to the west of the survey area, and from less well provenanced contexts at Mortimer, Sulhamstead Abbotts (a *bout coupé* handaxe), and Wasing (Wymer 1968; 1988), although quantities are very small (Fig. 12).

Most of the artefacts from these gravels are in sharp condition and are thought to represent casual losses on the surface. Some are rolled, but Wymer (1968, 127; 1972) suggests that this probably implies that the terrace has been at least partially resorted during the Wolstonian Age. Thomas suggested that the Kennet at this stage may have joined the Thames to the west of the Reading high level terraces (1961, 435) but Gibbard (1982, 381) disputes this and suggests that the confluence is more likely to have been further downstream at Henley, possibly linking with the Blackwater–Loddon system.

The Boyn Hill and Lynch Hill terraces of the Middle Thames area, dating to the period between the Hoxnian and the Ipswichian, are not recognised in the upper part of the survey area and may have been completely eroded away during the last glaciation (Wymer 1968, 113). However, a few artefacts produced using the Levallois technique, more commonly associated with the Lynch Hill Gravels, have been found at Enborne Gate Farm to the west of Newbury (Wessex Archaeology 1993). The Levallois flake, found during fieldwalking at Burghfield between the Hamstead Marshall terrace and the floodplain terrace, is therefore of some interest but of uncertain significance. In the Reading area, Boyn Hill or Lynch Hill gravels have produced large numbers of artefacts of Acheulian handaxes and of evolved Levalloisian industries, particularly at sites like Grovelands Farm, which is one of the few sites to produce faunal remains, and Denton's Pit (Fig. 12). Taplow terrace gravels are recognisable to the west of Newbury but not further east and have been dated in the Middle

Table 27 The Kennet terrace sequence, nomenclature, and suggested date. Heights are in metres above the present floodplain

Thomas 1961	Chartres 1975	Height (m)	Date
Higher gravel spreads	High terrace remnants	80	?Anglian or earlier
Harefield terrace		70	–
Rassler terrace		61	–
Upper Winter Hill terrace		52	
Lower Winter Hill terrace	Hampstead Marshall terrace	47	Late Anglian Black Park (Gibbard 1985)
Taplow terrace	Thatcham terrace	9–18	Wolstonian
Floodplain terrace	Beenham Grange terrace	2–3	Late Devensian

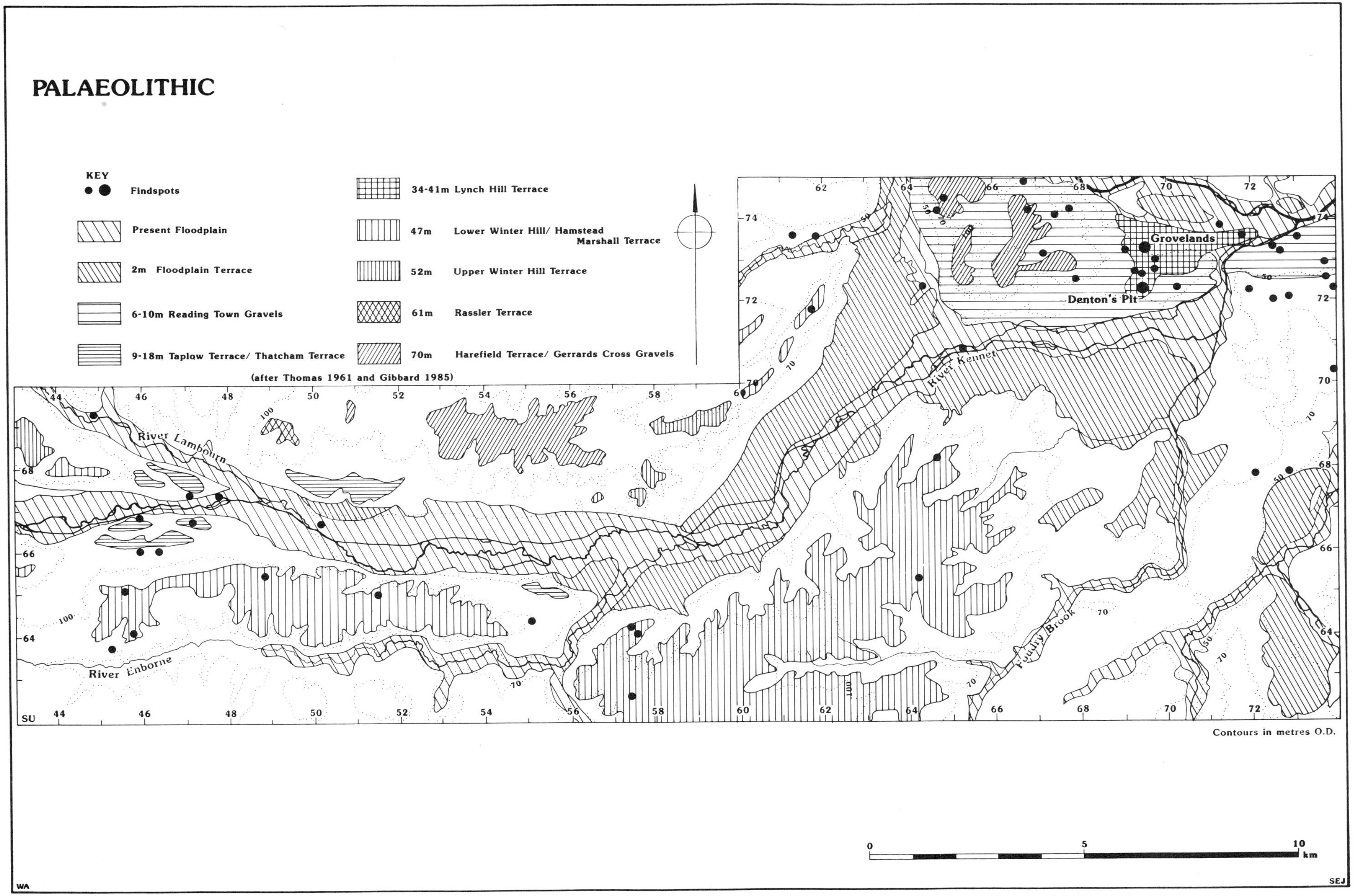

Figure 12 Distribution of Palaeolithic finds from the survey area

Thames area to the Ipswichian or Devensian phase (Wymer 1988, 90). The few palaeoliths from this terrace and below in the survey area, are nearly all very rolled and likely to be derived (Wymer 1968). The Reading Town Gravels are 6–10 m above the modern floodplain, below the Taplow Gravels, and are thought to date to the Devensian (Gibbard 1985); they have produced very few artefacts, most of which were very rolled and probably derived (Wymer 1988, 90).

In the Middle and Lower Kennet Valley, with one or two exceptions, only small quantities of finds have been made from a few find spots. Continued erosion, re-sorting, and deposition of the gravels have diminished the possibility of Palaeolithic working floors surviving in this area (Wymer 1968, 26–27). The palaeoliths are invariably in secondary contexts, derived from one terrace and redeposited in another, or resorted in the same terrace. Most of them are very abraded and rolled, although those from the Hamstead Marshall Terrace are in sharper condition, indicating relatively close sources.

There is clearly more work to be done on defining and dating the terraces in this area. Wymer (Wessex Archaeology 1993) touches upon the problem of dating and argues a Late Anglian Age for palaeoliths found on Silchester gravel based on previous research (Chartres 1976; Cheetham 1980, and Gibbard 1985). The few hand-axes which have been found on the surface of the Silchester gravel, Wymer believes can be explained by the loam filled channels which form part of the braided river system responsible for the Silchester Gravels. He highlights the necessity for future investigation in areas where these loamy channels occur, should these areas come under threat. This would include sites such as Hamstead Marshall, Wasing, and Englefield. As regards the Lower Terrace Gravel, Wymer states that the dating of the various gravels still remains a problem. He is reluctant to give all the gravels in the valley a Late Devensian origin. He stresses the need for more geological investigation regarding dating, and until then, any isolated palaeoliths that may be found in these gravels would be of limited significance.

The study of the gravel terraces at Woolhampton has demonstrated the potential for the survival of organic horizons within the lower gravel terraces which are useful for environmental and dating information. However, in view of the absence of the Boyn Hill and Lynch Hill terraces in the survey area, and the obviously derived nature of the artefactual material from the lower terraces, the greatest archaeological potential is perhaps to be found in the Hamstead Marshall and other high level terraces. Although, towards the edges, these gravels are considerably eroded, the central plateau areas are frequently very extensive (notably south of the Kennet) and apparently not degraded by later melt-waters or solifluction (the ground is fairly level). The remains of palaeosols, formed during the Hoxnian Interglacial and later, suggests that disturbance cannot be so great (Chartres 1975). Certainly, some of these gravels appear to have been resorted during the Wolstonian glacial but the presence of unrolled surface finds on this terrace suggests that any working floors that might exist may have been disturbed only by the action of permafrost, which will have mixed the palaeoliths

with the surface gravel. Deposits of loam in some areas (eg Gibbet Piece at Mortimer and on Padworth Common) might have provided additional protection if formed during the Wolstonian rather than the Anglian Glacial as Jarvis suggests (1968, 82).

Surface finds have been found on high ground in the Kennet and Middle Thames regions away from the gravel areas, such as from Brickearth at Wickham and Upper Basildon just to the north of the survey area (Wymer 1968, 111–20). The discovery of working floors at high levels in other parts of southern England (eg in brickearth at Caddington, Bedfordshire (Smith 1916)) emphasises the potential importance of these areas, which must include the uneroded surfaces of much of the plateau gravels. However, the survival and discovery of Palaeolithic material in this area remains very much a matter of chance. *The Southern Rivers Project 1991–1992* stresses that the Kennet Valley is likely to remain subject to mineral extraction planning applications. However, any new minerals plan is likely to require a Public Inquiry. Furthermore, valley bottom sites in Berkshire may be preferred to terraces for extraction purposes.

Upper Palaeolithic

Evidence for the Late Glacial and Early Post Glacial period is inevitably sparse. The lower terraces, the Beenham Grange Terrace and the Thatcham Terrace, were perhaps deposited during the Late Devensian and were crossed by a braided river system in a period when the peak discharge of the river was considerably greater than today. The change to the current meandering system is likely to have occurred by Early Flandrian times (Cheetham 1985). Woodland vegetation appears to have developed, at least on higher ground, towards the end of the Devensian, although the floodplain at this time was open (Holyoak 1980). At Theale, clay was deposited above the gravel in Late Devensian Zone III and associated pollen indicated a cold, dry, open environment (Wilkinson 1985), with vegetation dominated by grassland.

An important site, characterised by a prolific and undisturbed knapping floor containing the products of a long blade industry, was found at the edge of the floodplain at the junction of a small valley with the main valley at Avington VI further west in the Kennet Valley at SU 377671 (Barton and Froom 1986). The long blade horizon was at a depth of approximately 1 m below the surface, within largely colluvial deposits overlying the gravel. Limited pollen evidence suggests that the site was occupied at the end of the Late Glacial Zone III when conditions were open (Holyoak 1980, 135). The flint industry is characteristic of a kill and butchery site, and because of the homogeneity and completeness of the assemblage, the site is thought to have been short-lived.

Elsewhere in the valley, isolated finds of this period have been identified only at Hungerford (SU 330693), where a small group of flints was recovered, including a scraper made on a crested long blade characteristic of this period, from the edge of the floodplain (Ford 1988); and possibly at Englefield (SU 645721) where several long blades were found on the surface (information from the SMR). Further excavation at Hungerford did not produce any *in situ* flints.

The good preservation of the site at Avington VI, and the lack of disturbance through wind or frost action, suggests that the knapping floor was either rapidly sealed or well protected. The other two find spots were also in similar topographical locations at the base of fairly steep slopes. Colluviation in this period (during Pollen Zone IV) has been identified at the edge of the floodplain at the base of the steep valley side at Avenell's Cottages, Thatcham (SU 526656) by Cheetham (1975) and Holyoak, (1980, 147) and perhaps indicates the potential for further well preserved sites in similar well protected areas of the valley. Discovery of these sites, however, is made difficult by the fact that they are likely to be well buried.

Mesolithic

The transition from the Upper Palaeolithic to the Early Mesolithic should not be seen as an abrupt change but more a process of continuing adaptation to Late Glacial conditions (Jacobi 1987). The Kennet Valley offers great potential for further study of this period. The presence and potential of Upper Palaeolithic sites has already been referred to, and there is considerable evidence for Mesolithic occupation in the Kennet Valley.

A vegetational history is available for the Flandrian stage, largely owing to the research by Holyoak (1980) augmented by palaeo-environmental work associated with the excavations at Thatcham (Churchill 1962; Scaife in Healy *et al.* 1992). In the Pre-boreal period, the weather became warmer and is indicated by the lack of alpine plants. On the floodplain, a peaty soil developed on the wet ground and the vegetation was predominantly that of open fen with some *Salix* (willow) scrub. On the higher ground of the valley sides *Betula* (birch) grew in small woods but gradually declined as *Pinus* (pine) and *Corylus* (hazel) woodland became more extensive, with the later addition of *Ulmus* (elm) and *Quercus* (oak). The open fen conditions, with sandy and gravelly areas, on the floodplain appears to have persisted, at least in the Thatcham area, until after 9700 BP and it has been suggested that this lengthy duration may in part be due to the effects of grazing by large animals (Holyoak 1980, 263). Remains of *Cervus elaphus* (red deer), *Bos primigenius* (aurochs), *Sus scrofa* (wild boar), *Equus* (horse), and *Alces* (elk) have all been recovered from the peat on the floodplain relating to this period, and certainly the first two species were represented at the Thatcham site (Wymer 1962).

In addition, there is evidence for the burning of the fen vegetation in this period at Thatcham (Holyoak 1980) and at Theale (Wilkinson 1985) which is probably attributable to man and may have been deliberate management to improve grazing and encourage the herds (Holyoak 1980, 297).

'From Woolhampton to Hungerford is one of the richest areas of Mesolithic occupation in lowland Britain' (Wymer 1978). Work over the last 30 years has established the great importance of this part of the Kennet Valley in Mesolithic studies. Froom has recorded over 50 possible sites in the Wawcott region and has

excavated a number of them (Froom 1963; 1965; 1970; 1972; 1976; Barton and Froom 1986). Other excavations have been carried out at Thatcham (Wymer and Churchill 1962; Healy *et al.* 1992) and at Greenham Dairy Farm (Sheridan *et al* 1967). Consequently, there is now evidence for a large number of sites in the valley, many within the survey area (Fig. 13), with radiocarbon dates ranging from 10,365±170 BP (Q-659) at Thatcham (Wymer 1962; Gowlett *et al.* 1987, 127; Healey *et al.* 1992) to 5260±130 BP 4360–3780cal BC (BM-449) at Wawcott (Froom 1972a).

The sites at Thatcham were in small, grassy clearings on the edge of a gravel terrace overlooking the floodplain. The most recent excavations have indicated that occupation in this area continued into the Late Mesolithic period, suggesting an extremely long period of activity (Healy *et al.* 1992). This is matched in the Wawcott area where both early and late flint industries, associated with radiocarbon dates, have been recovered (Froom 1970). The Wawcott sites are in three main locations: on the lower slopes of the valley bordering the floodplain; on the edge of the floodplain terrace, but associated with a covering layer of flood loam; and on the floodplain, frequently sealed by a varying depth of peat.

The fieldwalking distributions hint at the possibility of similar extensive lithic scatters in the Enborne Valley (Mf. 3 and 9), although it has not been possible to distinguish definitive Mesolithic types and it is likely that some of the material may represent Early Neolithic activity as well (Mf. 4 and 10). The cluster at Wasing Lower Farm is of particular interest because of the large size of the scatter, which includes a number of cores suggesting knapping on a more industrial scale than is indicated by the smaller, isolated find spots elsewhere (Mf. 9).

This wealth of information reflects, not just the level of fieldwork in the area, but also the significance of the valley during the Mesolithic period. Firstly, the area as a whole would have acted as a natural routeway to the chalklands in the west and to the East Anglian and Wealden sites (Wymer 1978; Jacobi 1979, 68) for the central location of the area in relation to his Wealden and Midland/East Anglian 'social territories'. The density of sites in the Thatcham/Newbury area and the longevity of occupation, indicates at least a semi-sedentary lifestyle. This is supported by the evidence for structural remains at both Thatcham and Wawcott. Several hearths were identified at Thatcham and the presence of impermanent shelters, perhaps constructed of branches and hides, was also suggested (Wymer 1962, 336). A broad subsistence base, relying on vegetable sources as well as hunting, is suggested (Healy *et al.* 1992). Among the Wawcott sites, several hollows or pits were identified, some of which have been interpreted as sunken dwellings (Froom 1972; 1976).

The riverside base camps would have been perfectly placed to exploit the diversity of resources of both the river and the forest environments. The occasional stray finds on higher ground away from the river, which was presumably heavily wooded, perhaps reflect hunting forays from the riverine base camps. This may be compared to the situation in east Hampshire, where fieldwork found evidence for a low level of activity over a

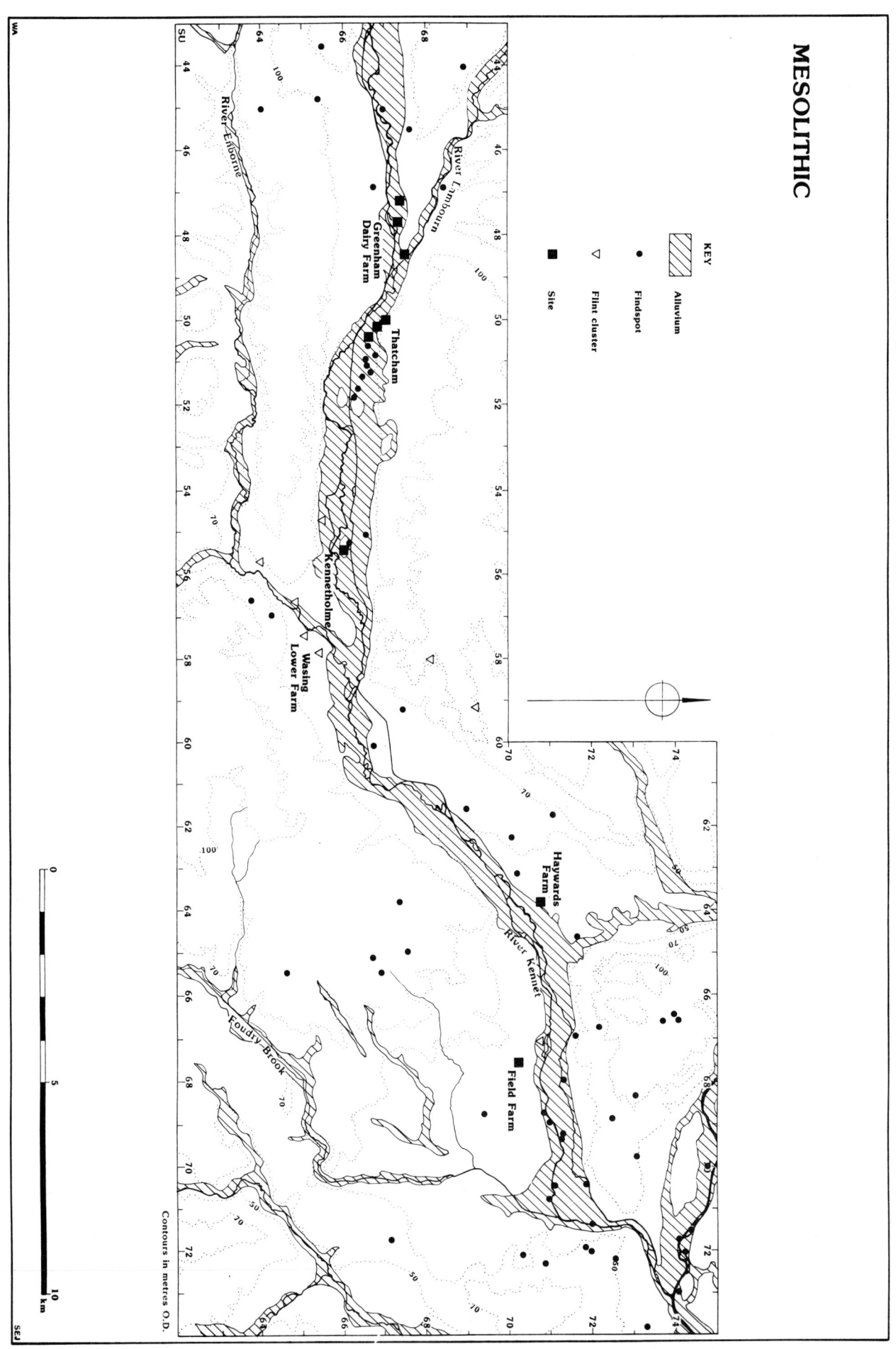

Figure 13 Distribution of Mesolithic sites and finds from the survey area

range of areas while confirming the known density of occupation at the edge of the Lower Greensand heathlands (Shennan 1981, 111). The lower reaches of the river, downstream from the confluence of the Kennet and the Enborne, may well have fallen within the 'territory' of the people based in the Newbury area. No large flint scatters have yet been identified in this area and those find spots that have been recorded appear to be very small in area. A small flint scatter was excavated at Field Farm, Burghfield (SU 676704) which was on a low gravel mound adjacent to a now abandoned stream (Butterworth and Lobb 1992). Similarly, a possible scatter was found during an evaluation at Kennetholme (SU 56586600), on the edge of the gravel terrace overlooking the Kennet (Farwell 1986). A small group of blade material was recorded recently at Haywards Farm, Theale (SU 635705), on the floodplain, sealed beneath alluvium (Hopkins pers. comm.). All three sites are very small (less than 10 metres square) and may represent single episodes. The lack of material from the Berkshire Downs where good quality flint may have been available (Richards 1978), remains surprising.

In summary, two models can be suggested for the context of the settlements on the valley floor; they may be more or less permanent settlements, exploiting the rich resources of the Kennet Valley and immediate environs, or they may be the temporary bases of more widely ranging groups exploiting the Lower Kennet as part of a periodic cycle. Each model may be applicable at different times. It has been suggested that an ecologically rich zone, such as the Kennet Valley, would have been able to support a high density of settlement and would have provided conditions which allowed a reduction in group mobility (Care 1979; Bradley 1978b, 98). This may well be the case, although the apparent intensity of activity seems less marked when measured against the time span involved.

Later in the Boreal period, the valley appears to have become inundated, possibly leading to the abandonment of the area and resulting in the growth of peat over the occupation levels at Thatcham, and the development of silts over some of the sites at Wawcott. Alder carr had developed on the floodplain in the Lower Kennet by about 7500 BP (Holyoak 1980; Healy et al. 1992), possibly as a result of reduced human intervention, while the higher ground was well wooded dominated by elm and lime.

Early Neolithic

The transition between the hunter/gatherer communities of the Late Mesolithic and the agriculturists of the Neolithic period, remains indistinct in the archaeological record and some continuity of traditions is indicated (Care 1979; Pitts 1978). Increasingly, sites demonstrating some overlap between the two groups are being recorded in the Thames and Kennet valleys. The site at Thames Valley Park (SU 744745), near the confluence of the Thames and the Kennet, has produced a flint assemblage which has been described as Late Mesolithic. The pollen sequence shows no substantial clearance prior to the elm decline but some of the flint assemblage is stratified within a colluvial deposit which

is unlikely to have accumulated prior to clearance in the vicinity (Hawkes et al. forthcoming). At both Cannon Hill, near Maidenhead (Bradley et al. 1976) and at Remenham, Hurley, in the Thames valley in east Berkshire (Holgate and Start 1985), pits have been excavated containing Neolithic pottery and flint industries of Mesolithic character.

Within the Lower Kennet Valley a similar pattern is emerging. A hearth in the top of a silted up pit containing Mesolithic flints at Wawcott I, produced a radiocarbon date of 5260±130 BP, 4360–3780 cal BC (BM-449) (Froom 1972a), and a flake from a ground flint axe was found at Wawcott IV, although the context of this piece is uncertain (Froom 1972). This radiocarbon date is very similar to that obtained from the pit at Cannon Hill, already referred to, (Bradley et al. 1976) of 5270±110 BP 4350–3810 cal BC (HAR-1178), and overlaps the earliest date from Lambourn Long Barrow of 5365±80 BP, 4350–4000 cal BC (GX-1178) (Wymer 1966). The lack of distinctive flint tool types of both periods within the fieldwalking material has already been referred to and is not necessarily unexpected in this period if continuity of traditions is assumed (Care 1979; Case 1969; Pitts 1978). Only one leaf-shaped arrowhead was found during fieldwalking at Rookery Copse (63) in the transect (in association with a predominantly flake assemblage) on the edge of the gravel terrace, in the same area which had previously produced Late Mesolithic material (Holgate 1988, table 1). Similarly, ground axe fragments were found at Donnington Castle (105) in the Middle Survey area, and at Field Farm (99) in the Burghfield area, although these need not be diagnostically Early Neolithic (Holgate 1988, 9–13). A few leaf-shaped arrowheads, and several axes of Early Neolithic type (Holgate 1988, table 14, map 22), have been found previously in the survey area (Fig. 14) but these appear to be isolated finds, many of them on higher ground above the floodplain and lower gravel terrace. However, some small blade clusters were also identified in similar locations in the fieldwalking transect (Mf. 9), and may indicate greater exploitation of this topographic zone than was previously believed.

The lack of Early Neolithic pottery from fieldwalking is matched by a lack of monuments and apparent domestic sites by contrast with the Upper Kennet. However, occupation sites of this period appear generally to be fairly insubstantial in physical remains (Holgate 1988, 27; Whittle 1977). The ephemeral nature of occupation features in this area is indicated by the shallow remains of an isolated pit at Field Farm, Burghfield, which was found to contain a few blades, and a single sherd of plain pottery (Butterworth and Lobb 1992), and suggests a mobile population in this area, despite the apparent more settled pattern in the Upper Kennet.

There is little environmental evidence for this period in the middle and lower reaches of the Kennet and no radiocarbon dates associated with periods of clearance. A single grain of emmer wheat, found in sand and gravel silts, immediately above the glacial gravels on the bank of the Kennet at Crane Wharf within Reading, is dated by associated radiocarbon dates to the 5th millennium (4950±80 BP, 3970–3530 cal BC (HAR-7028); 4990±60 BP, 3970–3640 cal BC (HAR-7027); 4740±70 BP,

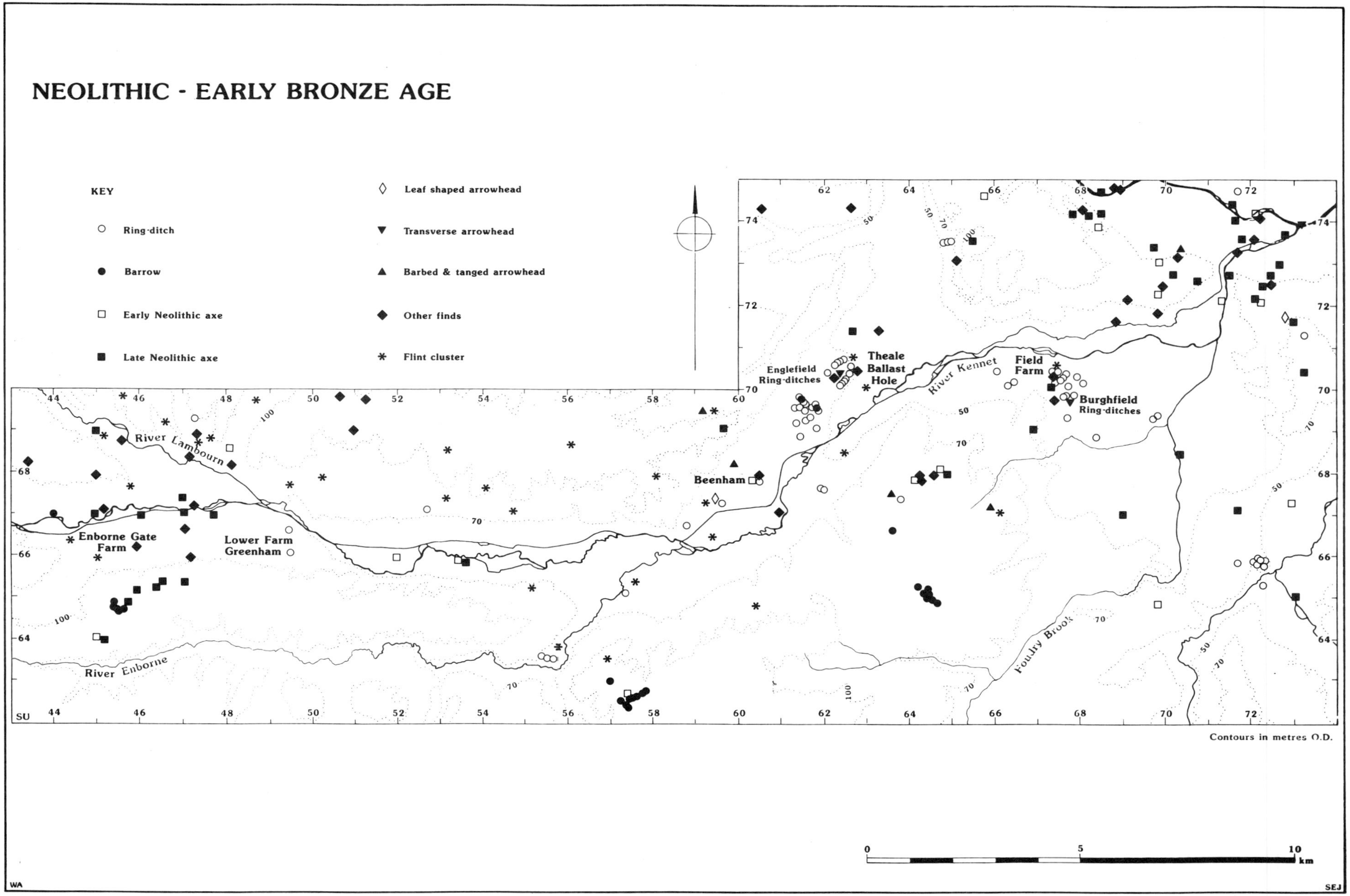

Figure 14 Distribution of Neolithic–Early Bronze Age sites and finds from the survey area

3690–3360 cal BC (HAR-7020)) and may indicate some arable cultivation at this time (Hawkes *et al.* forthcoming). On the chalk downlands adjacent to this area, in the Upper Kennet Valley and on the Berkshire Downs, large-scale woodland clearance appears to have been taking place at this time. In the Upper Kennet, it has been demonstrated that the valley was dry at this time and alluviation only began after woodland clearance in this period (Evans *et al.* 1988). Several of the long barrows in the Avebury area were constructed in open environments (Holgate 1988, 21–4 for a summary of the environmental evidence for this area). The long barrow at Lambourn was constructed in an open grassy environment (Wymer 1966). By contrast, the sites on the floodplain and adjacent terrace edges in the Middle and Lower Kennet valley, appear to have been abandoned, possibly due to inundation. Pollen records indicate that alder carr persisted on the floodplain until after the elm decline (Holyoak 1980, 238), although some signs of clearance within the region are evident. At Snelsmore Common, on the northern side of the valley, the pollen record shows a clearance episode coinciding with the elm decline, although this was followed by woodland regeneration (Waton 1982), and at Thames Valley Park, the presence of colluvial deposits suggests clearance at this period (Hawkes *et al.* forthcoming).

Late Neolithic/Early Bronze Age

As with the other traditionally defined periods, the division between the Late Neolithic and Early Bronze Age is artificial and unhelpful. Our knowledge of this period in the survey area is limited and the finds from fieldwalking diagnostically indistinguishable, particularly because of the low density of flint scatters and the lack of tool types. The flint assemblages are of flake industries which continued throughout the Late Neolithic and Early Bronze Age. Pottery finds are few and include Late Neolithic Peterborough types, as well as Beaker, which may span both periods.

It appears that it is only in the Late Neolithic period that the area began to be settled, after an apparent gap, during which time there is little or no evidence of any human activity. Prior to fieldwalking, chance finds amounted to flint and stone axes, flint artefacts, occasional sherds of pottery, and other finds (maceheads and jet sliders, the last particularly in the environs of Newbury (Fig. 14)). Three sites had been excavated which produced Late Neolithic material, all on the river gravel terraces. A pit at Enborne Gate produced three sherds of Peterborough Ware and two flakes (Hardy 1937), and two ring-ditches were associated with material of this date. Salvage recording at Beenham ring-ditch produced a small flint collection (Holgate 1988, table 29) as well as sherds of Grooved Ware and Beaker pottery (Anon 1964, 99). At Englefield ring-ditches, the excavations revealed the remains of at least six vessels of Peterborough pottery and Grooved Ware associated with a flint industry (Anon 1964), all of which are thought to pre-date the construction of the monument (Healy 1991–3). A Late Neolithic flint scatter, interpreted as domestic in character, has been collected from the area surrounding these ring-ditches (Ford 1977;

Holgate 1988, table 4). Two transverse arrowheads from the excavations at Burghfield ring-ditches, are thought to pre-date the ring-ditches (Lobb 1985, 13–14). Excavations at Field Farm, adjacent to Burghfield ring-ditches, exposed a Mortlake Ware bowl and a hearth, the latter dated by archaeo-magnetic dating to between 3900 and 3000 cal BC (AJC-63) in contexts pre-dating the construction of the ring-ditch (Butterworth and Lobb 1992). The buried soil beneath the monument also contained sherds of Beaker and Collared Urn.

Several clusters of flint flake material were identified during fieldwalking (Mf. 4, 10, and 30). Often these were associated with a diversity of tool types indicating domestic sites. Associated cores were generally sparse but the slightly higher density recorded along the Enborne Valley (Mf. 11) perhaps suggests easy access to a good source of raw material. There are limitations to the interpretation of landuse patterns as represented by the distributions and densities of the flint clusters. The flints may have been discarded over hundreds of years but the picture they present tends to be two dimensional, giving no insight into possible sequences and episodes of use; furthermore, they may have been discarded through a variety of activities. However, more extensive use and exploitation of a wide range of topographic zones, including the river valleys and the poorer drained soils of the valley sides and plateau edges overlooking the valleys, is indicated. This appears to contrast with the suggested pattern in the Upper Kennet, where a general trend towards abandonment of higher ground and settlement in the lower parts of the valley is indicated (Holgate 1988, 135). However, it is true that in the survey area, the more extensive and diverse scatters were found on the gravels. The less well defined and smaller scatters elsewhere suggest a low but widespread intensity of use. A period of expansion and experimentation throughout the area may have been followed by consolidation, partly as a result of the failure and impoverishment of some soils, and partly due to the fuller use of soils that are more productive in the long term.

As yet, there is a lack of environmental data to which to relate the evidence. Evans recognises two main types of forest exploitation and landuse during the Neolithic and Bronze Age: small, temporary clearings for cereal growing and cattle grazing, and the clearance of large areas for mixed agricultural use, perhaps incorporating sheep (Evans 1975, 129). The limited environmental evidence available suggests that, at a local level, the former model may apply, while the latter may have been taking place at a more regional level, perhaps beyond the Kennet Valley. In the Burghfield area, at Field Farm, the later Neolithic activity appears to have taken place in a small grassy clearing at the edge of forest, while at Anslow's Cottages, alluvial silts had begun to accumulate on the floodplain prior to the later Bronze Age, presumably as a result of soil run off following clearance and arable agriculture further upstream, and possibly on higher ground.

The distribution of flint and stone axes may be relevant to this picture. For other areas it has been suggested that axes most frequently occur in 'areas with less durable or extensive cultivation' and can be seen as 'a measure of repeated but limited onslaughts on forest or cultivated land' (Bradley 1978, 13). The axes of Early

Neolithic type have been plotted separately but have a similar distribution to the later ones, both in the valleys and on the higher ground of the plateau gravels. Although modern activities are probably responsible for most of these discoveries (especially in Reading and Newbury), the high proportion from the plateau gravels may indicate clearance of the type suggested. The large number of axes at Reading may be significant, perhaps attaching some importance to the position at the confluence of the Kennet and the Thames.

Dimbleby has shown that many of Britain's heathlands, both in Highland and Lowland zones, were the direct result of prehistoric forest clearances which led to the degrading of acid soils and the formation of podzols supporting heathland vegetation (1962). The impoverishment of the areas that are now heathland (or were until recently), is likely to have been general throughout southern England in the earlier Bronze Age (Barrett and Bradley 1980, 250, 254). An example from Berkshire is Ascot, where the buried soil beneath a barrow provided evidence for both cultivation and podzolisation (Bradley and Keith-Lucas 1975). The situation on heathland in the survey area is likely to be similar but it must be stressed that there is no environmental evidence, as yet, to test this.

The barrows themselves of course, are evidence for earlier Bronze Age activity on the heathlands. Three main groups survive as earthworks (Fig. 14): a group of five at Wash Common (SU 575625), and eight at Mortimer Common, Stratfield Mortimer (SU 643650), with three isolated examples nearby to the north in Ufton Nervet. Other isolated extant barrows have been recorded on the river gravel terrace. These barrow groups have parallels in groupings of ring-ditches which are widespread on the river gravels (Fig. 14). It is assumed that the majority of the ring-ditches are the remains of ploughed out barrows, although it is clear that some at least continued in use, or were constructed, in the Middle Bronze Age, and at least one is believed to be a Late Bronze Age house structure (Bradley *et al.* 1980; further discussion in the next section). There are two linear cemeteries within 450 m at Englefield (SU 624702, SU 623707, Gates 1975, map 7) each with four ring-ditches. At Ufton Nervet, there is a group of ten ring-ditches at SU 615695 (Gates 1975, map 8). These examples are on the broad floodplain terrace in the eastern part of the area. Elsewhere the ring-ditches appear to be more dispersed.

Several ring-ditches in the survey area have been excavated. The ring-ditch at Beenham (SU 604678) was associated with Late Neolithic material (Wymer 1964; Holgate 1988) but it is not clear if this is residual, as has been suggested for other sites in the valley, at Englefield (SU 624702) (Healy 1991–93), Burghfield (SU 677696) (Lobb 1985), and Field Farm (SU 686706) (Butterworth and Lobb 1992). The Englefield ring-ditch was the smallest of four conjoining circles, while the Beenham site was isolated and was much larger, 54 m in diameter, with a ditch 3 m wide. The other two ring-ditches were part of a larger group, many of which appear to date to the Middle Bronze Age; however, both these monuments were constructed in the Early Bronze Age (the

Field Farm ditch produced a radiocarbon date of 3650±80 BP, 2280–1780 cal BC for the construction of the monument). Only the Field Farm ring-ditch, with a diameter of 41.5 m, produced evidence that it was constructed as a barrow (Butterworth and Lobb 1992). Two other ring-ditches in the Burghfield area, at Heron's House, did not provide direct dating evidence, although one of them provided evidence of Middle Bronze Age activity in a secondary context (Bradley and Richards 1980). Other ring-ditches have been excavated but these are discussed below in the later Bronze Age section.

Evidence from elsewhere in the country suggests that barrows and ring-ditches on the chalk and the river gravels tend to be in areas where there are indications of activity both before their construction and subsequent to it, whereas on the heathland this is not apparent (Bradley 1978a). The river gravels and chalk appear to be preferred areas for long term settlement. Certainly the excavated ring-ditches mentioned above on the river gravel terrace, were all constructed in areas previously occupied. Intensive fieldwalking around the ring-ditches at Englefield, has suggested that there may have been extensive occupation in the area in the Late Neolithic (Ford 1977; Holgate 1988). As on the Bedfordshire gravels (Woodward 1978, 50), the ring-ditches can perhaps be seen as one element in a closely related settlements complex, with the secular and spiritual side by side in the landscape, although on the periphery of occupation areas.

The context of the barrows on the plateau gravels is unclear. Each group of barrows or ring-ditches along the valley may relate to specific communities and their related land. Some models may be suggested to explore this relationship further. The location of barrows on the plateau gravel and river gravel may imply the existence of separate communities and settlements on the higher ground as well as on the river gravels. Alternatively, the two locations may reflect two areas of landuse of a single community: the barrows on the plateau gravels may relate to upland grazing used by settlements on the river gravels or on the valley side. Thirdly, the siting of the ritual monuments may vary, sometimes being on the plateau gravel, sometimes on the river gravel, but in each case relating to a land unit which transects the valley.

The settlements need not be restricted to the river gravels in the first two models but this may have been a favoured position. It is likely that the barrows on the plateau gravels were being established on land that was becoming increasingly marginal. If this is the case, then it would seem that the broad patterns of landuse evident in later millennia were already becoming established by the end of the Early Bronze Age. The settlement sites themselves remain difficult to identify. This may be partly due to the lack of positive definition in the surface flint assemblages. The only distinctively Early Bronze Age flint artefacts recovered are barbed and tanged arrowheads and they are likely to reflect non-domestic activities. The number recorded from the valley is too few to draw any conclusions (Fig. 14) but it is interesting that they have mostly come from the higher ground which, if they are assumed to be hunting tools, suggests at least some woodland.

Large parts of the survey area are likely to have remained uncleared, or would have seen little intensive activity. The ring-ditch at Field Farm, Burghfield was constructed in a small grassy clearing in the oak and hazel woodland with some evidence for arable cultivation (Butterworth and Lobb 1992). At Snelsmore Common (SU 463704, a small bog on plateau gravel, just to the north of the survey area), there was minimal disturbance of the forest cover until the Early Iron Age (Waton 1982). The low density of flint clusters, identified by fieldwalking on the alluvium, suggests that either silts had already accumulated by this period but flints were not being discarded onto it, or more likely that much of the alluvium has formed subsequently. Certainly at Anslows Cottages it is indicated that the alluvial silts began accumulating, presumably as a result of clearance and arable agriculture, after the end of the Neolithic (Butterworth and Lobb 1992).

The evidence for fieldwalking is frequently ambiguous when applied to the explanation of patterns of landuse. The most urgent need for the archaeology of this period is the definition and investigation of sites combined with detailed environmental work to establish vegetation and landscape history at different types of location throughout the area. The most likely sources of environmental evidence will be buried soils under barrows on the plateau gravels and waterlogged deposits on the valley floor.

Later Bronze Age

Recent work in the Lower Kennet Valley has identified and investigated many new settlement and burial sites of the Middle and Late Bronze Age periods and the distribution map indicates a notable intensity of occupation (Fig. 15). These sites are also accompanied by a number of radiocarbon dates.

This distribution may be distorted, not only by the concentration of gravel workings in certain areas which have exposed sites, but also by the fact that sites of this period are difficult to identify from both surface collection and aerial photographs. They are unlikely to be identified as cropmarks as linear ditches are, for the most part, rare, and open settlements consisting of small ill-defined features are often invisible from the air. Nor will they be identified on the gravels as scatters of flint. Fewer than 100 flints were found in the excavations at Knight's Farm while, conversely, the pottery assemblage consists of some 2700 sherds (Bradley *et al.* 1980). Some sites should present themselves as surface scatters of pottery but the nature of the fabrics means that exposure to frost, ploughing, and topsoil weathering will mostly either destroy or reduce sherds to small and unrecognisable fragments. Indeed, the pottery scatters identified by the surveys (Mf. 5; 14; 24; 32) are generally very diffuse and statistically insignificant. However, at Smallmead Farm, subsequent excavation of areas where a low density pottery scatter had been identified, confirmed the presence of Late Bronze Age occupation

features (Dawson and Lobb 1986; Lambrick 1990; Moore and Jennings 1992). Most of the other sites identified were not fieldwalked prior to discovery.

Sites dating to the Middle Bronze Age are few in number and consist mostly of cremation burials, occurring both singly and in cemeteries. Occupation features have been identified at Brimpton on the bank of the Enborne but the nature of the site remains enigmatic as most of the finds, consisting of pottery sherds and a fragment of a socketed side-looped spearhead, were collected from an amorphous layer filling the depression created by an old river channel (Lobb 1991). There was clearly some occupation at Knight's Farm/Field Farm in the Early Bronze Age, as indicated by the radiocarbon dates, but the settlement appears to have become established in the Middle Bronze Age (from about 3200 BP) continuing in use into the later part of the period (2515 BP) before being finally abandoned after 2240 BP (Bradley *et al.* 1980). The nearby site at Pingewood was dated by the pottery to the period of transition between the Middle and Late Bronze Age (Johnston 1985). At both sites, the evidence takes the form of scatters of pits and post-holes. At Moores Farm, adjacent to Pingewood, recent investigation suggested either small-scale settlement or activity (Moore and Jennings 1992, 120).

Several cremation cemeteries and single cremation burials have been identified in the eastern part of the survey area. At Sulham (Shrubsole 1907), Shortheath Lane (Butterworth and Lobb 1992), and possibly at Tilehurst (Barrett 1973), the cemeteries were both on higher ground overlooking the valley and were unassociated with any monuments. At Field Farm, the cremation burials were found in association with ring-ditches and a possible barrow (Butterworth and Lobb 1992). Other single cremation burials have also been recorded in the area along the valley floor (Barrett 1973; Bradley and Richards 1979/80; Theale Ballast Hole, Piggott 1936). Cremated bones were placed generally in Deverel-Rimbury Urns, although at Field Farm, Collared Urns were used alongside the Deverel-Rimbury Urns.

The distribution of metalwork and other finds from the area suggest a more extensive human presence, particularly in the area of the confluence of the Kennet and the Lambourn, although as yet, no settlement site has been identified here. It is possible that the concentration of metalwork in this area may reflect an alternative form of burial ritual as has been suggested for the Upper Thames area (Bradley 1980, 66).

The lack of settlement evidence would appear to be at odds with the distribution of burials, cemeteries, and other finds and perhaps indicates that the period of experimentation and expansion of the earlier Bronze Age continued into this period. The limited environmental evidence for the period comes from the Burghfield area, where it suggests that much of the gravel terrace on the valley floor had been cleared by this time, although some mature oak woodland still existed. At the same time, secondary clearance of scrub was taking place in the environs of other ring-ditches, as at Heron's House, where the clearance horizon was dated by radiocarbon to 3040±90 BP, 1510–1020 cal BC (HAR-2749).

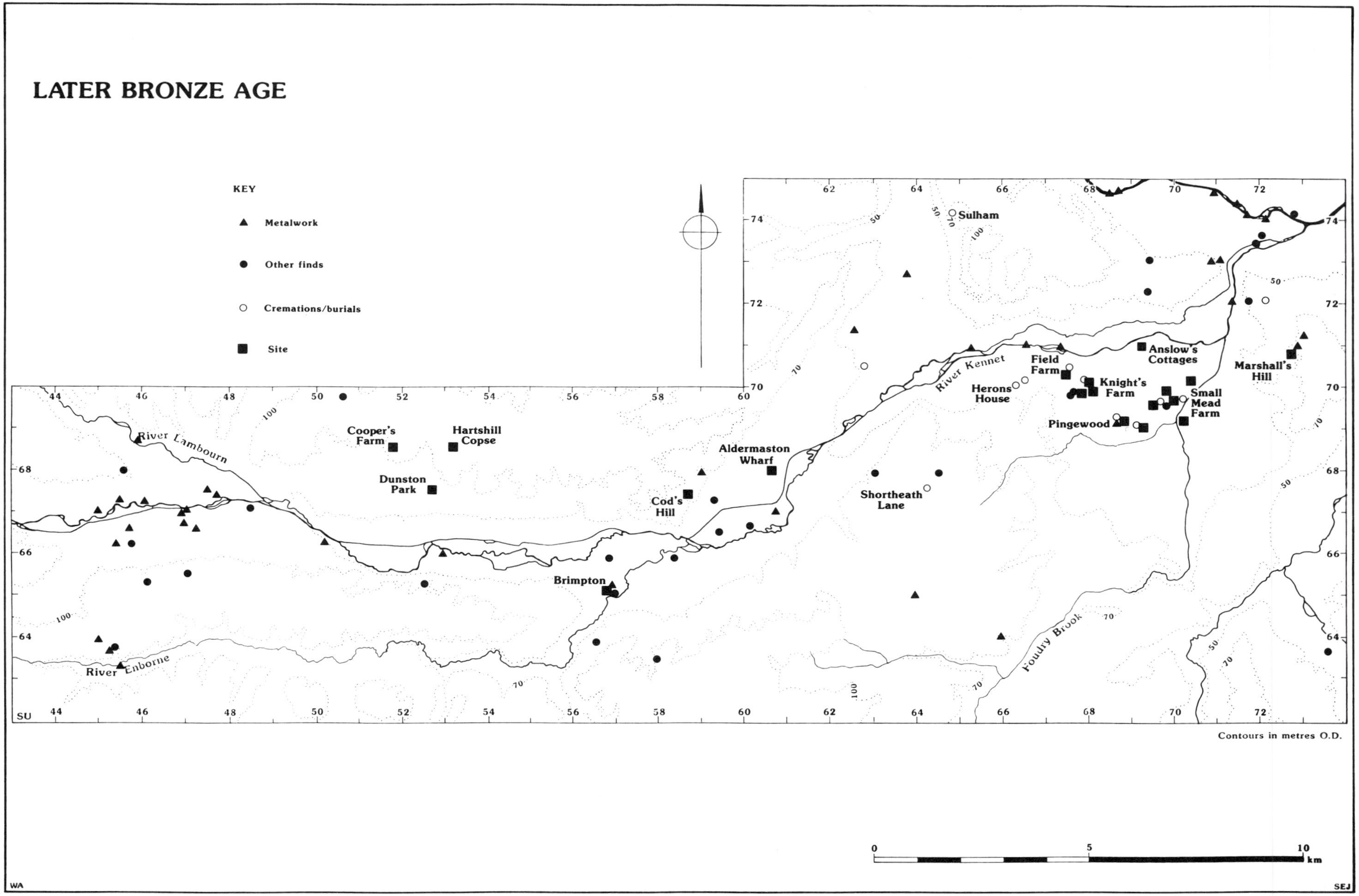

LATER BRONZE AGE

Figure 15 *Distribution of later Bronze Age sites and finds from the survey area*

The botanical remains from Field Farm indicate that both arable and grazing were being practised (Carruthers in Butterworth and Lobb 1992), and the location of settlement sites in very wet areas suggests that intensification was already taking place with all available land in the valley being utilised (Bradley *et al.* 1980; Bradley 1986). The cemetery at Field Farm, Burghfield appears to have been on the periphery of the settlement features (at Knight's Farm), while the other large cemeteries in the area were apparently well away from settlement areas in very prominent positions on the edge of the plateau gravels overlooking the valley. Whether this is due to social reasons, or to the deliberate location on marginal land to avoid tying up permanently large areas of valuable agricultural land, is not clear (Butterworth and Lobb 1992).

The large number of Late Bronze Age sites identified along the valley floor (Fig. 15) emphasises the intensification of landuse in the later part of this period. The excavations of the settlement sites at Aldermaston Wharf, Beenham, and Knight's Farm, Burghfield, have been described and discussed elsewhere (Bradley *et al.* 1980). The latter site is part of a concentration of sites on the broad gravel terrace at Burghfield, towards the confluence of the Kennet and the Thames, which include a number of small settlements within 1.5 km of each other in the environs of Smallmead Farm and Pingewood (Lambrick 1990; Moore and Jennings 1992; Oxford Archaeological Unit 1989; Johnston 1985), and the riverside site at Anslow's Cottages (Butterworth and Lobb 1992). All these sites were on the terrace gravel of the valley floor but in areas which were liable to seasonal flooding. Recent discoveries include two sites on the more clayey soils on higher ground at the edge of the gravel terrace and the valley side at Dunston Park and Cooper's Farm (Barnes and Lobb 1989; 1990; Barnes *et al.* 1995) and at Hartshill Copse on the edge of the plateau gravels overlooking the valley (Miles and Collard 1986). A similar site is indicated at Cod's Hill, Beenham, on a ridge overlooking the valley (Ford, Thames Valley Archaeological Unit). These sites are all in areas which have previously been little investigated and may reflect increasing pressure on land, perhaps because of soil exhaustion and population increase, necessitating expansion onto the poorer soils and into new areas. The pottery scatters from the surveys confirm the preference for valley floor locations but the recovery of stray sherds on the higher ground (Mf. 14) provides further evidence for more widespread exploitation of marginal soils.

On Snelsmore Common, to the north of the survey area, a clearance horizon within a peat deposit was dated by radiocarbon to 2570±190 BP, 1220–210 cal BC and provides evidence for primary clearance in this period (Waton 1982). There is also some evidence for clearance and reoccupation of land which had previously been cleared and left to regenerate. At Aldermaston Wharf, the limited pollen evidence may suggest that the settlement was established in an area high in scrub (Bradley *et al.* 1980) and the clearance horizon within the fill of the ring-ditch at Heron's House, Burghfield, dated to this period, indicated clearance of scrub regeneration (Bradley and Richards 1979–80).

The sites are characterised by post-built roundhouses with associated four-post structures, pits, ponds, and fences. At Knight's Farm, these cover an area of at least 2.2 ha and is perhaps more like a small village, although not all of this area need to have been occupied at any one time. The size of this site is also a reflection of its longevity with occupation occurring from 3630±50 until 2240±120 BP (Bradley *et al.* 1980). The other settlements in the valley appear to have been short lived and consist of a few round-houses with associated structures representing single family units or farmsteads. The site at Dunston Park, however, occupies a larger area (at least one hectare), although only six houses were identified, which is more akin to the size of the Knight's Farm settlement, although the lack of artefactual material from the former site suggests that the site was not very long lived (Barnes *et al.* 1995). At Anslow's Cottages, a small timber jetty was found at the edge of an old river channel of the Kennet and indicates some exploitation and perhaps control of the river itself, although the size of the structure suggests that only small craft would have been used (Butterworth and Lobb 1992).

Field boundary ditches of this period were identified at Smallmead Farm, where they defined paddocks which were subsequently built over (Lambrick 1990; Moore and Jennings 1992), and at Anslow's Cottages, where they post-date the use of the jetty (Butterworth and Lobb 1992) and were clearly excavated to drain marshy ground. At Smallmead Farm, the varying size of the fields may indicate different uses and it is suggested that the smaller fields may have been associated with flax production (Moore and Jennings 1992, 120). At Knight's Farm, a pair of parallel ditches may be the remains of a field system marking a droveway between fields (Bradley *et al.* 1980). It is likely that fences, and perhaps hedges, were used instead to mark field boundaries. The lack of ditches is surprising as drainage of surplus water must have been a problem at certain times of the year but it is possible that they were not necessary if the animals were grazed here only seasonally, or on a rotational basis, or simply moved to new ground when land became unusable; the settlement at Smallmead Farm may have been built over the paddocks because they had ceased to be productive. It is possible that some of the field systems seen on aerial photographs in the valley (Gates 1975) may have begun life in the Bronze Age as they often occupy similar locations to the settlements, but as yet there is no evidence to support this.

Some form of bronzeworking was being carried out on a small-scale at Aldermaston Wharf (Bradley *et al.* 1980) and possibly at Pingewood (Johnston 1985) and presumably represents production for the needs of each settlement only. By the very end of the period, as indicated by the pottery, ironworking was beginning to be carried out at Cooper's Farm where relatively large quantities of iron slag were found in a dry valley deposit on the clay soils of the valley side, well above the level of the river but close to water sources, and may indicate production on a more industrial scale. The number of burnt flint concentrations in the vicinity of this site to the north, perhaps indicates further industrial workings in this area.

By the Late Bronze Age the ritual associated with the burial of the dead appears to have changed from a preference for cemeteries around the edge (or away from) settlements, to a more haphazard arrangement within the occupation areas. A few burials, mostly of cremated individuals (often unaccompanied) but including one or two inhumations, were discovered in among the settlement features at Field Farm (Butterworth and Lobb 1992.), at Small Mead Farm (Moore and Jennings 1992), and at sites in the Pingewood area (Johnston 1985; Oxford Archaeological Unit 1989) but these clearly represent a small part of the population. It is possible that bodies were simply buried in the river courses and it could be suggested that some of the metalwork from wet contexts in the area represents a burial rite. There are notable concentrations of bronzes, many of them weapons, from areas around the confluence of the Thames and the Kennet and, similarly, in the area of the confluence of the Kennet and the Lambourn.

The interpretation of the Bronze Age landscape and society in the Burghfield area is discussed in more detail elsewhere (Butterworth and Lobb 1992) and only general observations need to be made here. In the lowlying area of the Burghfield settlements, the occupation sites appear to be confined to slightly higher and better drained gravel areas. The botanical evidence from all of the sites indicates that an exclusively pastoral economy was being practised with grazing and, in some cases, hay making being carried out on the lower ground. Faunal remains do not survive well in these conditions but the little evidence there is suggests that cattle, sheep, and pig were all being reared, with red deer possibly supplementing the diet. Despite proximity to the river, there is very little evidence to suggest that fish were being eaten in any quantity. The spindle whorls and loomweights from the Burghfield sites suggest production of fabrics and there is some indication that flax was being grown as a crop at Smallmead Farm (Moore and Jennings 1992). The area was clearly prone to flooding and this has led to the suggestion that the sites may have been occupied on a seasonal basis, with herds being moved in the winter to higher ground (Bradley *et al.* 1980), perhaps on the plateau gravels. Cereals were clearly being consumed and must have been imported from sites situated on better drained and more fertile soils further west in the valley.

By contrast, the quantities of burnt cereal grain, and the capacity of the storage pits found at the site at Aldermaston Wharf about 8 km to the west, indicate that the economy of the site was predominantly arable and the output was clearly more than was required for consumption on the site (Bradley *et al.* 1980). A similar degree of specialisation is perhaps indicated by the site at Dunston Park, where the lack of domestic debris contrasts dramatically with the other sites in the valley. Unfortunately, the lack of environmental evidence from these newly discovered sites makes speculation of the landscape and landuse in the western part of the survey area impossible.

If the plateau gravels supported grass or heathland at this time, following impoverishment of the soils during the earlier Bronze Age, it is possible that the larger tracts were used for pasture by peripheral specialised settlements in the same way that the Burghfield settlements used the lowlying pastures of the valley floor; such a site has yet to be identified. An alternative model would be that the plateau gravels provided seasonal grazing for sites like Aldermaston Wharf, where the emphasis on both arable and sheep farming suggests a site catchment that could have cut across a range of environments or by lowlying sites like those in the Burghfield area, where adverse winter conditions would have made it difficult to maintain animals close to the settlement areas.

It has been argued that the contrast between the large numbers of find spots of prestigious metalwork in the Thames Valley, and the lack of them in the Kennet Valley in general, suggests that the survey area formed part of a productive hinterland supporting an elite in the Middle Thames Valley (Bradley 1980b) where large numbers of quality metalwork have been found. Bradley (1986) argues that the site at Marshall's Hill, on the plateau gravel overlooking the Thames/Kennet confluence, which was originally interpreted as a disc barrow, may have been a high status site which controlled both the produce of the poorer farms and settlements of the Kennet Valley and the passage of metalwork along the Thames. It is possible that the concentration of bronzes and other finds at the confluence of the Kennet and the Lambourn at Newbury may signify a similar situation, although no obvious site has yet been identified.

Occupation appears to have lingered into what has been traditionally considered the Early Iron Age period in parts of the Burghfield area with no discernible change in tradition before being abandoned, although many of the sites had ceased to be occupied well before the end of the Bronze Age. The late radiocarbon date from Knight's Farm is associated with sherds of Late Bronze Age type, and the furrowed bowls, associated with other sherds of finer fabric from Field Farm, indicate that occupation here continued until the 4th century BC. At Anslow's Cottages, the Late Bronze Age jetty was abandoned and the area became inundated, sealing the site with alluvium before an old land surface developed in more stable conditions. Two boundary ditches cutting through this land surface were thought to be Late Bronze Age in date on the basis of the pottery, although it is possible in this context that the pottery was residual. Elsewhere in the valley the evidence is less clear. The ironworking site at Cooper's Farm has been too little investigated to make any positive comment but the associated pottery is typical of the Late Bronze Age pottery of the region, although this may be very early for the production of iron. At present, there is no indication what the product of the industry was. The decline appears to have been gradual and the reasons for the breakdown of the social and economic system are unclear. One can only speculate about collapse due to over exploitation of the land.

Iron Age

Discussion of the earlier part of this period is hampered by the chronological terminology and the apparent lack

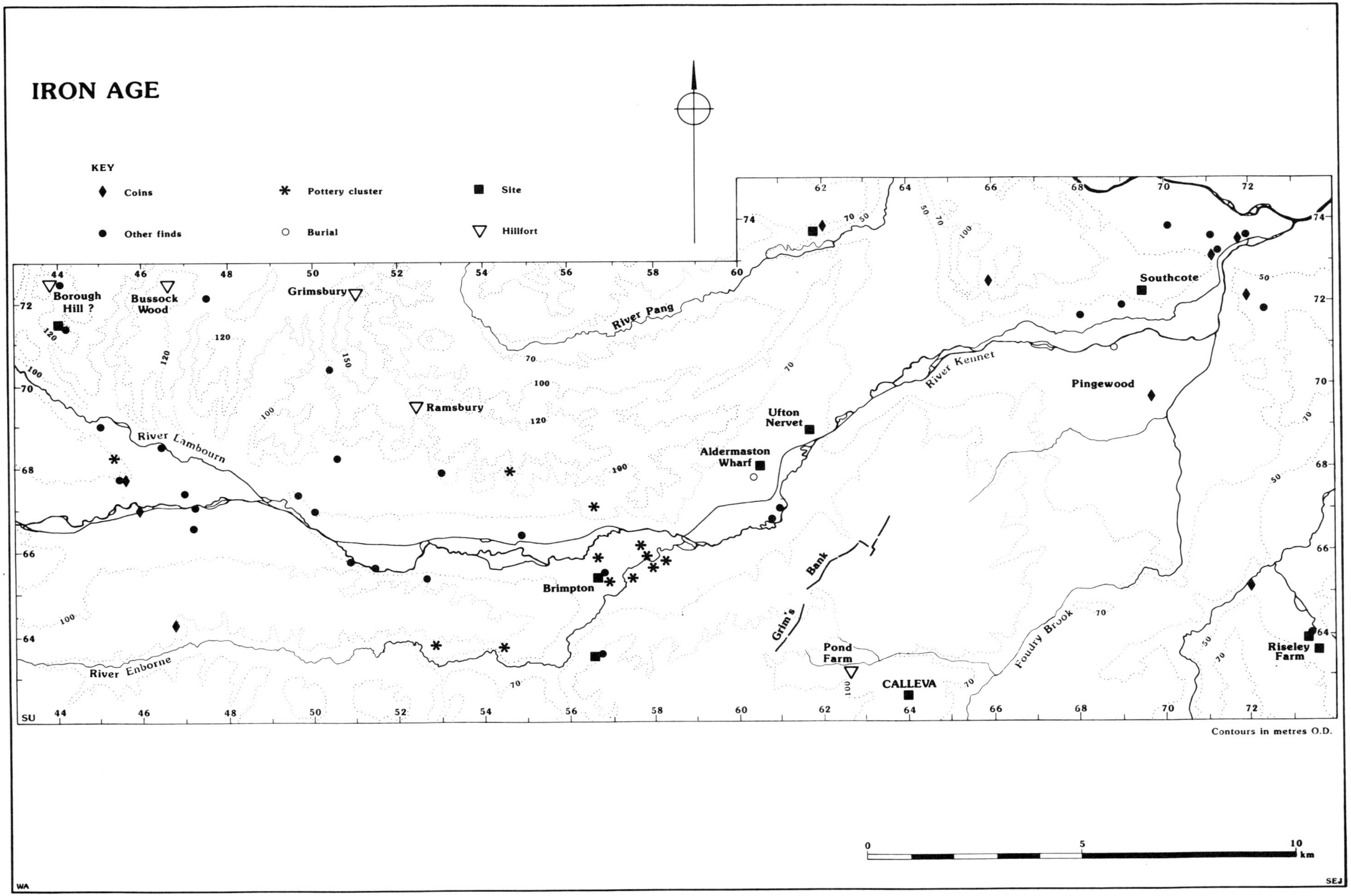

Figure 16 Distribution of Iron Age sites and finds from the survey area

of known sites. Some areas of settlement clearly continued to be occupied unchanged from the Late Bronze Age into this period. The discovery during an evaluation of the ironworking site at Cooper's Farm, provides some tantalising evidence. It is unclear whether the apparent lack of sites represents a real pattern but the contrast with the large number of sites from the previous period suggests that there was a shift in settlement. The Burghfield area, which had supported occupation over several centuries in the Late Bronze Age Period, was clearly abandoned and not reoccupied for perhaps two centuries, although the late radiocarbon date from Knight's Farm suggests that some small-scale occupation may have lingered on.

The settlement features recorded at Southcote, on the edge of the plateau gravels to the north of the Kennet, provide the earliest evidence for reoccupation in the region (Fig. 16) (Piggott and Seaby 1937). The nature of the occupation at this site is unclear as only a small part of the site was investigated, consisting of pits and segments of ditches containing pottery of Middle Iron Age type. At Pingewood, on the floodplain in the same area, two cremations were associated with pottery of Middle–Late Iron Age date (Johnston 1985) and provide further evidence for occupation in the area. A settlement of Middle Iron Age date in the region has been investigated on valley gravels at Riseley Farm in the Blackwater Valley to the south-east (Lobb and Morris 1991–93). At this site, an enclosure was investigated and interpreted as being of non domestic function, possibly associated with pottery production, and it was suggested that a complex air photo site in the close vicinity may have represented the focus of the settlement. This has not been investigated, but a Middle Iron Age date is suggested on the basis of the morphology of the cropmark features which comprise a complex of hut circles with associated compounds, such as is found in the Upper Thames, for instance at Farmoor (Lambrick and Robinson 1979) and Ashville Trading Estate (Parrington 1978). The cropmark sites of the Kennet Valley tend more to rectangular enclosures with associated enclosed fields and trackways (Gates 1975), although like the Upper Thames Valley, much of the area must have remained unenclosed (Robinson 1984, 5). Excavations of some of the latter type of cropmark site have suggested that these are generally Late Iron Age in date. Interestingly, the pottery from the Middle Iron Age enclosure at Riseley Farm has more affinities with that from the Upper Thames, while the other Middle Iron Age sites in the Kennet Valley indicate contacts with sites to the south.

Many cropmark sites, with rectangular enclosures and associated field systems, are known on the river gravels along the Kennet Valley (Gates 1975; fig. 5 for extents). By analogy with sites in the Upper Thames Valley, many of these enclosures may date to this period, although the lack of excavated sites makes confirmation uncertain. The evidence from the sites at Ufton Nervet and Pingewood suggest that these are more likely to be Late Iron Age and later in date (see below). However, some field systems at least may have earlier Iron Age

(or even Late Bronze Age) origins. At Aldermaston Wharf, part of a field system dating to the Middle Iron Age was revealed and partly excavated during topsoil stripping in advance of gravel extraction. This site was subsequently occupied in the mid 1st century AD, although the nature of the site could not be interpreted; a scatter of pits and post-holes, a possible tank or pond, and several ditches and gullies were recorded (Cowell *et al.* 1978). At Brimpton, a very small part of what may have been an agricultural settlement, with associated field ditches dated to the Middle–Late Iron Age, was examined prior to gravel extraction, but the nature of the site remains unclear (Lobb 1977–78). Neither of these sites showed on aerial photographs, even though other cropmark enclosures are known in the vicinity.

Two possible Iron Age sites already known are close to the edge of the plateau gravel at Crookham (SU 525654) where 1st century sherds were found (Peake 1931, 79 and 234), and at Brimpton (SU 567634), where an Early Iron Age vessel was found in a pit (Underhill 1937) but excavations at Boxford Common (SU 440715) have shown that settlements can be expected on the plateau itself, although the excavators suggested that the site may only have represented summer grazing; here a series of pits and hearths, containing domestic debris, was recorded (Anon 1930–8, 103; Peake and Coghlan 1932–5, 12– 14). A sub-rectangular enclosure, found on Padworth Common (SU 61886456, Appendix 2), has parallels in size and shape with other Iron Age enclosures but is otherwise undated. Late Iron Age sherds were found close to a rectangular cropmark enclosure on a small knoll of plateau gravel, on a spur of Bagshot Beds at SU 6556366 (PRN3639, Appendices 1 and 5). The enclosures at Ufton Nervet (SU 617690) are the only settlement features of this period in the Kennet Valley to have been excavated to any extent. Here, the site was occupied from the Late Iron Age to the 4th century AD. The earliest enclosure was built in the Late Iron Age, just before the Roman Conquest, and the apparent lack of any structure within it led to the interpretation of the site as a stock enclosure, which implies that there was occupation somewhere in the vicinity (Manning 1974). At Riseley Farm, in the Blackwater valley, a rectangular enclosure of Late Iron Age date was excavated and found to have several phases of occupation, with the final phase associated specifically with ironworking (Lobb and Morris 1991–3).

By the end of the 1st century BC, the river valley terrace clearly supported dense occupation with a structured system of settlements, often in rectangular enclosures surrounded by fields and approached by trackways. These sites suggest a marked increase in population from the earlier Iron Age. Most of the sites are on the river gravel terrace and the floodplain, but exploitation of the high level terrace on both sides of the river is suggested by the presence of several sites in this locality. This is supported, to a certain extent, by the distribution of the pottery clusters recorded by field-walking, many of which are found on the floodplain in the area of the Enborne/Kennet confluence, but others are sited on the edge of the plateau gravels along the

Enborne valley, and to the north of the Kennet (Fig. 16). Some suggestion of organisation and control in the landscape is indicated. The concentration of sites at the Enborne/Kennet confluence, in the area where the subsequent Roman Road crosses the rivers, may suggest a pre-existing route in the later Iron Age forming a focus for these settlements. Similarly, the site at Riseley Farm is adjacent to the later road running eastwards from the Roman town at Silchester. Equally, the clustering of finds at the three river confluences in the survey area, may also indicate the continuing importance of the rivers for the passage of commodities and people. The number of Iron Age coins, found in the area of the Kennet/Thames confluence at Reading, suggests a site of some importance in the area, although no specific site has been identified. Grim's Bank is a linear earthwork, possibly dating to this period (Astill 1979/80), which may mark a territorial boundary of the sort seen on the Berkshire Downs (Bradley and Richards 1978) or possibly associated with the developing *oppidum* at Silchester. There is some suggestion that this feature may have been more extensive, making use of natural features such as streams, instead of an earthwork wherever present (Trott 1988).

Another class of Iron Age site which occurs in the Kennet Valley is the hilltop enclosure, generally referred to as hillforts, although it is not certain whether all the sites in this area would have served this function. There are several in the area, sited on plateau gravel ridges or spur ends; four to the north of the Kennet at Ramsbury, Grimsbury, Bussock Camp, and possibly at Borough Hill and one to the south of the river at Ponds Farm (Fig. 16). Borough Hill, Ramsbury Hillfort and Pond Farm are all univallate, enclosing areas of c. 2.25 ha, and c. 1.5 ha respectively. Bussock Wood, c. 5 ha in size, is largely univallate but bivallate on the eastern and southern sides, perhaps suggesting two phases of fortification. Grimsbury is the largest and most complex and is clearly a hillfort enclosing an area of c. 8 ha, with an elaborate system of defences of ramparts and outworks. Excavation at this site suggested two phases of occupation, with an earlier pallisade later fortified by a flint wall. Only very small quantities of pottery were recovered from admittedly limited excavations, but an 'Early Iron Age' origin was suggested (Wood 1959). The small excavation across the ditch at Ramsbury Hillfort did not provide any dating evidence and the ditch fills give no clue to the nature of the monument (Hadcock 1950); nor were any Iron Age sherds found during fieldwalking at Ramsbury but it is likely that any occupation levels within the earthwork would have long since been ploughed away as the rampart is now barely visible on the surface. The other sites have not been excavated but a small quantity of Early Iron Age sherds has been found at Borough Hill (information from the SMR).

The lack of excavation of these sites makes it difficult to assess whether they were contemporaneous and what was their status in the landscape. There is some suggestion that they may date to the earlier part of the Iron Age, although the more complex defences at Grimsbury, and possibly Bussock Wood, indicate that these two enclosures may have been fortified and continued in use into the later period. The excavations at Rams Hill on

the Berkshire Downs to the north, suggest that some of the univallate hillforts may have begun life as early as the later Bronze Age (Bradley and Ellison 1975). Indeed, the proximity of Ramsbury Hillfort to the later Bronze Age sites, including the ironworking site at Cooper's Farm, leads to the speculation that this hilltop enclosure may have been constructed by an elite who controlled this specialised production. If these enclosures all served a defensive function, or represented power bases, their frequency suggests a politically fragmented social organisation which contrasts with the centralised control of the *oppidum* at *Calleva,* and suggests that they relate to an earlier pattern. Because the hillforts occupy a particular niche in the settlement hierarchy, their siting need not have been tied down by the factors which determined the location of other settlements. The strategic value of the site is likely to have been a priority, but it is also possible that these sites were placed to exploit the extensive areas of potential grazing available, assuming the parts of the plateau gravels were predominantly open rather than scrub or forested. At Highclere on the Tertiary gravels, about 6 km to the south of Newbury, a 'celtic' field system covering at least 2 ha has been identified (Corney pers. comm.). The clearance of woodland on Snelsmore Common to create pasture (Waton 1982) is further indication of expansion onto heavier soils in this period. The numerous springs on the plateau gravels in the vicinity of these hilltop enclosures would have provided sufficient water for the needs of herds. It has been suggested that these hilltop enclosures might represent communal management of livestock with areas of common pasture (Cunliffe 1984), although generally they are associated with linear boundaries for which there is little evidence in this area.

An important factor which must have influenced the pattern, nature, and economy of settlements in the Lower Kennet Valley, is the rise in power of the *oppidum* of *Calleva Atrebatum* at Silchester on the plateau gravels to the south of the river. The pre-Roman occupation began in the mid 1st century BC, consisting of densely packed round-houses, pits, and wells, covering an area estimated to be approximately 32 ha by the end of the century. It is suggested that the size of the settlement, and the poor quality of the land round about, indicates a powerful elite who are likely to have been the Atrebates, with Silchester at the centre of their territory. Before the end of the 1st century BC, a more formal layout was adopted consisting of a regular street pattern with houses at right-angles to the streets, and is seen as evidence of Romanisation among the elite in Britain. The site may have been abandoned for a short period in the latter half of the 1st century AD, prior to the construction of the Roman town (Fulford 1987). The surrounding countryside, including the Kennet Valley, must have come under the domination and control of this tribal centre, which may also have acted as a market and distribution point.

Environmental evidence for the period is sparse. The site of the *oppidum,* and the subsequent Roman town at Silchester, is a broad promontory of plateau gravel in an area which in itself is likely to have offered limited return on agricultural activity. For a settlement of this status such factors are unlikely to be important. The place name suggests a wooded environment (Rivet and

Smith 1979, 291) but this may refer to forest cover on the surrounding slopes, rather than the general character of the area. The Grim's Bank linear earthworks north of Silchester remain undated, but an Iron Age date for some of the earthworks is at least as likely as a late or post-Romano-British date (Astill 1979/80). Pollen evidence from a section at Aldermaston indicates that, at the time of construction, the land was open pasture, probably used for rough grazing, with hazel scrub and sporadic stands of trees in the wider environment (Sheddon 1979/80, 62). If Grim's Bank is Iron Age in date it can be suggested as having served more than one function. At one level, the banks control access to the centre of the chiefdom of the Atrebates. But, at the same time, they would serve to enclose and defend a very large area of rough ground where the mobile wealth of the tribe could be safely grazed. The pollen evidence from Pingewood indicates an open grassland environment, largely unchanged from the Bronze Age to the Romano-British period, with an emphasis on a pastoral economy.

Romano-British

There is much in common between the Iron Age and Romano-British patterns of landuse and settlement, with many of the sites continuing in use with little or no change. However, there is some evidence for expansion during this period into more marginal land and re-occupation of land which had been abandoned during the Iron Age, perhaps due to a population increase and to a greater degree of organisation in the landscape in order to maximise the use of all types of soil and topographic zones. Figure 17 inevitably presents a simplified picture of the settlement pattern during this period. Not all individual finds and finds clusters have been included. In many cases it is difficult to know whether these find spots represent sites or manuring scatters, such as were identified on the Maddle Farm Project on the Berkshire Downs (Gaffney and Tingle 1985). Many of the cropmark complexes recorded along the valley probably date to this period but lack of excavation makes definite assignation uncertain, and for reasons of clarity, they have not been included (see Gates 1975 and the Berkshire SMR for detail; extents of cropmark complexes shown on Fig. 3).

The distribution and economic base of settlements may have been influenced by the presence of Roman Roads and by the proximity and authority of the Roman town at Calleva Atrebatum (Silchester). Boon saw the area which might have come under the direct control of the town as being quite restricted (up to 15 km radius) (Boon 1974, 245), and this would have included much of the survey area. The Roman town would have provided a ready market for consumables which might have encouraged the profitable production of surpluses in this immediate hinterland. One can almost see a loose parallel with the situation suggested for the later Bronze Age (Bradley et al. 1980, 292), with surpluses and specialised production supporting a social elite peripheral to the area.

The survey area is crossed by two main Roman Roads from Silchester; to the north-west, the road to Cirencester (Corinium) and Gloucester (Glevum) and to the north, the road to Dorchester-on-Thames, although it is likely that a network of minor roads and tracks operated in the countryside. The Roman town at Cunetio at Mildenhall is located approximately 45 km to the west of Silchester, close to the river in the Upper Kennet Valley and it is possible that the river, or at least the valley, provided an important communication route; the river would have been navigable by light craft, certainly in the lower reaches of the river. The concentration of sites and finds, including many coins, at Newbury and at Reading, particularly the latter where there is no clear evidence for a road link with Silchester, may lend further weight to this theory. Indeed, it has been suggested that Reading may have acted as a river port for Silchester, with the Kennet and the Thames providing a cargo route to and from London (Rivet 1964, 140), although no site which might have served this function has yet been found.

The nature of the occupation of the Reading area is unclear as many of the finds were made during the last century, with little systematic excavation since, and the area is now built-up. Several sites, possible farmsteads, are suggested by concentrations of finds covering large areas, both on the higher terrace of the plateau gravels overlooking the river and along the valley itself (Fig. 17). Traces of buildings at Rose Kilns by the Kennet to the south of the town (SU 714714), were suggested as possibly representing a villa site, although it is equally likely that this site was a large farmstead with slightly more pretentious buildings than similar settlements elsewhere in the valley. The economy and status of these sites, and their relationship to each other, cannot therefore be suggested. The finds from the Reading area suggest occupation throughout the Romano-British period, although the coin hoards of the area largely date to the 4th century. The upper part of a skeleton was found in alluvial silts at the Crane Wharf site in Reading and is dated by radiocarbon to the earlier Romano-British period, but there is no evidence to suggest that this was a formal burial (Hawkes and Fasham forthcoming).

Large numbers of finds have been recorded around Newbury. South of the Kennet, these probably represent at least four settlement sites within 2 km along the floodplain terrace. One of these is represented by a cemetery of 100 inhumations with 1st and 2nd century AD pottery (SU 475668) (Peake 1931, 100, 214). Another site, to the west of Newbury, can probably be regarded as a villa; this is suggested by walls, tiles, plaster, and a hypocaust covering an area of approximately 8 ha. No date has been suggested for this occupation but a later Romano-British date is indicated. Twenty cremation burials were associated with this site (SU 46106629) (Peake 1931, 100, 214).

A Roman station called Spinis is recorded in the Antonine Itinerary but its exact location remains unknown. Its distance from Cunetio (Mildenhall, Wiltshire) in Iter XIII of the Antonine Itinerary suggests a location at Woodspeen (general area SU 4469), west of

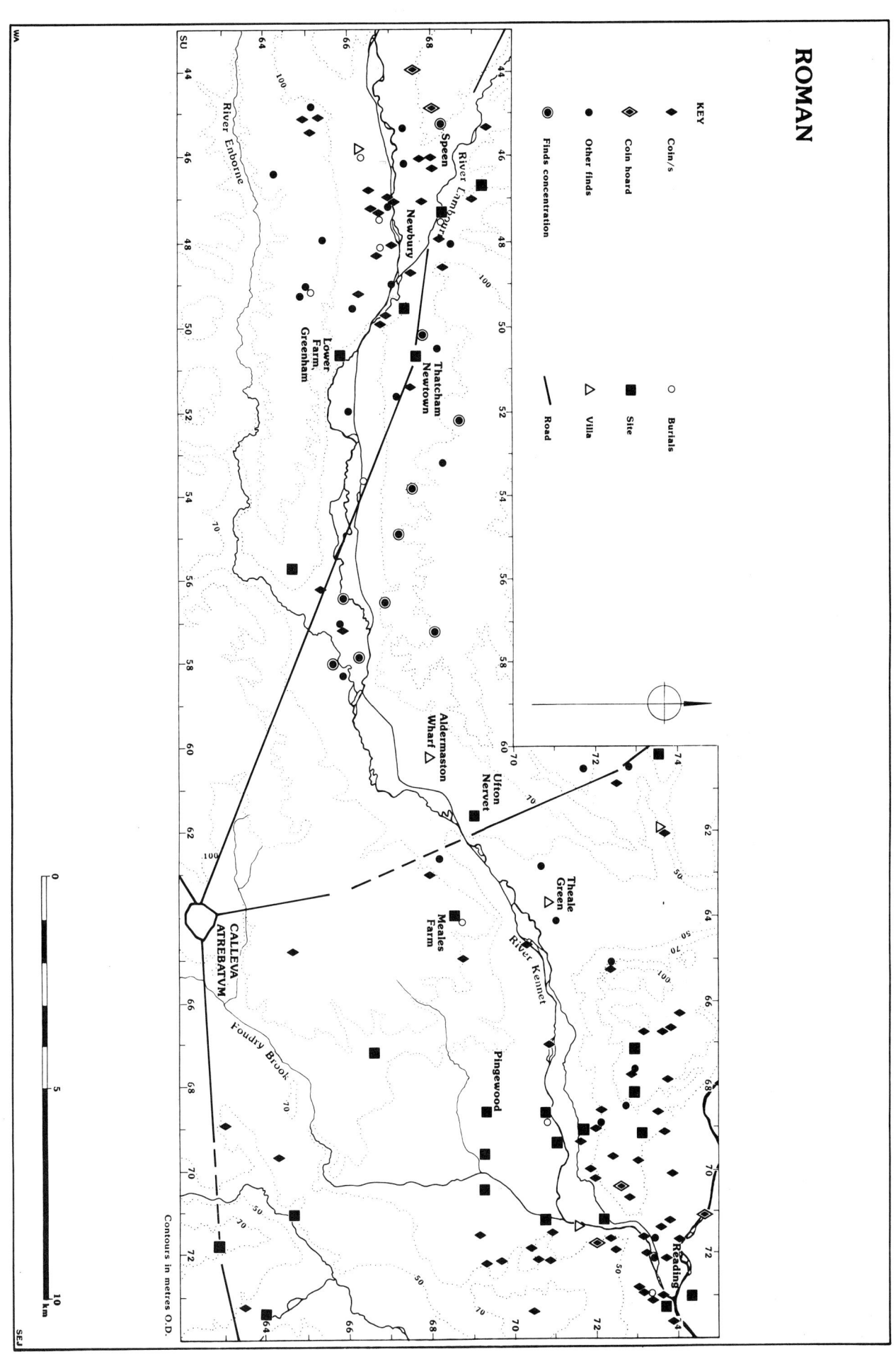

Figure 17 Distribution of Romano-British sites and finds from the survey area

the present village of Speen (Rivet and Smith 1979, 176), but the concentration of coins and finds further east, suggest that this may be a more likely location and the place name of Speen is very suggestive as a survival of the name *Spinis*. A roadside settlement on Reading Beds and river gravel at Thatcham Newtown (SU 505676), observed in the 1930s during building work and by trial trenching (Harris 1937), stretched for at least 700 m on either side of the Roman Road to *Corinium*, 15 km from Silchester. The nature of the settlement is unclear because of the way in which it was discovered, but the finds are tantalising, including stone foundations, tiles, and building stone; a column base; a pottery waster; evidence for ironworking and bronze-working, and six wells (with good preservation of organic material). The pottery suggests 3rd and 4th century occupation. On the basis of its size, and the evidence for craft specialisation, it is suggested that this is a small town rather than a purely farming settlement. The site has largely been destroyed by the expansion of Thatcham but cropmark and fieldwalking evidence suggests that there may be some survival of features to the west. With the development of this site, other settlements nearby may have been abandoned; there are probable Late Iron Age/early Romano-British sites to the south-west at SU 496674 (Peake 1931, 79, 234), and to the north at SU 505682 (Harris 1939, 118).

In the countryside, the character of the settlements appears little changed from the farmsteads of the Late Iron Age. Although the number of sites and finds in the Reading and Newbury areas can be explained, to a large extent by the accident of discovery during construction work in this century and the last, they must also reflect the density of settlement in the area. It is possible that the density of sites in these two areas may reflect the importance of the two river confluences but it does also give some idea of the likely intensity of occupation along the valley as a whole. The distribution of excavated and air photo sites indicates a preferred location on the valley floor, both on the floodplain and on the lower gravel terrace, although the plateau gravels were equally popular in the Newbury and Reading areas, and this may suggest that sites on this topographic zone have yet to be discovered. Indeed, the fieldwalking results suggest a number of new sites on the valley side and the edge of the plateau gravels to the north of the river.

The nature of these rural settlements is very similar throughout the survey area. The farmsteads were generally enclosed by rectangular ditches, were surrounded by fields, and associated with trackways. Very few of these sites have been excavated. At Ufton Nervet, two Romano-British enclosures replaced the Late Iron Age one in the 1st and early 2nd centuries AD, and occupation continued until the early 4th century. One of the enclosures at this site was clearly reserved for habitation; the excavator interpreted three sets of gullies in a rectangular layout as drip gullies of huts. In addition, a scatter of post-holes and pits was recorded. The other enclosure may have been used for stock (Manning 1974). The finds from the site indicated that the occupiers were not wealthy, although some degree of Romanisation is indicated by the rectangular plan of the houses and the find of a dump of Roman roof tiles

nearby (Manning 1974). The site at Pingewood in the Burghfield area, of 1st–2nd century AD date, was very similar, although perhaps less prosperous, consisting of an enclosure containing pits and post-holes, although no structure was identified, surrounded by fields and trackways, with ditched boundaries, and a well. The environmental evidence from this site suggested that it was situated in open grassland and had an economy based on livestock, predominantly cattle. It has been suggested that the ephemeral nature of structures at the site may indicate a specialist pastoral function with seasonal occupation (Johnston 1985). The limited excavations of a 1st century AD rectangular enclosure at Riseley Farm in the Loddon valley to the south-east, provided evidence for a grassland environment, with no hint of arable agriculture throughout its occupation (Lobb and Morris 1990–3). Most of the farmsteads occupy generally well drained sites on the lower gravel terrace above the floodplain, for instance at Ufton Nervet. In the Burghfield area, several farmsteads have been identified on gravel islands within a generally lowlying area, on the edge of the valley terrace, close to the clay soils of the valley side.

Expansion of occupation onto the floodplain in this period is indicated by a number of stray finds and sites which have been recorded on the river bank and investigated within the region. At Lower Farm, Greenham, an archaeological evaluation on the southern bank of the river revealed a 1st century AD occupation site, apparently continuing on from the Late Iron Age settlement. Not enough of the site was excavated for clear interpretation of its nature and status (Farwell and Lobb 1987). At Burghfield, occupation levels were recorded within an old river channel (Boon and Wymer 1958). At Anslow's Cottages, 400 m to the east of this last site, a ploughsoil was dated to the Romano-British period and the quantities of artefacts within it indicated occupation in the near vicinity; within the adjacent river channel, a timber structure, which has been interpreted as a trap of some sort, was dated by radiocarbon to 1670±60 BP, cal AD 230–540 (HAR-9179). The associated environmental evidence indicated that the floodplain had been cleared and was used for grazing and hay making (Butterworth and Lobb 1992). Clearly, at least part of the gravel terrace in this area was used for arable agriculture, although pastoralism appears to have been the dominant practice along the valley.

Evidence for the use of the floodplain at this time is an important result of the fieldwork. Previous find spots are known from the Kennet peat and were very much on the edge of the alluvium, perhaps in some cases slightly overlapping onto the floodplain terrace. If these represent sites which were liable to flooding, they may have been not permanent, but seasonal settlements associated with the summer grazing of the floodplain. Many of the finds clusters from fieldwalking came from the surface of the alluvium and confirm that these flood deposits had accumulated prior to the Romano-British period. It is apparent from the excavations at Anslow's Cottages, that alluvium in this area started to accumulate on the floodplain prior to the later Bronze Age, presumably as a result of woodland clearance for agriculture. However, in parts of the valley, conditions on the floodplain were wet enough for peat to accumulate after this period; at Bellwood, near Newbury, evaluation of a site on the floodplain exposed a peat deposit, 0.50 m deep, overlying the gravel which may post date the Romano-British period, although the dating evidence for this relies on a single sherd of Romano-British pottery sealed beneath the peat (Lobb 1986). In Reading, alluvial deposits continued to accumulate after the early Romano-British period (Hawkes and Fasham forthcoming). A similar pattern of alluviation has been recorded in the Upper Thames Valley and is likely to have been common to many lowland valleys in southern Britain; in the Thames Valley it is suggested that seasonal flooding of the floodplain began in the later Bronze Age or Iron Age and alluviation continued, with increasingly higher ground water levels, throughout the Iron Age and Romano-British periods (Robinson and Lambrick 1984).

Meales Farm is a recently excavated site on less productive land at the edge of the plateau gravels. The site was discovered after the topsoil (and some subsoil) had been removed prior to gravel extraction and there was only limited opportunity for excavation. The nature of the Romano-British occupation could not be fully defined, but pits and ditches of this date were recorded and large quantities of building materials, including Roman roof tile, and floor tiles, as well as limestone slabs which were probably used for roofing, were found in one area of the site, suggesting that there had been a substantial building on the site in this period. The pottery indicated occupation throughout the Romano-British period. Three cremation burials in urns, at least one of which was 1st century AD in date, were found in a group on the edge of the settlement area (Lobb *et al.* 1991). Evidence from fieldwalking by the *Calleva* Field Research Group, and from pollen analysis, has suggested a predominantly pastoral landscape around Roman Silchester (Fulford 1982, 406). If this reflects a maximisation of the potential of the surrounding land, then the plateau gravels in general are perhaps likely to have seen similar or less intensive use for grazing.

On the higher ground, almost all the fieldwalking sites found are on the valley side rather than on the plateau. However, fieldwalking around the town of Silchester suggests that there must have been fairly dense settlement on the plateau gravels, certainly in this case around the immediate environs of the town (Corney in Fulford 1984). A high proportion of these sites on the valley side are on Bagshot Beds, which form a generally narrow band between the plateau gravel and the London Clay, mostly rather less than 200 m wide. It is improbable that the sites were situated specifically to exploit the Bagshot Beds; more likely they are there because the Bagshot Beds act as an interface between the London Clay and the plateau gravel, and because of the spring line. Most of the sites are on gently sloping spurs between two breaks in slope and closer to the downhill, rather than the uphill break.

The pottery scatters, found by fieldwalking on the valley sides, suggest small settlements, perhaps single isolated farmsteads, while the concentrations on the valley floor might indicate larger, nucleated settlements, although still of an agricultural nature as no building materials were generally recovered. Those sites which did produce building material were all off the valley floor, except for the finds cluster at Wasing Lower Farm (33, Mf. 14), where there may have been a site adjacent to the Roman Road crossing of the River Enborne. However, the scatter of cropmark enclosures and the scatter of sites found by fieldwalking, might suggest a dispersed rather than nucleated pattern of settlement. It appears that settlements do cluster in certain areas, for instance in the Burghfield area and around the river crossings and river junctions.

The size of the settlements and their dispersed distribution, suggest that they would have farmed their immediate locality, rather than exploiting a range of resources right across the valley. But from the present distribution, it remains possible to argue that there was predominantly valley side settlement where the valley floor, or in particular the floodplain terrace, is restricted in size. Conversely, there was predominantly valley floor settlement where the river gravels are more extensive, but in each case with the settlements, whether on valley side or valley floor, making use of a range of farming potential from floodplain to plateau. There is likely to have been considerable variety according to locality. More intensive fieldwalking may define the extent of low density scatters of pot associated with individual settlements and presumably the result of manuring. This will not necessarily tell us how the land was being used. The potential of the areas as we know them now suggests that the floodplain would have been used for grazing or meadow, and the river terrace for cultivation. But in the Romano-British period, their use may have been determined by other factors. This is clear, for example, from environmental work at Farmoor, Oxfordshire, where an Iron Age and a Romano-British site were both found to have been in a grassland environment, even though the first was on the floodplain and the second on the floodplain terrace (Robinson 1978).

Pottery production in the 1st and 2nd century AD was dominated by Silchester Ware which must have been produced on an industrial scale in the Silchester area (Charles 1979; Fulford 1982, fig. 3). The exact location of the kilns of this productive industry is unknown. Two small updraught kilns were recorded in 1909 in a field to the north-east of the town (John Hope and Stephenson 1910, 327–8) but the exact site is not known. Fieldwalking in the Silchester area revealed kiln debris to the west of the amphitheatre but this is not thought to be the site of the 1909 kilns (Corney in Fulford 1984, 246). Other kilns have been recorded or suggested in the survey area and were probably for more local pottery production. At Ha mstead Marshall, just to the west of the survey area (SU 410660), several kilns of updraught type were investigated and it is suggested that they were in use from the mid 2nd century to the 4th century (Rashbrook 1983). At Shaw in the Newbury area, certainly two, and possibly three, circular kilns of 1st/2nd century AD date were found and, because of the quantity of associated material, it was suggested that they may have been producing mainly roof and box tiles (the Kennet Valley Survey (KVS) archive contains the

SMR info.). Several kilns were observed during the construction of the M4 at Bradfield (SU 603738); two were excavated and the main product was suggested as grey storage jars (KVS archive contains the SMR info.). In the same area, at Pangbourne (SU 618737), a chalk floored rectangular building with a kiln was found beneath a 1st century AD villa building (KVS archive contains the SMR info.), suggesting pottery production at an early date, although this may have been purely for use by a single settlement.

Given the apparent intensity of occupation throughout the Romano-British period in the area, the number of recorded burials seems remarkably few (Fig. 17), although it is likely that each settlement had its own cemetery. The largest cemetery was found at Newbury (SU 47536684), where about 100 skeletons were found as well as several cremation burials sited on a gravel bank; the associated artefacts indicate a 1st or 2nd century AD date. These burials must have been associated with a settlement of significant size and status but none has been definitely identified in the close vicinity, despite the number of stray finds from the general area of Newbury. The villa to the west of Newbury had an associated cemetery of 20 cremation urns (apparently in Upchurch Ware) laid out in rows (KVS archive contains the SMR info.). Elsewhere in the valley, single or small groups of cinerary urns have been found, sometimes with associated ashes and artefacts, mostly in coarse local pottery but at Greenham, a 2nd–3rd century samian vase was found with associated coins (SMR No. 2900).

There appears to have been little resistance to the colonisation of the Romans in this area, although most of the agricultural settlements show little evidence of Roman influence. Evidence for Romanisation in the countryside is found on the sites of several villas within the area. These richer sites are largely found along the valley gravel terrace, notably at Theale, Aldermaston Wharf, Thatcham, and Newbury (Fig. 17). Finds of pottery and *tesserae* suggest the site of a villa at Theale Green (SU 636707) (Peake 1931, 99 and 234), although this could simply be a wealthy farmstead with one prestigious building. Excavation at Aldermaston Wharf identified a probable late 3rd–4th century villa in an area which had previously supported a field system in the Middle and Late Iron Age (Cowell *et al.* 1977–78). There may be an exception to this pattern on plateau gravel at Brimpton, where hypocaust tiles and Roman bricks are said to have been built into the church in the 18th century, but the circumstances of the discovery leave the nature of the site obscure (*c.* SU 557647) (Peake 1931, 100, 184). Other possible villas on the higher plateau gravel terrace have been noted just to the north of the survey area at Eling (SU 52407495), Hermitage (SU 52347258), Bucklebury (SU 52907380), and possibly at Frilsham (SU 5507130), where a Roman altar to Jupiter was said to have been found in 1730, although the antiquity of this report makes the interpretation a little suspect (*see* Berks. SMR in the KVS archive); these are all sites which have produced evidence for stone buildings (Information from the SMR). A large villa (KVS archive contains the SMR info.) with an aisled and a corridor building, a hypocaust, and corn dryers has been excavated at Pangbourne (SU

618737), at the edge of the valley known as the Sulham Gap which links the Kennet and the Thames valleys. These villas may have been deliberately placed to control estates which exploited both the Kennet Valley to the south, and the large agricultural area of the Berkshire Downs to the north. The limited environmental evidence from excavations of the rural agricultural sites in the valley, suggests a predominantly pastoral economy with very limited arable, and it is possible that the products of arable agriculture were provided by the sites on the Berkshire Downs, which would have been more suited to cereal growing; it has already been suggested that the downland fell within the agricultural hinterland of Silchester (Richards 1978, 45).

These villa sites must represent a range of status and wealth but the lack of excavation makes further definition impossible. However, some of them are likely to have been supported by substantial estates and Thatcham Newtown may also have fitted into this sort of framework. The frequency of these settlements and estates remains to be established but it is suggested that the strip pattern of estates, so clear in the medieval period, is likely to have been equally pronounced at this earlier date. This is inferred from the complementary distribution of these sites along the valley, assumed from the likelihood that the estates would have been sizeable and would have been established in an environment comparable to that of the early medieval period, and under comparable restraints presented by the availability of particular types of land. This is not to say that there need be continuity of the estates or their boundaries from the Romano-British period through to the medieval, only that the factors determining the outline of the estates are likely to have been very similar. Small farming settlements of the type found during the survey should probably be seen as existing within estates of this type. The effect of the development of these suggested estates and estate centres on the general pattern of settlement, and the relationship between these sites and the humbler farming settlements, are problems that can be tackled by further fieldwork. One should perhaps expect a wide range in the detailed pattern of settlement along the valley in response to different regimes of ownership and estate management.

The deposition of several coin hoards in the 4th century at Reading and Newbury bears witness to troubled times, perhaps resulting from economic or political uncertainties. This is confirmed, to a certain extent, by the evidence from Silchester itself. The town walls were constructed in the late 3rd century (Fulford 1984, 236) and, while the occupation of the site expanded beyond the walls in the late 3rd–4th centuries, by the late 4th century the coin evidence suggests some retraction within the walls itself, perhaps for defensive reasons (Corney in Fulford 1984, 288–89). It is also at this period that the south-east gate was blocked (Fulford 1984, 237). The town at *Cunetio* in the Upper Thames was also massively fortified in this period (Burnham and Wacher 1990, 340). Within the countryside, the evidence for occupation at this period is not clear, as there are too few excavated sites to provide secure dating and the nature of the settlements is unclear. Occupation at Ufton Nervet continued until the early 4th century and at several of the villas it is likely that occupation lingered

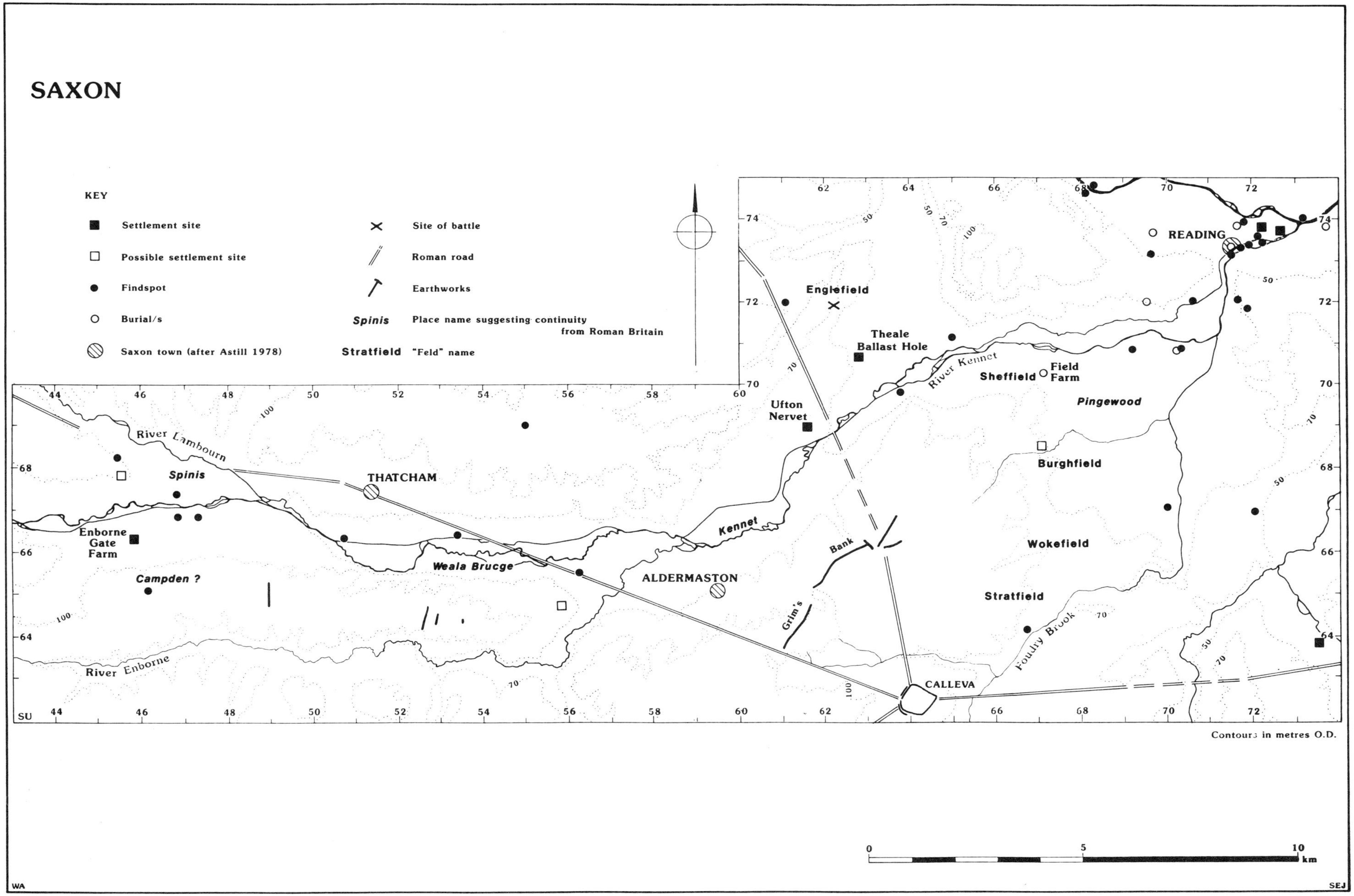

Figure 18 Distribution of Saxon sites and finds from the survey area

on (eg at Aldermaston Wharf and at Pangbourne, the KVS archive contains the SMR info.). At Silchester, occupation does seem to have continued within the walls of the town into the 5th century (Boon 1974, 73) and it is possible that the town at Thatcham Newtown may also have continued to function in some capacity (Harris 1939). It seems likely that most of the rural settlements would have been abandoned well before the end of the 4th century but the number of stray 4th-century coins, as well as the hoards, signify continued habitation in the area, and a slow decline of the established way of life is indicated.

Post-Romano-British to Medieval

Despite the early Saxon settlement in the Upper Thames, evidence for the 5th–8th centuries in the survey area is scant (Fig. 18). Interpretation depends much on limited archaeological and place name evidence, together with inference from the previous and subsequent better known periods. The 5th century finds in the Reading area must necessarily be seen in the context of the migration of the Saxons into the Upper Thames region with the Thames forming the main access route for both people and commodities. The 4th century defended town at Dorchester-on-Thames continued to be occupied through the 5th century, with an influx of Saxon mercenaries, and is seen as being central to the defence of the Thames. The Saxon settlement at Reading in the 5th century, may have been strategically placed to control the confluence of the Thames and the Kennet (Hawkes 1986, 71–5), and the early 5th century spearhead from Pangbourne (Swanton 1974, fig. 7), may also reflect this defence of the river. The nature of the settlement at Reading is unclear. A mixed cemetery at Earley near the Kennet mouth was partly excavated in 1891 and is dated by the grave-goods to the 5th and 6th centuries but one grave at least is earlier, containing a number of late or sub-Roman buckles, all of probable early 5th century date (Stevens 1894). Early–middle Saxon metalwork and pottery were found in pre-Abbey levels (Slade 1973), and the stray find of a 5th century coin from the Reading area provide further evidence of settlement here (information from the SMR). To the south-west of Reading, on the Kennet floodplain at Smallmead, a logboat coffin containing a skeleton was discovered during gravel extraction; there were no associated grave-goods but the tree trunk was dated by radiocarbon to the early 5th century (Chadwick 1981–82, 104).

The mid to late 5th century cemetery at East Shefford in the Lambourn valley, with Frankish imports, has been assumed to be connected with settlement of the Kennet (Meaney and Hawkes 1970); as the Lambourn is a tributary of the Kennet one might have expected a migration route along the Kennet from the Thames but there are no other Frankish finds known from the region. Hawkes sees the cemetery at East Shefford more as expansion of settlement from Dorchester-on-Thames (Hawkes 1986, 77). Other evidence for settlement in the Kennet Valley in this period has been provided by a recent evaluation at Beenham, which uncovered a nearly complete cremation urn (with cremated remains); this vessel has been dated by comparison to sites in the East Midlands and East Anglia to the late 5th century (Newman and Lovell 1992).

The role of Silchester during the 5th–7th centuries is crucial but remains obscure. The duration of occupation into the 5th century, or later, has yet to be firmly established. Boon concluded that the town continued to be occupied into the earlier part of the 5th century, with recognisable town life gradually declining before final abandonment by the middle of the century (Boon 1974, 74, 82). The suggested late 5th/6th century Ogham stone now appears to be a fake (Fulford and Sellwood 1980). If there was indeed little use of Silchester beyond the middle of the 5th century, its concentric boundary may have been fossilised as such by the survival of the surrounding estates, as by any continued importance of the *territorium* itself.

More than once the suggestion has been advanced that it was the centre of a sub-Roman enclave. For O'Neill (1943; 1944), the northern extent of this enclave was defined by Grim's Bank. There is still much uncertainty about the date and purpose of the Grim's Bank earthworks, particularly the relationship with the Silchester to Dorchester-on-Thames Roman Road (Astill 1979–80). These earthworks, and the suggested blocking of the Roman Road, have been seen as defensive measures against the rising dominance of the Saxons based in Dorchester (Hawkes 1986, 77). Recent work has not established a firm date for the monument, which could be placed in the Iron Age, the late Romano-British, or the post-Romano-British periods, and it is possible that prehistoric earthworks were modified or extended at a later date (Astill 1979/80, 65). A further series of linear earthworks on Greenham and Crookham Commons have been described by O'Neill and Peake (1943); excavation of one of the banks produced late Roman pottery in the lower silts of the ditch. They suggest a 5th or 6th century date for the earthworks and argue that these linear earthworks are the demarcation lines or frontier of Silchester in that period. A late Romano-British, rather than post-Romano-British date, would not be out of place and Boon cites Bokerly Dyke in Wiltshire as a parallel for both these earthworks, and Grim's Bank (Boon 1974; 1979–80). A late Romano-British date for the use of the earthwork seems to be the simplest explanation for the large fragments of two late Roman pots found in the ditch.

More recently, the evidence for a sub-Romano-British enclosure has been seen in a different guise. Silchester sits in the centre of a circle formed by county and parish boundaries. Biddle suggests that this circular boundary represents the *territorium* of Roman Silchester; its incorporation into Saxon administration divisions is due to the protracted survival of Silchester as a sub-Roman or British political entity (Biddle 1976, 334–5). A different line of argument has been adopted by Gelling (1976, 809), who concludes that the local administrative landscape evolved at a time when Silchester was no longer an important centre. This argument (followed by Dickinson 1977, 408) depends on explaining the drastic kink of the county boundary around Silchester as the result of a 19th century alteration, but this is not the case; the boundary is shown much as it is today on Rocque's map of Berkshire

(1761). The boundary around Silchester remains very striking.

During the 6th and 7th centuries, we begin to see settlement being established along the Kennet Valley, although the evidence is again rather sketchy. Settlement at Reading, and in the valley to the south-west, is indicated by the cemeteries at Earley (Stevens 1894) and at Field Farm, Burghfield (Butterworth and Lobb 1992), and by two isolated burials, one inhumation and one cremation of the late 6th century from the west of Burghfield (Astill 1978, 77). There was clearly occupation in the Burghfield area from the 7th century, although no settlement site has yet been identified. The inhumation cemetery at Field Farm contained at least 50 graves, many of them containing artefacts consisting largely of weaponry and other items in common everyday use; it was by no means representative of a wealthy population (Butterworth and Lobb 1992). The banks of stream or river channels associated with the Kennet in this area, appear to have been revetted and utilised for fishing or trapping. Timber stakes forming parts of structures have been identified at Anslows Cottages from which a series of radiocarbon dates suggests occupation from the 7th until the 10th centuries, and a stake reveting the bank of a river channel at Coley produced a comparable date in the 7th century (Hawkes and Fasham forthcoming). Three sites have produced pagan Saxon pottery, probably no earlier than the 6th century. At Theale Ballast Hole, sherds of an urn with stamped decoration were recovered, together with fragments of annular loomweights (Piggott 1936). At Ufton Nervet, a sunken-featured building was excavated and associated with 6th century pottery (Manning 1974). A few sherds of pottery from a pit at Enborne Gate gravel pit may also date to this early period (Hardy 1974). Sherds of grass-tempered pottery have been found at Brimpton (SU 563653) but this type of pottery could have been used into the late Saxon period (Lobb 1991). Similarly, a few sherds of pottery associated with loomweights from Aldermaston, near the confluence of the Kennet and the Enborne, is broadly dated to the Saxon period but cannot be dated more specifically (KVS archive).

Environmental evidence has been obtained from only a few sites and the information is generally of a very local nature. At Anslow's Cottages, there is some evidence for woodland or scrub regeneration on the floodplain in the 7th or 8th centuries, although damp grassland continued to predominate. The evidence from sites in Reading, at Anslow's Cottages, and at Theale, may point to climatic deterioration, or at least much wetter conditions in the late Saxon period. At Anslow's Cottages, use of the suggested watermeadow system appears to have come to an abrupt end when the channel containing the timbers was filled with a coarse deposit resulting from rapidly flowing and increased volume of water. A similar deposit filled an old channel sealing a Saxon timber bank revetment (dated by radiocarbon to the late Saxon period) at a nearby site at Theale (Butterworth and Lobb 1992). Subsequently, peat developed at both sites, signifying much wetter conditions on the floodplain and the edge of the gravel terrace. In Reading

itself, Late Saxon revetments of the edges of watercourses may be seen as a response to increased inundation, although the problem may not have been resolved until the 14th century (Hawkes and Fasham forthcoming).

In Berkshire, the place name evidence relating to this period has been thoroughly examined by Gelling (1973–76). Place names hinting at interaction between the sub-Roman and Roman populations fall into two main categories. Firstly, there are complete or partial survivals from the Romano-British period. Complete names include Kennet, Speen (Roman *Spinis*) (Gelling 1973, 266), and Pingewood (primitive Welsh **penn*, 'end', and **ced*, 'wood' (ibid., 209). The name Silchester may be a partial survival (Rivet and Smith 1979, 292). Secondly, there are elements of English place names which suggest contact with a sub-Roman population. The examples in the survey area are rather tentative. *Campden*, Newbury (lost but perhaps surviving as Camp Close on the Tithe Apportionment (SU 472653)), contains the element *camp*, a Latin loan word which may refer to stretches of open, uncultivated land. Gelling notes two 'Wickham' place names in this area (*see* Appendix 2), but both are minor names without early forms and it is very uncertain whether they belong to the class of *wic ham* names, identified by her as an English term given to substantial sub-Romano-British settlements which had not been taken over or obliterated by Germanic people (Gelling 1976;1977). The *Weal a Brucge* ('bridge of the Britons' or 'serfs' or 'foreigners'), mentioned in the 10th century charter for Brimpton, is perhaps more likely to refer to the survival of a pre-Saxon bridge on the line of the Roman Road, rather than implying the survival of a British community there. The context of the place name evidence is illustrated by Thomas (1981, fig. 47) where the study area is seen to fall within a broad, east–west belt across Britain in which it may be possible to infer a substantial survival of Roman-descended British, 'certainly in the late 5th century and, to an appreciable degree, up to AD 600 (or later)' (ibid. 262).

Certainly the evidence from fieldwalking suggests that at the end of the Romano-British period, the landscape would have been settled with a scatter of farms and hamlets, which probably fitted into a system of estates with their centres suggested by some of the richer or more substantial building remains at villas such as Aldermaston Wharf and Beenham. The lack of archaeological evidence for a Saxon presence in the 5th century is possibly genuine, rather than misleading negative evidence. A long history of gravel quarrying and construction work in the Lower Kennet Valley has produced finds of many periods including, for example, large numbers of Romano-British finds. If pagan Saxon cemeteries exist, it is surprising that they have not yet been brought to light in the same way. On the other hand, the cemetery at Field Farm, Burghfield may well have gone unnoticed by the machine drivers during topsoil stripping as very little skeletal evidence survived and the finds were largely of mineralised iron which blended into the subsoil and could easily have been overlooked by the unpractised eye. The negative evidence upstream contrasts with the finds from the Reading area and the Upper Thames but finds a parallel in the absence of cemeteries in Hampshire to the south of Silchester (Meaney 1964; Meaney and Hawkes 1970, fig. 1). As the place name evidence seems to confirm, there are good reasons to suppose that a British population maintained an identity in the Silchester area through the 5th century and quite possibly through the 6th century as well.

If farming communities continued to operate beyond the end of the Romano-British period, the land units within which they functioned may well have continued with them to be taken over in due course by the Saxons. It is clear from the charter evidence that by the 10th century at the latest, the area was divided into estates which formed the basis for the medieval manors and parishes. At how early a date were these divisions established? The evidence is mostly ambiguous or inadequate. There are three adjoining 'Stratfield' parishes: Stratfield Turgis, and Stratfield Saye in Hampshire, divided from Stratfield Mortimer in Berkshire by the county boundary which runs along the Roman Road. Presumably, this was originally one large estate, or common land, which pre-dates the county boundary, at least on its present line. Hampshire was certainly in existence as a county by the mid 8th century (Hinton 1981, 63) and the Stratfield estate could, therefore, date to the 7th or 8th centuries; however, we do not know that the county boundary was on the same line then as now.

Gelling (1976) suggests that a large number of parishes in the area relate to land units that were organised and formed before the coming of the English, or even earlier. She suggests that the way in which they straddle the Roman Road, rather than abut it as a boundary, implies that they pre-date the road. But this need not follow. The boundaries may well be later and determined by topographic and environmental features as well as the potential and resources of an area, rather than by a Roman Road, whether or not it was still in use or had been redundant for time out of mind. Gelling contrasts this situation with that slightly to the east, where the Roman Road is used as a boundary by estates established in the Saxon period, and she suggests that this contrast is related to the element -feld in the place names of this area. A band of eight parishes share this element (Fig. 18) — Bradfield, Englefield, Burghfield, Wokefield, Stratfield, Swallowfield, Arborfield, and Shinfield. In this context, Gelling suggests that -feld is a settlement term referring to open land used as common pasture and only divided into land units after the Romano-British period. Gelling also points out that the open land contrasted with the forest to the east and may have marked the boundary between the kingdom's of Wessex and Mercia. The -feld parishes are, for the most part, on London Clay and river gravel, between two areas to the east and west that are more predominantly Bagshot Beds and plateau gravels, which are likely to have supported heath and wood then as now. Perhaps the -feld names refer to open land with large areas under cultivation, as would be appropriate for land which included a considerable acreage of river gravels, rather than referring simply to extensive pastures as Gelling

suggests. In this case, the Roman Road may be adopted as a boundary, not as a convenient line ready provided through rough ground, but as a prominent feature in a fairly uniform landscape lacking natural topographic divisions. However, if the band of -feld names represents a border of open country between the Middle and West Saxons (Gelling 1978), then political factors may well have determined, or perhaps reflected, the pattern of landuse here. These points could be investigated by fieldwork, for example to see how populated was the area during the Romano-British period.

A case could be made to suggest that the large manor of Thatcham is based on a pre-Saxon estate. If Kemp's suggestion is correct, that the minster at Thatcham was possibly established as early as the 7th century (Kemp 1967–8), it could well have been founded in an estate that a century earlier or less had belonged to the British. However, this cannot be demonstrated. Thatcham could nevertheless find a parallel in its functions and origins in the important estate centres at Ramsbury and Kintbury (Haslam 1980). The siting of the church at Thatcham is of interest. Firstly, it is on the valley floor which is unusual for churches in this area. Secondly, and more importantly, it is immediately next to the Roman Road from Silchester to Circencester and must have been fairly close to the eastern extent of the substantial Romano-British settlement at Thatcham Newtown (c. 600 m away). Rather than relating closely to an early medieval context, its siting may suggest that it was established at a time when the use of the Silchester–Cirencester road was still a relevant factor, although there is very little evidence to support this argument. It is tempting to speculate that the minster church could have been situated here (in the 7th century?) because of some continuing importance of this locality, both as a centre of population and of administration and, if this were so, it leads to speculation about continuity of Christian worship from the late Romano-British period. Late Roman Christianity is well attested at Silchester (Boon 1974, 173–84; Thomas 1981, 169). Early Christian sites are known to have been established in the late Romano-British cemeteries that flanked the roads outside other Roman towns (Thomas 1981, 170–5). The minster church at Thatcham is adjacent to a Roman Road and is peripheral to the apparent small Roman town at Thatcham Newtown. However, there is little evidence to indulge this speculation. The area around the church is now almost entirely built-up and no discovery of late Romano-British burials has been reported, nor is there any other evidence of late Roman Christianity at Thatcham Newtown, or a place name indicative of continuity.

For the present, the limited evidence requires us to keep an open mind about developments in the 5th–8th centuries. After all, the place names indicating contact or continuity are rare; the great bulk are English names. Saxon settlement in the 6th and/or 7th centuries could have been into an area where the population had been very considerably reduced by ceaseless warring, emigration, and possibly disease. Continuity of estate units remains a possibility, though undemonstrated, but continuity does not preclude change. Troubled and uncertain times may have seen frequent amalgamations or redivisions of land, eventually producing quite a

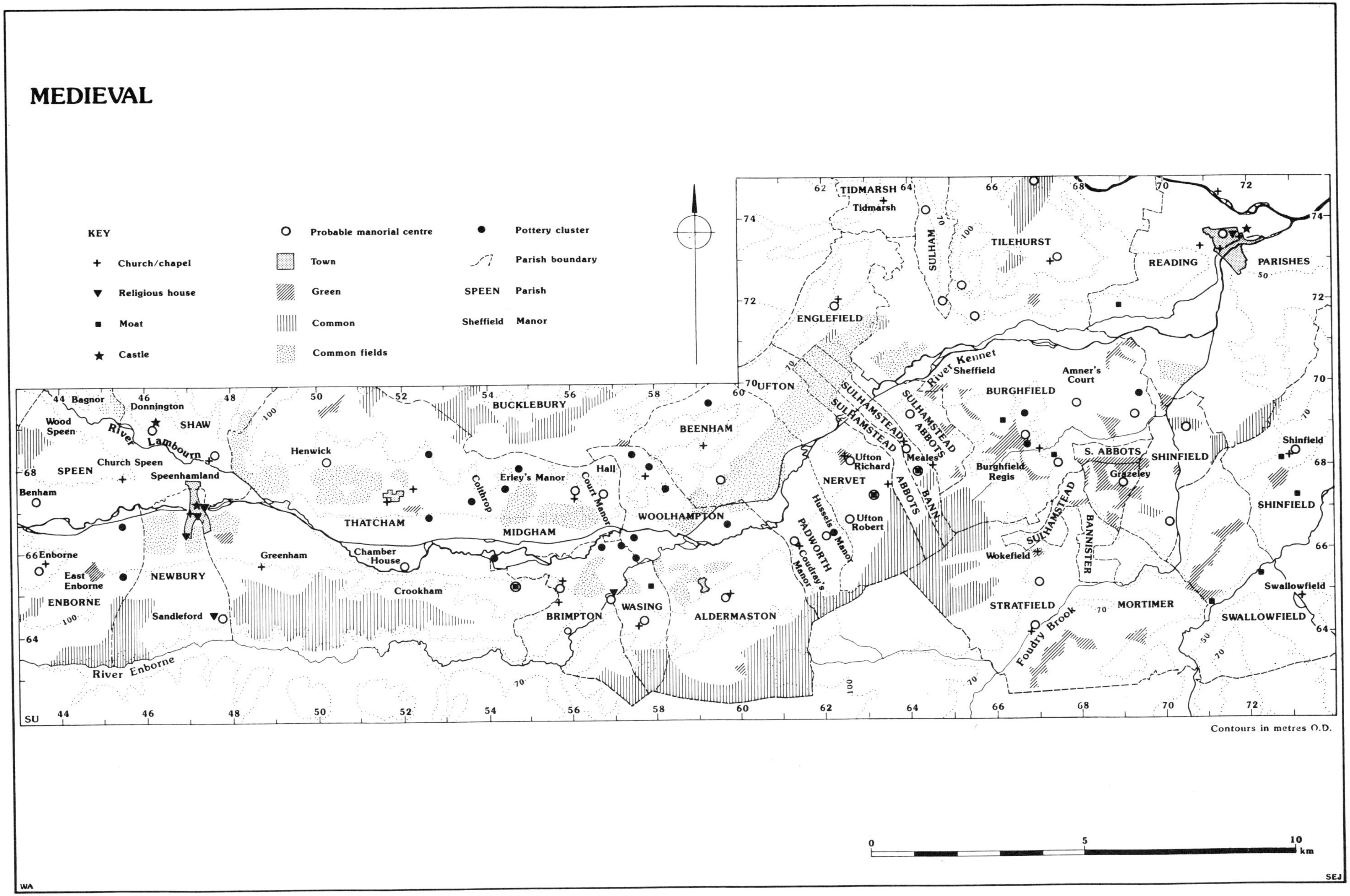

Figure 19 The medieval landscape within the survey area

different pattern while still being the product of continuity. The boundaries of Saxon land units need not have followed precisely the same lines as the Romano-British ones, and indeed, in terms of the history of landuse, this is perhaps not the most important consideration. What is important is the likelihood that, in both periods, the division of land would have followed a very similar pattern, determined by the desire, or need, to incorporate a range of resources within each land unit, and resembling the valley floor to valley top, strips or blocks, that are certainly apparent by the 10th century.

This is a murky period but there are areas on which further work would shed light. Settlement archaeology of this period remains totally obscure; other than chance discoveries, the most promising starting point is the excavation of late Romano-British sites which, as has been suggested above, may well have continued in use to a later date. There is also an urgent need for an environmental sequence to establish the character of landuse in this period; indeed with the absence of finds from fieldwalking, and the absence of settlements, this is likely to be the only way that this can be achieved. Is there, for example, evidence for regeneration of the woodland at this time as there is at Snelsmore Common at some time near the end of the Romano-British period (Waton 1982), or does the landuse continue much as before? Also required is the long overdue recording of the Grim's Bank earthworks.

The Lower Kennet Valley had many of the elements that one would expect in a medieval landscape: the parish churches and minor religious houses; boroughs and markets; moats and manors; parks; fishponds, and mills; a mixture of nucleated and dispersed settlement; and the open fields, meadowland, heath, and woodland that supported it all (Fig. 19). In contrast to the earlier periods, many of these elements remain as features in the countryside today. We also have the advantage of documentary evidence to place these elements within the context of parish and manor. Evidence for the character of the landscape and the form and distribution of the settlements, can come directly from medieval documents, more indirectly from post-medieval maps and documents, and also from fieldwork and topographic studies. The medieval archaeology of the Lower Kennet Valley has received little attention except for excavations in the towns of Reading and Newbury. A general survey of the development of all medieval towns in the area has also been carried out (Astill 1978). The scope of the present survey has not extended to an examination of medieval documentary sources; basic secondary sources, such as *Victoria County History*, have been used.

In the late Saxon period, urban centres were beginning to develop at Aldermaston, Reading, and Thatcham (Astill 1978), while settlements of unknown character and status are also indicated from documentary sources at Brimpton, Speen, and Burghfield. Bucklebury, which is on the fringes of the survey area to the north of the valley, may have had urban status in this period as it was the centre of a *Domesday* hundred, and the place name suggests a fortified place but there is no evidence to substantiate this (Astill 1978, 6).

Elsewhere in the countryside, the evidence is slight. An isolated pit containing late Saxon metalwork and pottery was excavated at Ufton Nervet, suggesting continued occupation at this site (Manning 1974). The Danes are known to have wintered at Reading in 870/71, and a battle was fought between the Danes and the Saxons in 871 at Englefield, but the archaeological evidence for these events has yet to be identified; indeed, the political upheavals of this period, which must have affected the survey area, are little understood in the archaeological record. The river margins and the floodplain appear to have been carefully maintained in this period, at least in the Burghfield and Reading areas, prior to a period of much wetter conditions, during which deep deposits of peat and alluvial silt accumulated above the 10th century timbers (Butterworth and Lobb 1992; Hawkes and Fasham forthcoming). This may indicate some pressure on open land in an otherwise heavily wooded area, which may have been subject to forest law. In Reading, similar pressure on land is indicated by the evidence for the cultivation of a pre-Abbey soil at the Abbey Stables site, despite its poor agricultural potential (Hawkes 1991).

In the late Saxon period, Wallingford was the county town for Berkshire and presumably dominated the economic network but Reading and Thatcham may have operated as secondary exchange centres. While there was a manor at Newbury in this period, it is not until the 11th century that the town developed as a commercial centre, ultimately at the expense of Thatcham, although the latter did achieve borough status in the 14th century (Astill 1984). Aldermaston, Thatcham, and Reading also had minster churches and were late Saxon royal manors. A similar pattern is seen in other known and potential late Saxon urban settlements in Berkshire (Astill 1978, 6). In the Upper Kennet, there are indications of the way in which urban functions may have developed at major estate centres (Haslam 1980) and this has been clearly argued for the Berkshire sites (Astill 1984). We know very little about these early settlements in the Lower Kennet and not a great deal about their later character and economy. For example, what proportion of the livelihood of the inhabitants depended on farming rather than commercial or industrial activities? This may have some bearing on their relationship with the surrounding settlements, a question which also needs further explanation.

With the boroughs we can be rather more confident than we can about most settlement sites in the area, that their form and location derive from the medieval period, although Astill suggests post-medieval movement of the settlement at Aldermaston (1978, 18). The medieval towns in the area, and their archaeological potential, are fully discussed elsewhere (Astill 1978). After the 14th century, Thatcham declined as a market centre and by the 16th century it was no longer a borough. Similarly, Aldermaston became a borough in the 14th century but apparently went into decline as an urban centre after this period. Newbury thrived as a market centre and the town developed rapidly during the 12th and 13th centuries. The town appears to have survived a decline in the 13th and 14th centuries and became extremely prosperous in the 15th and 16th centuries, largely due to the wool and cloth trade. With the foundation of the Abbey in Reading in the 12th century and subsequently, the town became an important economic and administrative centre and had replaced Wallingford as the major town in the County by the beginning of the 14th century. The relationship between these two market centres and the settlements in the countryside in between, is unclear and it is interesting that the pottery from fieldwalking, even in those areas closer to Reading, show more affinities with the assemblages from the excavations at Newbury than those at Reading. It is possible that Newbury was more of an agricultural market, drawing on the west of the county, while Reading was a more commercial centre with a local catchment area to the east along the Thames and to the south.

The earliest evidence of estate boundaries is found in the Anglo-Saxon charters (Brimpton, Padworth, Wokefield, and Speen). From these, it would appear that the estates described coincide, more or less, with the form of the present day ecclesiastical parishes, suggesting continuity of the boundaries over at least a thousand years. Assuming the situation to be much the same for the other parishes in the area under study, we have a good idea of the nature of the land units in the late Saxon period and later. It is clear that the form of the land units is closely related to the Kennet Valley. Generally, the parishes are roughly rectilinear and lie at right-angles across the line of the valley, with one boundary on the valley floor and the opposing boundary along the gravel plateau or ridge. This is most marked in the group of strip parishes in the middle of the area (Sulhamstead, Ufton Nervet, and Padworth) but a similar relationship to the valley is apparent in the other parishes.

Almost all the parishes comprised two or more manors at the time of *Domesday Book* and many of the manors, particularly the larger ones such as Thatcham, were further subdivided during the medieval period. There is some indication that like the parishes, these small land units generally ran across the valley from floodplain to gravel plateau. For example, the manors of Thatcham are strung out along the valley on either side, while the two manors of Padworth, Cowdray's and Husseis', were divided by the north–south road running up the valley side (Clinton 1911). The present parish of Sulhamstead comprises the two former parishes of Sulhamstead Abbots and Sulhamstead Bannister, which formed two adjacent, very narrow strips up the side of the valley. This is a further indication of the nature of the division of land within what must have originally been a single larger unit. In Tilehurst parish, there appears to have been four likely manors, two on the high ground of the plateau gravels at Tilehurst and Kentwood, and two close together on the river gravels at Pincents and Beansheaf, suggesting that the division in these cases was based on single topographic zones.

This pattern evidently reflects the landuse of the area, with each land unit cutting across a varied topography, thus providing a diversity of resources. It is clear from the estate, Inclosure, and Tithe maps of the 18th and 19th centuries that the river gravels formed the core of the post-medieval and presumably the medieval, open fields. In some cases, the fields are simply named as common. In others, detail of the strips is given, notably for Greenham, Midgham, Newbury, Ufton Nervet, and at Smallmead, near Reading. The open fields must have formed a virtually continuous band along the length of the valley, with the common meadowland running alongside on the floodplain. One consequence of this seems to have been the intermixing of land between the parishes on the valley floor. For example, before the Inclosures, there was no clear boundary between Woolhampton and Aldermaston. By contrast, whereas there is every indication of intensive medieval cultivation of the river gravels, the plateau gravels probably remained predominantly heath but by no means entirely so. Certainly, much of the plateau gravels are common or heath on Rocque's map of 1761; and in the Anglo-Saxon charters there is reference to heathland on the higher ground at Brimpton and Wokefield. The land was essentially marginal in character but, although it would appear to have been largely heath in the 10th century and in the 18th century, it is possible that some areas may have been broken in at some point in the intervening centuries, only to yield again to heath and scrub. It does seem likely, moreover, that gradual encroachment on the common did occur, as it certainly did during the post-medieval period. In some cases, it appears from the field boundaries, eg around Shortheath Firs, Sulhamstead (SU 645678), that the edge of the common had been pushed back and the area cleared and enclosed; but it is not known when this occurred. It is also possible that areas that were heath in the 18th century were formerly more intensively wooded but had been allowed to degenerate to heathland and scrub through overgrazing and the decline of woodland management. Although, in Figure 19, the areas of common fields, commons, and greens are based on post-medieval information, they can be taken as at least a guide to the medieval situation.

On the valley sides, the field boundaries are frequently irregular and evidence of open fields is unusual. These seem to be old enclosures and on some maps are referred to as such. In some cases, they may have been carved out of woodland. Indeed, the valley sides still present a well wooded appearance and the form of fields around the surviving woodland is often suggestive of encroachment and clearance, though of unknown date. The woodland, of course, would have been a valuable asset, used for building timber, fuel, forage for pigs, and for hunting. The poorer drainage of soils on the valley side (Jarvis 1968) may have encouraged their use for pasture rather than cultivation.

The study area lies on the edge of the royal forests of Windsor to the east, Savernake to the west, and Pamber to the south, although in the early 13th century, most of the rest of the county of Berkshire was known as the Forest of Berkshire which would also have come under the restrictions of forest law. After 1227, there was extensive deforestation in this area and several parks were created (Hatherly and Cantor 1979–80). Hatherly and Cantor note a concentration of medieval parks in the Kennet Valley and list at least 16 in this area, most of which were created in the 13th century or later. In most cases, their general location can be identified from field and place names. As would be expected, the parks avoid the land most suited to cultivation, that is the river gravels, and are instead found on the London Clays and plateau gravels of the valley side and top. Parks at Aldermaston and Ufton are both largely on plateau gravels. In 1338, Richard Paynel was given licence to enclose a park of 300 acres of pasture and wood at Ufton (Hatherly and Cantor 1979–80, 78). In 1262, William Achard received permission to impark his thicket at Aldermaston (ibid., 73). This must give some indication of the landuse of at least some areas of plateau gravel in the 13th and 14th centuries. Three parks in Thatcham, one at Chamberhouse, two at Crookham, were probably in quite well wooded areas across the valley sides. The imparking of large blocks of the valley may have had the effect of intensifying the use of the remaining areas. It may also have preserved for us pre-park features of cultivation and settlement.

Each parish then, contained areas of open fields on the river gravels; meadowland on the floodplain, pasture, woodland, and cultivated fields on the valley side, and predominantly common heathland on the plateau, though large areas around the edge were probably enclosed now, if not earlier, for cultivation and pasture. Each land type played an important role in the overall economy; note, for example, how the boundaries of Brimpton project to the south-east to include an area of heathland.

It is apparent from fieldwork elsewhere (eg Wade Martins 1975; Taylor 1978; 1983), that medieval settlement need not remain static, nor can the present day or post-medieval pattern be taken as a direct guide to the medieval scene. Nevertheless, with direct evidence lacking, the picture presented by 18th century maps (particularly Rocque 1761) should be considered. It is evident that there are nucleated settlements recognisable as villages, notably Aldermaston, Speen, Shaw, Donnington, and Woolhampton but also, though not so clearly defined, at Brimpton, Beenham, Burghfield, Englefield, Sulham, Theale, Tidmarsh, and Tilehurst. More striking, however, is the large number of smaller settlements. Churches are mostly either associated with only one or two buildings, or are peripheral to villages. Manorial centres tend to be relatively isolated or next to churches. Other isolated farms and buildings are very numerous. Sometimes the smaller settlements are spread out along the line of a road or roads, often in no coherent grouping; in other cases they are grouped around greens or dotted along the edge of the heath. Settlements along the edge of the heath, or actually within it, are a common feature of the post-medieval pattern, presumably reflecting encroachment onto heath as well as the need or desire for access onto the common. Whether this is a purely post-medieval phenomenon, or one with medieval roots, is unclear. The greens are found mostly in the east of the area, particularly at Burghfield and Grazeley, where they are quite extensive. They are frequently irregular in shape and sometimes lead one into another, funnelling to a narrow neck before opening onto the next green. In form they

often resemble small areas of heath and give the impression of areas of heath or pasture that have been left unenclosed. Perhaps settlement here was developing in a fairly open environment, consistent with Gelling's explanation of -feld (Gelling 1976; 1978). Similar settlements on the edge of common land have been identified elsewhere (Taylor 1983, 131).

Settlements are generally more common on the valley sides than on the river gravels, in spite of, or perhaps because of, the value of the gravels as cultivatable land. This is quite marked in Ufton Nervet, Sulhamstead, Wasing, and Brimpton but is not the case at Burghfield where farms are dotted over the extensive gravels; and the medieval boroughs of Newbury, Thatcham, Aldermaston, and Reading are all on the river gravels.

Most moated sites and parish churches are likely to be genuinely medieval elements in the landscape and they are are not uncommon in the area. Moats are more common in the eastern part of the survey area. The 10 or 11 examples include three suggested by cartographic evidence during the survey (Appendix 2). Chamberhouse, Thatcham could well be 12th, having had a licence to crenellate in 1446, but there is no surface evidence for a moat. At least five of the sites were very probably manorial: Burghfield, Brimpton, Crookham, Sulhamstead, and Ufton, and the remainder could also have been; Shinfield, on the edge of the survey area, is another example. None of the moats is associated with a concentration of settlements; all are now isolated or associated with one or two buildings. This need not reflect the medieval situation, but where the opportunity was taken to walk fields close to two of the moats (at Brimpton and Ufton Nervet), no evidence for more extensive settlement was found. It is likely that many of the moats may have been associated with the parks in the area and tended, therefore, to be separate from other settlements. To some extent, the location of a moated site will be affected by the desired result, a water-filled moat, but the drainage of the area is such that many sites are suitable. The distribution is more likely to reflect the pattern of settlement, perhaps in the 13th century, when a large proportion of moats were constructed (Clarke 1984, 54). Six are on river gravel, three on London Clay, and two on plateau gravel, both at the head of gullies at the plateau gravel edge.

The position of the medieval churches is also of interest. Of the 24 parish churches, 10 or 11 are high up on the valley side, either on the edge of the plateau gravel or not far from it. Ten churches are on the plateau gravel, two on Bagshot Beds, and three on London Clay. The factors determining their siting fall into perhaps three categories. Firstly, the churches may reflect the existing settlement pattern and be placed for convenience of access for the lord of the manor or the parishioners, or both, and it is noticeable that they are mostly situated fairly centrally within the parishes. Secondly, the siting may depend on the availability of land, both for the church itself, and for the priest, and this may have encouraged the building of churches on more marginal land. Other factors may relate to the site itself, such as a conspicuous location, or a traditionally venerated spot, although there is no evidence for the latter. It is, however, unlikely that the distribution of the churches is consistently unrelated to the pattern of settlement. Those churches which have not been rebuilt, almost invariably contain 12th and sometimes 11th century fabric. The results of excavations in churches elsewhere (Rodwell 1981) show that a 10th century date is not unusual and it is likely that the churches in the Lower Kennet Valley would have been established in the 10th and 11th century, or even earlier.

The use of the valley side was clearly well established at an early date and the distribution of the churches may reflect a scatter of settlements on the spring line of the upper valley side, perhaps also coinciding with the junction of the heath and the enclosed land. The tendency to site the churches on the valley sides and higher ground is striking and it is suggested that this reflects the main focus of settlement in the centuries before the Norman Conquest. Initially, it is surprising that there are not more churches (and settlements) on the fertile river gravels but this is partly explained when it is recognised that the open fields provided only one facet of the farming economy of the valley. Firstly, settlements on the valley side would have been more centrally placed within the parish. Secondly, it appears that some of the churches may have been on the edge of areas of heath. This may indicate a tendency to establish settlements in areas where more marginal land is available, perhaps in association with the colonisation of areas of the valley side and plateau, or else because of the importance of the grazing provided by access to the heath. Settlements are also likely to have been established in those areas where the greatest investment of labour was being made. If the river gravels were fully exploited and parcelled out as open fields by this time, any expansion of the arable acreage would most likely have occurred on the valley sides, with clearance of woods and heath and more intensive use of existing fields. Furthermore, the reorganisation of the subdivided arable, or its partitioning for the first time, might have coincided with a deliberate removal of the settlements from the more fertile land.

In the 18th century, churches were within towns or villages (all on river gravel), peripheral to villages (some on lower ground), or they were associated with small settlements of three buildings or fewer (all on higher ground). Further work is needed to establish whether this reflects the medieval pattern or whether, for example, churches are peripheral to settlements because there has been a shift from an original focus around the church, whilst the small settlements adjoining most of the churches may originally have been larger. Near Padworth church, 'there are many traces under the surface of foundations of buildings all around the house (Padworth House), especially on the north side' (Clinton 1911). These may represent a village just below the church but no earthworks remain. Some hamlets have shrunk since the 18th century, for example, at Enborne Street and at Ufton Green Church, where houses were shown on the 18th century estate maps. Earthworks at Ufton Green, recorded by Wilkey (1977), are therefore likely to be post-medieval but may derive from an earlier pattern. There are some indications of medieval shrinkage of settlements suggested by documentary evidence. In 1349, at Cowdray's Manor, Padworth, and at Crookham, Thatcham, the land was worth nothing, as all the free tenants and peasants were said to be dead (Clinton 1911; *Victoria County History*). Inclosure in the 15th and 16th centuries may also have had an effect. Desertion on a small-scale, involving only one or two households, is recorded for Greenham, Burghfield, and Woolhampton (Leadam 1897). These may not have been long term or major changes. Only three settlements appear to have been deserted altogether: Henwick in Cold Ash parish, at Bucklebury, and at Sheffield.

9. Review

Summary

One of the recurring themes in the archaeology of the Lower Kennet Valley is the way in which the pattern of settlement and the character of landuse relate to the valley's topographical and geological diversity. Against the environmental constraints must be weighed the broader social and economic factors, the villa owner's cash crop policy or the lord of the manor's penchant for a little hunting.

In the medieval period it is clear from documentary evidence that the settlements stood within land units which ran across the valley from floodplain to plateau and within which landuse was closely related to the topography and potential of the varying localities. This was the case from at least the 10th century, but how far back does this pattern go and at what point did the varying potential of different areas become a determining factor in the location and economic base of settlements? What was the relationship between settlements in different locations across the valley and how did this change through time? For example, are they a series of more or less independent farming settlements, or components of an economic and/or social unit?

In the Romano-British period, similar units to those in the medieval period may be implied by a series of substantial buildings (villas?) along the valley. Within these units or estates we see a dispersed pattern of settlements, probably farms and hamlets, with larger settlements on the valley floor and smaller on the valley side, probably reflecting the topography and the available resources. A dispersed pattern is also seen in the medieval period. Romano-British and medieval landuse may have been broadly similar but there is some indication of medieval intensification of use on the valley side and also of some movement of settlement from the river gravels. This is seen, for example, in the contrast between the positioning, on the one hand of the Roman villas and the larger settlements on the valley floor and, on the other hand, the medieval churches on the higher ground. At the same time, the medieval use of the river gravels may have been more intensive than ever before. In both periods, there are also settlements with specialised, non-agrarian functions: Newbury, Thatcham, and to some extent Aldermaston in the medieval period, and in the Romano-British period, the settlement at Thatcham Newtown. If *Spinis* is another such settlement, and this remains entirely unknown, then the spacing of these urban sites also becomes comparable. In both periods, the area is also within the hinterland of a major urban centre, *Calleva* and also Reading.

There appears to have been a decline in population and exploitation of the valley in the Early Iron Age, possibly as a result of the intensification of the Late Bronze Age. The pattern of settlement in the Late Iron Age appears, superficially, to be very similar to that of the Romano-British period but the structure behind it could be quite different. Evidence for Iron Age land units is difficult to establish but the degree of specialisation in the Late Bronze Age certainly suggests that individual settlements were working within a wider framework.

In the Late Neolithic/Early Bronze Age, settlements are more difficult to find but activity is demonstrated by extensive flint finds, though in small quantities, and by the barrows and ring-ditches. Although large areas are likely to have remained wooded at this time, the field-walking results suggest fairly widespread activity on all geologies but perhaps with more emphasis on the use of the river gravels. By analogy with other areas in southern Britain, it was probably in the Bronze Age that the soils of the plateau gravels were degraded to podsols, supporting only rough grass, heath, or scrub. This impoverishment of the plateau gravels may have been one of the factors leading to higher densities of flints on the river gravels, but this may always have been the preferred locality. It was quite probably at this time that the persisting character of the valley was developing. In the earlier Bronze Age, the groupings of barrows/ring-ditches along the valley, sometimes on the river gravel, sometimes on the plateau gravels, may relate to a series of land units running across the valley, although other models can also be suggested (*see* above).

As yet there is no evidence for intensive Early Neolithic activity, no ritual monuments, and few finds. If this distribution is genuine, rather than apparent, it may be because Early Neolithic activity was concentrated in areas where extensive light, well drained soils were available on the chalklands or the more extensive gravels of the Upper and Lower Thames. Perhaps the early use of the Lower Kennet was as a component in the economy of other areas, for example, for hunting or grazing.

The evidence from the Early Neolithic contrasts strongly with the wealth of evidence from the Mesolithic. It remains to be established whether the valley formed a more or less self-contained unit, with relatively permanent base camps on the valley floor, enjoying the rich resources of the valley as a whole, or whether these settlements were only one component of a cycle of settlement in central southern England.

Floodplain

This is an area of great archaeological potential, partly because of the important role it played at many times in the past, and particularly because of the potential of waterlogged deposits and remains sealed by peat. Mesolithic sites are certainly sealed in this way and their main focus is on the floodplain and the floodplain terrace. There is local variation in the date of the floodplain deposits. However, it is striking that very few Neolithic/Early Bronze Age flints were found on the alluvium, whereas Iron Age/Roman finds are common. This is most likely due to the development of floodplain deposits during prehistory, perhaps in part because of hillwash induced by agriculture either here or upstream. From recent excavated evidence, it appears that alluvial deposits began to accumulate in the Neolithic continuing throughout the Bronze Age; further-more, in some areas, peat and alluvium continued to develop in the Romano-British and Saxon periods and man's intervention in the flow and direction of the river in the medieval and post-medieval periods has resulted in further accumulation. The later Bronze Age, Iron Age, and Roman sherds from the alluvium are generally found just off the floodplain terrace, sometimes on slightly higher ground than the rest of the floodplain. Presumably, these sites are exploiting the grazing potential of these lowlying areas. Medieval sites are found in similar locations; does this reflect a similar use? The floodplain was evidently used as more than just the common meadowland; some settlements on the floodplain may have used drainage to support mixed farming. Sites sealed by floodplain deposits are difficult to find by ordinary survey methods but the evaluations carried out recently have demonstrated the need to investigate this topographic zone.

River Gravels

Because of the discovery of archaeological sites during gravel extraction and the susceptibility of the soils to cropmark formation, the archaeological potential of the river gravels has become relatively well known compared to other parts of the study area. There is a wealth of archaeological remains on the river gravels and the potential here is reinforced by the identification of some waterlogged deposits containing environmental data, although most archaeological sites in this zone are on dry land.

Mesolithic sites can be expected, particularly on the river gravel edge, in a similar context to those on the floodplain. As yet, there is little evidence for Early Mesolithic activity but from the Late Neolithic onwards it was probably the river gravels that offered the greatest potential for agriculture. In the Late Neolithic/Early Bronze Age this is indicated by greater densities of flints on the river gravels than on other geologies but the densities are still not high and concentrations or settlements are difficult to pinpoint. This may be partly because of the character of the raw material and the low intensity of the fieldwalking, but may also reflect the character of the settlements. Also obscure is the economic base of these sites. Environmental evidence suggests that by the later Bronze Age, the gravels had been very largely cleared of woodland, although with secondary scrub in places. From the later Bronze Age to the Romano-British period, the river gravels were clearly intensively settled. As yet, it is not possible to reconstruct the appearance and organisation of the contemporaneous landscape. Associated with the presumed Iron Age and Romano-British cropmark enclosures there are trackways and some indications of field systems, but these seem to be rather restricted in extent (Gates 1975, eg map 11). Further investigation may reveal whether this merely reflects the present level of air photo coverage or a genuine indication of the nature of Iron Age and Romano-British boundary systems. Does it mean, for example, that only an area quite close to the settlements was enclosed for fields, or is it simply that the majority of the fields were defined only by ditchless, organic hedges?

It is on the river gravels that the villas tend to be found, possibly because the wealthier landowners sited their estate centres in the middle of their most productive land, or did particular Iron Age farms prosper into villas because of the potential of the surrounding land? In the medieval period, the intensive use of the river gravels as the basis for the open fields may be accompanied, in some places, by a shift in settlement to the higher ground, although at the same time, it is on the river gravels that the boroughs were situated.

Valley Side (London Clay, Bagshot Beds, and Plateau Gravel Edge)

At present, archaeological investigation here is restricted by the rarity of sites identifiable as cropmarks and by the lack of ground disturbance on the scale of the quarrying on the river gravels. However, fieldwalking suggests that, for much of prehistory, the valley side could have been quite as intensively settled as the valley floor.

No evidence had been found for Mesolithic settlements: quite probably the valley side and top, and perhaps a wider area still, were exploited from the base camps on the valley floor. In the Late Neolithic/Early Bronze Age, the widespread finds of flints suggest general activity on the valley side, though not perhaps as intensive as on the river gravels. It is evident that in the Iron Age and Romano-British period, settlements were quite as common on the valley side as on the valley floor and the situation may well be similar in the later Bronze Age as well. The settlements seem to be small, perhaps reflecting the topography and the Bagshot Beds may be a preferred location, probably because they are on better drained soils on the spring line at the interface between the London Clay and the plateau gravel. The medieval pattern is perhaps a continuation and intensification of the earlier situation, although at the same time, the wooded character of the valley side and the use of the valley side and plateau for medieval parks reflects the different potential and character of the area compared to the river gravels.

Plateau (Plateau Gravel)

This is an area which is still relatively under studied because of the present landuse and the full potential may not be known. It is on the plateau gravels that there is the greatest chance of finding relatively undisturbed Palaeolithic sites, unlike the river gravels where the palaeoliths will invariably be in resorted deposits. In the Mesolithic and Neolithic, the use of the plateau may have been much the same as the use of the valley side. The fieldwalking evidence for the Late Neolithic/Early Bronze Age, when flints are found equally on the plateau and the valley side, contrasts with the evidence for the Iron Age, Romano-British, and medieval periods. Sherds of these periods were only occasionally found on the plateau gravels. This contrast may reflect the impoverishment of the plateau gravel soils, perhaps in the Early Bronze Age. This change is a significant aspect in the development of the valley which will have had important consequences on the subsequent pattern of settlement and landuse. Extensive areas of grass or heath may well have been an important element in the economy at any date, as a valuable resource for grazing and for fuel. There may also have been episodes of clearance and cultivation at any period, when pressure on land was particularly acute and large areas of the plateau edge, perhaps better drained and closer to suitable water supplies, may have been more intensively used from an early date. The essential character of the area, established in the Bronze Age, continued beyond the medieval period and is still apparent today, though heavily disguised by more recent developments.

Conclusion

In the integration and critical assessment of all the available data for the study area, the survey initially created a broad framework on which the results of extensive and detailed field survey could be built. These results, despite the problems of interpretation posed by low surface artefact levels, provide the first indications of a range of past activities formerly under-represented within the archaeological record as well as enhancing the existing record. Although some types of site and specific activities may be expected to retain subsoil features associated with the identified surface traces, it is likely that for others the surface artefacts represent the sole surviving evidence. The problems for the curation and management of such sites are considerable.

Despite the intensity and extent of the survey, gaps still remain in our understanding of the development of the landscape from the Late-Glacial onwards. Some of these gaps, perhaps more a function of site visibility than of genuine absence, are shared by almost all studied areas within the British Isles. Others contrast strongly with evidence from adjacent blocks of landscape. A number of specific themes which would benefit from further investigation can be identified and have been discussed within their respective period sections. The hints of activity dating to the Upper Palaeolithic suggest that this period may be worthy of further investigation. While there is a wealth of information available for the Mesolithic period in the survey area, the Neolithic period as a whole remains poorly understood. However, the Kennet Valley does appear to offer great potential for the study of changing culture and economy at the time of the Early Neolithic transition. In the later prehistoric period both the Early and Middle Iron Ages are similarly poorly represented. The problems of the decline of Romano-British occupation and influence and the subsequent Saxon settlement pattern are universal and no less so in the Kennet Valley. Finally, greater attention needs to be directed towards developing a greater understanding of the rural settlements and their economic relationship with the urban centres of the Kennet Valley.

The systematic methods of collection employed during the survey produced data of high quality, the analysis of which has allowed statements relating to past landuse to be made with confidence. The data base also provides the basis for valid comparison with other areas of the survey, in particular the Upper Kennet Valley, the Marlborough and Berkshire Downs, and parts of the Thames Valley. However, there are clearly improvements and refinements to be made in the methodology adopted. The fieldwork and related investigations carried out in the Lower Kennet Valley have clearly indicated the significance of localised topographical features as well as the nature of the soils themselves in relation to both the location and the recovery of surface finds. Future survey work may benefit from the closer examination of such features, employing aerial photographs and existing mapping alongside field survey, as well as augmenting surface collection with more detailed mapping in the field. The value of augering in the identification of buried topographic features such as old river courses as well as in providing extensive data concerning broad soil development has already been demonstrated. It may be considered an aid to the interpretation of surface assemblages to routinely employ this rapid method of prospection alongside surface collection within specific topographic zones. From a purely logistical viewpoint, greater emphasis should be placed on the mapping in the field of bulk finds such as burnt flint, although such an approach may present its own specific problems.

Within the last decade and despite the great increase in field investigation, environmental studies do not appear to have progressed at a rate which might have been expected. The potential of the survey area for providing relevant information is considerable and yet great gaps still exist for certain periods. This is perhaps partly owing to the nature of more recent excavations, many resulting from development proposals and intended to evaluate with minimum intervention.

Despite these gaps, the survey has confirmed the considerable human impact on the landscape of the Kennet Valley and also the great potential remaining within zones as yet little explored or exploited. The Kennet Valley has seen considerable development pressure within the past two decades, pressure which is likely to continue. In line with this pressure, the County Council developed enlightened planning policies relating to the archaeological resource which has resulted in routine evaluation of areas affected by development proposals. In this context, the data provided by this survey will be crucial in the development of strategies appropriate to the management of the remaining archaeological resource. As more sites are investigated both through fieldwalking and evaluation on development sites, the nature and significance of surface assemblages identified during this survey may be more clearly understood.

10. Appendices

Appendix 1   1976–77 Survey: new air photo sites

Reference	NGR (SU)	Parish	Description	Geology	Source
Soilmarks					
3862	64506675	Sulhamstead	Sub-rectangular enclosure formerly under woodland	PG	BCCC1969,8882
3863	57956512	Wasing	Light and dark rectangular marks possibly associated with moat at Wasing Lower Farm (Appendix 2)	RG	BCC 1969, 9055
3864	47166923	Donnington	Ring-ditch (20 m in diameter) fieldwalked 1977 (Appendix 6)	C	BCC 1969, 5082
Cropmarks					
3865	691682	Grazeley	Square enclosure with mark in interior and 2 linear features leading off to SE. Adjacent to Burnt House Farm	LC	BCC 1976, 4119
3866	655636	Mortimer	Probable sub-rectangular enclosure, walked 1977 (Appendix 6)	PG	BCC 1976, 6422. NMR SU 6536/17 165–66.
3867	61546955	Ufton Nervet	Possible additional ring-ditch to group defined by Gates (1975, map 8)	RG	NMR SU 6169/17, 238–41
3868	52906700	Thatcham	Sub-rectangular enclosure with a probable second enclosure <100 m away. Farmer had noticed pottery after ploughing	RG	NMR SU 5266/2 91–92
3869	51346818	Thatcham	Linear features now built over	RB	NMR SU 5767/1 364–65
3870	503677	Thatcham	Two parallel linear features with offsets and 2 small enclosures. Roman Road, Silchester–Cirencester. Adjacent to known RB settlement. Walked 1977 (Appendix 6)	RB	110–11
3871	458658	Enborne	Trackway and enclosures. Walked 1977 (Appendix 6)	LC	NMR SU 4565/1 133–34; 2/187–89; 3/190–92; 4/334–37
3872	443657	Enborne	Linear features and a group of large marks. Visited (Appendix 6)	RB	BAU 1977

104

Appendix 2 1976–77 Survey: field and place names

Names which may suggest the existence of archaeological sites are listed in groups sharing a common element.

1. With a possible element in *burgh* (gen. and dat. *byrig* — fortified place. Used in three senses: ancient fort, manor house, and market town (Gelling 1976, 854, 923).

Olderbury	SU 684697	Burghfield
Berry Hams	SU 665679	Burghfield
Arbour Pightle	?	Burghfield

Field (1972) suggests possibly land near or containing an earthwork

Aubery's Farm	SU 586690	Beenham

Field (1972): old earthwork. OE *ald* and *burgh*

Aubery's Meadow	SU 598665	Aldermaston
Berry's Copse	SU 545684	Bucklebury

Investigated without result

Dewberry Meadow	SU 54006560	Thatcham

Fieldwalking produced only a few sherds of Romano-British and medieval pottery

Berry Stiles Cottages	SU 52586742	Thatcham
Ramsbury Corner	SU 525696	Thatcham

Known hillfort (Hadcock 1950)

Bury's Bank	SU 490650	Grennham
Greyberry or Dryberry Copse	SU 496655	Greenham
Beamsbury Coppice	SU 438641	Enborne

Some of the 'berry' names, particularly those on alluvium, may have an element in *ieg* — land partly surrounded by water, dry ground in marsh, well-watered land (Gelling 1976). Other examples may refer to the flora, for example, Dewberry (Gelling 1973, 192).

2. With a possible element in *wic ham*. 'Wickham' or *wicham* names may indicate substantial sub-Roman settlements and are frequently close to Roman Roads (Gelling 1976; 1977).

Wickham Knights Bridge,		
Wickham Knights Meadow	SU 581663	Woolhampton
Wickhams, Wickham Tenacres,		
Five Acres Mount		
Hither and Further Mount	SU 669698	Burghfield

The former is on the floodplain about 1.5 km north of the Roman Road from Silchester to Cirencester. The second is 4.5 km from the nearest known Roman Road; it is on a tongue of London Clay projecting out onto the river gravel and 'Pingewood', a British place-name survival (Gelling 1973, 209), is 2 km to the east in the middle of extensive Iron Age/Romano-British cropmark complexes (Gates 1975, map 11).

3. References to pot or potters

Crocks Pightle	SU 66156755	Burghfield	plateau gravel
Crocker's Pightle (built over)	SU 481669	Greenham	river gravel
Potter's Piddle	SU 431649	Enborne	Reading Beds

For 'potter' field names, Field (1972) suggests 'land used or occupied by a potter', the use normally being for the provision of clay for pottery. None of the above locations are actually on clay, so perhaps these names merely indicate the small-holding of a potter (Le Patourel 1968); but the possibility of kiln sites or large scatters of pot cannot be ruled out.

4. Moat names

Moat Pightle	SU 676682	Burghfield

A narrow strip of water shown on the OS 1:10560 is no longer visible on the ground. There is a slight depression in the field to the south-west. The field adjoins the former manorial centre, Burghfield Place.

| Moat Close | SU 579651 | Wasing |

An L-shaped pond is shown on early maps. Nothing is visible on the ground, but see Appendix 1, PRN 3863. There was formerly a small mill at at Wasing Lower Farm; some of the equipment remained in the outhouse. Field (1972) suggests that 'moat' can also apply to millpools.

5. With an element in *totaern dun* — hill with a look-out building (ie hillfort) at Bussock Camp, Winterbourne (Gelling 1976, 910).

| Totterdown Hill | ? | Mortimer |

Although no earthworks were observed when this locality was visited, there is certainly an excellent view in an arc from north-north-east to south-south-west.

| | ? | Burghfield |

Totterdown

Field (1972) suggests 'land adjacent or containing an earthwork'.

6. Mill names

| Mill Field | SU 5 71658 | Brimpton |

No mill now exists, but on the Inclosure map, a stream is marked running north of the field. A scatter of medieval pot was found by the edge of the stream (Appendix 5.3, PRN 3578).

Appendix 3   1976–77 Survey: earthwork sites in woodland, heath, and plantation

Ref.	NGR (SU)	Parish	Description	Geol.
3875	62546625	Ufton Nervet	Slightly oval mound, *c.* 11 m in diameter and *c.* 1 m high. Gentle slope. Possibly associated with 'Brickcroft Copse' immediately to the north-east.	BB
3876	63046545–	Ufton Nervet	Low bank a few cm high, 600 m long, 2–3 m wide. Slight ditch to the south-east. Continues over the apparent course of the Roman Road. Cut by drainage ditches. Continues to the south-west into dense plantation.	PG
	63426574			
3877	62876616	Ufton Nervet	Low bank *c.* 50 m north of Grims Bank.	PG
3878	64536511–			
	64626534	Mortimer	Hollow-way, *c.* 3 m wide and 0.15 m deep. S. end disturbed by plantation ridges and furrows.	PG
3879	61886456	Padworth	Banked and ditched sub-rectangular enclosure, 40 x 30 m. One side destroyed. Bank *c.* 0.6 m high, ditch 0.4 m deep, mostly water filled.	
3880	61826470	Padworth	Low mound with slight flanking ditches, *c.* 25 m long, 8 m wide, 0.4 m high, tapering in height and width to north-east. ?pillow mound.	
3881	57786328	Wasing	Low oval mound, *c.* 10 m diameter Plateau edge overlooking gully	PG
3882	58206310	Wasing	Hollow-way. East end destroyed by quarry; extends 150 m to the west.	PG

Appendix 4 1976–77 Survey: fieldwalking results from cropmark sites

Gates's Map	NGR	Parish	Description	PRN	Finds
1	SU 568653	Brimpton	Roman Road and irregular linear features	3572	2 flints; 2 Roman sherds; 2 medieval sherds
1	SU 572656	Brimpton	Enclosures (destroyed)	3583	No finds from field to south-east
1	SU 573651	Wasing	Roman Road; ring-ditch; enclosure	3746	No finds from ring-ditch. 5 Iron Age sherds + 22 Roman sherds from enclosure
1	SU 580655	Aldermaston	Enclosure and linears	3531	9/10 prehistoric sherds, 76 Roman, and 12 medieval sherds in area of enclosure. 12 medieval sherds from cropmark to the south-east
1	SU 586653	Aldermaston	Linear features	3536	9 flints, 5 Roman + 2 medieval sherds
1	SU 593656	Aldermaston	Rectangular enclosure & linear features	3525	4 flints, 3 medieval sherds not from the area of enclosure
2	SU 565647	Brimpton	Elongated enclosure (2)	3588	42 flints; 1 Roman and 1 defining cleared wood medieval sherd (Tithe map)
8	SU 606681	Beenham	Linear features	3555	6 flints; 1 medieval, partly destroyed (old quarry) sherd
8	SU 620676	Ufton Nervet	2 ring-ditches; linears	3721	2 flints from ring-ditches; 4 prehistoric sherds from linear features
8	SU 630682	Ufton Nervet	4 small conjoined rectangular enclosures & linears	3736	1 flint
	SU 454658 (PRN 3871)	Ufton Nervet	Trackway & enclosures	3616	8 flints; 8 medieval sherds. Lower part of rotary quern ploughed up from depression in adjoining field (west).
	SU 471692	Donnington	Ring-ditch (PRN3864)	3614	Large numbers of flints to the south but few in the area of ring-ditch
	SU 503677	Thatcham	Roman Road, linear features; 2 small enclosures (3870)	3682	20 flints; 48 Roman sherds, 2 medieval sherds. Adjoins known Roman site (Harris 1937)
	SU 523686	Thatcham	Linear features (? fields)	3684	8 flints; 26 Roman and 7 medieval sherds. Part of former parkland.
	SU 655636	Burghfield	Enclosure (3866)	3639	9 flints; 2 Iron Age sherds 60 m south of enclosure

107

Appendix 5 1976–77 Survey: pottery find spots/sites

5.1 Prehistoric

PRN No.	NGR (SU)	Parish	No. sherds	Geol.	Topography	Area
Neolithic						
3545	61136458	Aldermaston	1	PG		
3745	57436477	Wasing	1	RG	Edge of floodplain	
3746	57346518	Wasing	1	RG	Edge of floodplain terrace	
Later Bronze Age						
3562	56486402	Brimpton	12 (Dev. Rim.)	BB	Hill slope above the river	40 m
3539	60286662	Aldermaston	1 (LBA)	RG	Edge of floodplain terrace	
3577	56786597	Brimpton	1 (LBA)		Edge of floodplain terrace	
Late Bronze Age/Iron Age						
3577	56786597	Brimpton	4		Edge of floodplain	100 m^2
3531	580656	Aldermaston	10		Edge of floodplain terrace	200x100 m
NB. cropmark site						
3532	58476577	Aldermaston	9		Floodplain	250x100 m
3533	57806590	Aldermaston	11–15		Floodplain	50x180 m
3625	56586705	Midgham	3/4	BB	Slope above sharp break	50 m
3630	54666788	Midgham	4/5	BB	Crest of gently sloping spur above break in slope	70 m
3658	45186820	Speen	4/5	PG	Side of small gully	70x50 m
3659	65526366	Mortimer	2	LC		
NB. 50 m south of cropmark enclosure (PRN3866 — Appendix 6)						
3671	52876372	Thatcham	8	BB	Crest and side of spur	120x70 m
3693	54406352	Thatcham	3/4	PG/BB	Slope above sharp break	50x40 m
3733 and 3721	62206770	Ufton Nervet	21	LC	Along break in slope	60x150 m
NB. cropmark site						
3746	57406530	Wasing	12		Floodplain terrace	100x300 m
3749	57676621	Woolhampton	19		Floodplain terrace	250x100 m

5.2 Romano-British

PRN No.	NGR (SU)	Parish	No. sherds	Date	Geol.	Topog.	Area
3531	579655	Aldermaston	76	2–4 C *3–4 C		Edge of floodplain	200 m
NB. cropmark site (Appendix 6)							
3533	578658	Aldermaston	106	3–4 C	All.	Floodplain	70 m
3576	565865	Brimpton	34	1–2 C	All.	Floodplain	100x30 m
3577	566869	Brimpton	42	2–4 C *4 C	All.	Floodplain	100x30 m
3601	660966	Burghfield	16	1–2 C	LC	Slope above stream	10x10 m
3625	565767	Midgham	34		BB	Slope above sharp break in slope	60x50 m
3658	451768	Speen	9	1–2 C	PG	Side of small gully	50x40 m

Nb. also produced Iron Age sherds

Appendix 5 (5.2) continued

PRN	NGR (SU)	Parish	No. sherds	Date	Geol.	Topography	Area
3682	502677	Thatcham	48	3–4 C	RB	Gentle slope	100x100 m

NB. adjacent to known Romano-British site at Thatcham Newtown (Harris 1937). Also cropmark site.

PRN	NGR (SU)	Parish	No. sherds	Date	Geol.	Topography	Area
3684	52326878	Thatcham	26	3–4 C	LC	Edge of break in slope	40x40 m
3689 and 3695	53766739	Thatcham	37	3–4 C	LC	On a spur adj. break in slope	80x30 m
3693	54406379	Thatcham	24	1–2 C	PG/BB	Sharp break in slope	40x40 m
3646	57326515	Wasing	22		RG	Edge of floodplain terrace	40x20 m

NB. cropmark site, see Appendix 6

PRN	NGR (SU)	Parish	No. sherds	Date	Geol.	Topography	Area
3749	57656617	Woolhampton	33	12 C	All.	Floodplain	100x100 m
3752	57036827	Woolhampton	21		BB/LC	Head of gully	60x50 m

The quantities of Roman and medieval pottery described are as collected in runs at 50 m intervals. Where the material came from only one run, assessment of the extent of the concentration was made by pacing out from the line of the run to the apparent edge of the scatter. The date range is given as, for example, 2–4 C (2nd to 4th century AD). * indicates predominant date.

5.3 Medieval

Probable settlement sites

PRN	NGR (SU)	Parish	No. sherds	Date	Geol.	Topography	Area
3578	57106594	Brimpton	42	13–15 C	RG	Edge of floodplain	60x30 m

NB. adjacent to 'Mill Field' (see Appendix 2)

PRN	NGR (SU)	Parish	No. sherds	Date	Geol.	Topography	Area
3594	55876387	Brimpton	22	14–15 C	RG	Next to hollow-way at edge of floodplain terrace	30x15 m
3617	45476538	Enborne	16	12–13 C	BB/LC	Edge of spur	30x30 m
		Enborne	72	12–16 C	BB/LC	Edge of spur	100x100 m

NB. associated with darker soil. Adjacent to a small green shown on 18th-century estate map

PRN	NGR (SU)	Parish	No. sherds	Date	Geol.	Topography	Area
3628	54616744	Midgham	42	13–14 C	LC	Side of a gully	40x30 m
3699	53636590	Thatcham	102	12–16 C		Floodplain	50x30 m

Possible sites

PRN	NGR (SU)	Parish	No. sherds	Date	Geol.	Topography	Area
3533	578658	Aldermaston	48			Floodplain	200x100 m (max)
3630	4666788	Midgham	22		BB	Small spur near break in slope	70 m
3649} 3650}	621562	Padworth	29				180x30 m

NB. associated with darker soil and slightly raised above the rest of the field. Also produced post-medieval pottery.

PRN	NGR (SU)	Parish	No. sherds	Date	Geol.	Topography	Area
3688	52486693	Thatcham	13	13–15 C	RG	Edge of floodplain terrace	15 m

NB. includes relatively large fresh sherds

PRN	NGR (SU)	Parish	No. sherds	Date	Geol.	Topography	Area
3688	52566682	Thatcham	15	11–13 C		Floodplain	40x40 m
3749	57656517	Woolhampton	30			Floodplain	150x100 m

Appendix 6, 1976–77 Survey: Recommendations

In recent years large areas of the Lower Kennet Valley have been drastically altered. This is a continuing process. The archaeological resource has already been seriously diminished and unless an adequate record is made there are many questions which it will become increasingly difficult to answer as further sites are destroyed. These sites are not a series of isolated phenomena, but must be seen as a component of a larger site, the historic landscape as a whole. This view may be a platitude nowadays but it is no less true for that.

The archaeological response to development in the valley must not be purely reactive, a series of *ad hoc* actions as emergencies arise. The threat is demonstrably long term and on a large-scale; the response must correspondingly be forward thinking with a planned course of action. In substance, this is the only recommendation that the writer believes to be imperative. In general it is recommended that further work in the Lower Kennet Valley should include the following aspects.

Environmental Work

Environmental evidence is crucial for an understanding of all periods and must be a major element in any programme of work in the Kennet Valley. The systematic collection of environmental data is likely to be the only way to examine satisfactorily and, in detail, the complex changes in the landuse history of the valley. The retrieval of environmental data should normally be a major aspect of any excavation in the valley, in particular on the valley floor where waterlogged deposits are likely to be found. On the floodplain it will be important to establish the depositional sequence and archaeological potential of the area. Many of the sources of environmental data are on the plateau gravel where earthworks may preserve buried soils. A sampling programme could be designed to establish key elements in the environmental sequence and should certainly be incorporated in project designs for any excavations carried out in this topographical zone.

Fieldwalking

The present survey has established the value of fieldwalking in the Lower Kennet in both identifying specific archaeological sites and outlining trends but it is also clear that low intensity fieldwalking has its limitations. Further work should aim to examine a larger sample using a gridded framework. Further survey should be concentrated primarily on potentially threatened areas, notably the gravels, but should also examine areas off the gravels to establish the broader archaeological context.

Survey of Earthworks

More detailed survey of earthwork sites at an adequate scale is required. In particular, scheduled sites should be re-examined, reinterpreted where relevant, and surveyed and planned at a large-scale. As an example, not all the earthworks of the Grims Bank linear feature seem to have been fully identified and surveyed. Survey is required to establish whether the present scheduling is adequate as well as to interpret the monument.

The potential of the heathland, woodland, and plantation areas needs to be assessed systematically. The density of vegetation in these areas makes survey difficult and many areas of heath or scrub will only really be accessible after they have been burnt off. This means that survey may have to be carried out as the opportunity arises. The extent and character of the ridge and furrow of the grassland areas of the valley side and floor needs to be mapped, making use of air photographs followed by ground checking. The Lower Kennet Valley contains large areas of parkland which may be expected to preserve relict features of the pre-park landscape, in particular traces of medieval agriculture. Identification survey is required to assess this potential. Settlement earthworks provide another subject that could be usefully surveyed.

Air Photography

The area would benefit from more regular aerial reconnaissance. Areas off the gravels need to be examined to establish whether cropmark formation can be expected. In particular, air photography of sites identified by fieldwalking may provide further evidence of their character and extent and allow comparison with sites identified on the river gravels. Cropmarks should be plotted analytically at a suitable scale to ensure the recording of interpretative detail. This is crucial if cropmarks are to be used for archaeological analysis and decision-making, rather than simply indicating the general character and location of the remains.

Geophysical Survey

The results of geophysical survey can be striking; where the conditions are right it provides a rapid and effective method of survey. Initially, geophysical prospecting should be undertaken in a range of localities to establish its potential in the Lower Kennet Valley.

Watching Briefs

Many sites are not easily identifiable by survey methods, either because of the nature of the site or because they are obscured by vegetation cover or deeply buried, for example, by floodplain deposits. Such sites may be revealed anywhere through disturbance of the ground but observation of such exposures can be concentrated in two main areas: the floodplain and the gravels.

Excavation

Excavation of sites in advance of destruction must clearly be an important part of future work in the Kennet Valley. Total excavation is required for many classes of site which have yet to be adequately invest-igated, but where there is a danger of merely gathering repetitive data, problem oriented sample excavation may be more appropriate. Provision will need to be made to investigate those sites that are discovered by chance. Some excavation will also be necessary on sites off the gravels, partly in response to long term erosion by agriculture and partly to provide a context for work on the gravels. This may be achievable by small-scale excavations linked to detailed field survey.

Preservation and Management

One of the major objectives of survey will be to provide guidelines for policies of preservation and management. Wherever possible, the first aim will normally be to preserve sites; excavation should only be employed as a last resort or for purposes of assessment.

There is little point in scheduling sites if they are not subsequently preserved by appropriate management. On most sites this may mean continued cultivation to an agreed depth. The management of sites in woodland or plantation requires closer liaison with forestry managers to agree appropriate policies for the long term management of archaeological monuments.

Presentation

The scope for archaeology in amenity and education should be fully explored. The development of public awareness of the value of archaeology in interpreting and appreciating the environment which people have created is also one of the most effective ways of securing the future of both the archaeological remains and of archaeology as a discipline.

Appendix 7 1982–87 Survey, transect, all finds

Field No.	Flint Cores					Flakes/Blades Unbroken			Flakes/Blades Broken					Tools							Bnt flint Mean wt/g	Pottery				Tile	
	Bl	Fl	Fr	Deb	Ch	Fl	Bl	Blt	Fl	Bl	Blt	Bnt	Ret	1	2	3	4	5	6	7		Ph	RB	Med. P. med.	RB med.	Fab. A	P. med pres mean wt/g
1	1	–	–	–	–	4	–	–	–	–	–	–	–	–	–	–	–	–	–	–	35	–	–	1	–	–	–
2+3	–	–	–	–	–	5	–	–	1	–	–	–	–	–	–	–	–	–	–	–	42	–	–	–	–	–	34
4	–	–	–	–	–	2	–	–	1	–	–	–	–	–	–	–	–	–	–	–	17	–	–	2	–	–	13
5	–	–	–	–	–	5	1	–	2	–	–	–	–	–	–	–	–	–	–	–	14	–	–	1	–	–	30
6	–	–	–	–	–	–	–	–	–	–	–	–	–	–	–	–	–	–	–	–	5	–	–	1	–	–	114
7	3	6	1	3	–	41	3	–	31	2	1	–	2	–	–	–	–	–	–	–	141	–	14	1	?	–	96
8	–	–	–	–	–	–	–	–	–	–	–	–	–	–	–	–	–	–	–	–	8	–	–	1	3	?	3129
9	–	–	–	–	–	5	–	–	9	–	–	–	–	–	–	–	–	–	–	–	56	–	–	2	14	–	27
10	1	–	–	–	–	5	–	–	11	–	–	–	–	–	–	–	–	–	–	–	60	–	–	–	37	–	104
11	–	1	–	–	–	5	–	–	3	–	1	–	–	–	–	–	–	–	–	–	83	–	2	–	44	–	95
12	–	3	2	–	–	51	1	–	32	1	2	1	–	–	–	–	–	–	–	–	52	1	1	2	71	–	45
13+	–	6	1	–	–	20	–	–	20	2	–	2	1	–	–	–	–	–	–	–	171	–	–	–	12	–	43
14	–	–	–	–	–	–	–	–	–	–	–	–	–	–	–	–	–	–	–	–	–	–	–	–	–	–	–
15	–	–	–	–	–	11	–	–	6	1	–	–	–	–	–	–	–	–	–	–	60	5	–	19	8	?	124
16	–	–	1	–	–	10	1	–	14	1	1	1	–	–	–	–	–	–	–	–	36	–	–	4	5	–	72
17	–	–	–	2	–	16	–	–	13	–	–	–	–	–	–	–	–	–	–	–	18	–	–	–	9	–	65
18	–	–	–	–	–	5	–	–	5	–	–	–	–	–	–	–	–	–	–	–	39	1	2	–	14	–	31
19	1	4	–	–	–	31	4	–	25	2	2	–	2	–	–	–	–	–	–	–	64	–	2	2	30	–	22
20	–	2	1	–	–	30	–	–	11	3	1	–	1	–	–	–	–	–	–	–	95	–	1	1	47	–	51
21	–	1	1	–	–	2	–	–	5	1	–	–	1	–	–	–	–	–	–	–	28	–	1	2	20	–	67
22	–	1	–	–	–	9	–	–	5	–	–	–	1	–	–	–	–	–	–	–	106	–	–	–	17	–	105
23	1	1	–	1	1	16	–	1	18	1	1	–	–	–	–	1	–	–	–	1	88	–	1	–	12	–	52
24	1	1	–	–	–	5	–	–	2	–	1	–	2	–	–	–	–	–	–	–	31	–	1	–	14	–	25
25	–	–	–	–	–	12	–	–	8	–	1	–	–	2	–	–	–	–	–	–	108	–	–	–	11	–	12
26	1	–	–	–	–	11	–	–	15	–	–	–	2	–	–	–	–	–	–	–	428	–	–	12	–	–	74

Appendix 7 continued

Field No.	Cores Bl	Cores Fl	Cores Fr	Cores Deb	Cores Ch	Unbroken Fl	Unbroken Bl	Unbroken Blt	Broken Fl	Broken Bl	Broken Blt	Bnt	Ret	Tools 1	2	3	4	5	6	7	Bnt flint Mean wt/g	Ph	RB	Med P. med	RB	Fab A	P. pres mean wt/g
27	1	6	1	—	—	86	2	—	65	—	—	3	1	1	—	—	—	—	—	—	348	—	—	—	29	?	—	48
28	—	—	—	—	—	3	—	—	1	—	—	—	—	—	—	—	—	—	—	—	11	—	1	2	—	?	—	52
29	—	6	—	2	1	42	1	—	26	2	3	1	2	1	—	—	—	—	—	—	183	—	3	26	?	?	—	204
30	2	—	—	1	1	6	—	—	10	—	—	1	1	—	—	—	—	—	—	—	45	1	—	—	20	?	—	136
31	—	—	—	—	—	1	—	—	—	—	—	—	—	—	—	—	—	—	—	—	15	—	4	—	5	—	—	48
32	1	1	—	—	—	4	—	—	6	—	—	1	—	—	—	—	—	—	—	—	35	—	33	11	59	?	—	62
33	23	16	1	7	2	188	14	6	166	11	2	10	11	5	—	—	—	—	1	—	125	12	31	6	180	?	?	60
34	—	—	1	1	—	3	—	—	2	—	—	—	—	—	—	—	—	—	—	—	9	—	—	—	22	—	—	177
35	2	2	—	—	—	9	—	—	6	—	1	1	—	—	—	—	—	—	—	—	132	1	—	1	27	—	—	50
36	(Flint combined with 35)					50	—	1	—	26	—	—	44	—	—	—	—	—	—	—	—	—	—	—	—	—	—	—
37	(Flint combined with 35)					32	—	—	1	73	?	—	30	—	—	—	—	—	—	—	—	—	—	—	—	—	—	—
38+	—	—	—	—	—	—	—	—	1	—	1	—	—	—	—	—	—	—	—	—	6	1	3	7	33	—	—	102
39																												
40	—	4	2	—	—	11	—	—	10	—	—	—	1	—	—	—	—	—	—	—	234	5	6	40	?	?	146
41	—	2	1	—	—	10	—	—	7	—	—	—	—	—	—	—	—	—	—	—	50	1	9	17	86	?	?	247
42	—	—	2	—	—	6	—	—	3	—	—	—	—	—	—	—	—	—	—	—	178	—	—	—	3	—	—	11
43	—	1	—	—	—	5	—	—	5	—	—	—	—	—	—	—	—	—	—	—	55	—	—	—	5	—	—	13
44	—	—	1	—	—	2	—	—	5	—	—	—	—	—	—	—	—	—	—	—	114	—	—	—	3	—	—	25
45+	—	3	2	—	—	15	1	—	7	1	—	3	3	2	—	—	—	—	—	—	58	—	—	—	10	—	—	23
46																												
47	—	1	—	—	—	10	—	—	6	—	—	1	1	—	—	—	—	—	—	—	33	—	1	6	—	—	32
48	—	—	—	—	1	5	—	—	8	—	—	—	—	—	—	—	—	—	—	—	49	—	—	—	12	—	—	27
49	—	—	—	—	—	18	—	1	4	—	—	1	—	—	—	—	—	—	—	—	204	—	—	2	90	—	—	105
50	—	2	—	2	—	—	14	—	1	—	18	1	—	1	—	—	—	—	—	—	—	344	1	27	2	127	—	—	75
51	1	4	—	1	13	—	—	16	—	—	—	—	—	—	—	—	—	—	—	—	147	—	1	4	66	—	?	143

Appendix 7 continued

Field No.	Flint Cores Bl	Fl	Fr	Deb	Ch	Flakes/Blades Unbroken Fl	Bl	Blt	Flakes/Blades Broken Fl	Bl	Blt	Bnt	Ret	Tools 1	2	3	4	5	6	7	Bnt flint wt/g mean	Pottery Ph	RB	Med P. med	RB	Tile Fab. A pres	P. med wt/g mean
52	—	—	1	—	—	6	1	—	3	—	—	—	—	—	—	—	—	—	—	—	162	—	1	10	—	—	83
53	—	—	—	—	—	5	1	—	1	—	—	—	—	—	—	—	—	—	—	—	18	—	1	1	16	—	41
54	—	—	—	—	—	5	—	—	1	—	—	—	—	—	—	—	—	—	—	—	12	—	—	—	8	—	95
55	—	1	1	—	—	10	—	—	5	—	—	—	1	—	—	—	—	—	—	—	8	1	—	1	61	—	83
56	—	1	1	—	1	7	—	—	2	—	—	—	—	—	—	—	—	—	—	—	18	—	—	—	6	—	31
57	—	—	—	—	—	4	—	—	—	—	—	—	—	—	—	—	—	—	—	—	37	—	—	—	1	—	47
58	—	—	—	—	—	18	—	—	10	—	—	1	—	—	—	—	—	—	—	—	12	—	—	—	33	—	73
59	—	—	—	—	—	—	—	—	1	—	—	—	—	—	—	—	—	—	—	—	20	—	—	—	29	—	241
60	—	1	—	2	—	27	1	—	22	—	1	—	—	—	—	—	—	—	—	—	160	—	—	5	61	—	?	260
61	—	3	—	1	—	35	2	—	32	1	3	—	—	1	—	—	—	—	—	—	233	—	2	9	111	—	118
62	4	2	—	1	—	19	1	—	8	—	—	1	—	1	—	—	—	—	—	—	50	1	1	1	115	—	80
63	—	8	—	2	2	64	1	—	48	1	—	2	4	1	—	1	1	—	—	1	374	3	—	3	39	—	182
64	—	1	1	—	—	28	—	—	19	—	—	—	—	—	—	—	—	—	—	—	110	—	4	1	5	—	75
65	—	1	—	1	—	12	—	—	8	—	—	—	—	—	—	—	—	—	—	—	505	—	2	—	18	—	293
66	—	—	—	—	—	—	—	—	—	—	—	—	—	—	—	—	—	—	—	—	12	—	4	1	2	—	69
67	—	1	1	—	—	23	—	1	28	—	—	2	2	—	—	—	—	—	—	—	140	—	—	—	39	—	179
68	2	—	—	—	—	6	—	—	7	—	1	—	—	—	—	—	—	—	—	—	96	—	2	—	5	—	55
69	—	—	—	—	1	2	—	—	—	—	—	—	—	—	—	—	—	—	—	—	19	—	—	1	2	—	57
70	—	1	—	1	—	16	—	—	9	1	—	1	—	—	—	—	—	—	—	—	11	—	—	1	10	—	23
71	—	—	1	—	—	8	1	—	4	1	—	1	—	—	—	—	1	—	—	—	10	—	—	1	3	—	33
72	—	2	—	—	—	11	—	—	10	—	—	—	2	—	—	—	—	—	—	—	37	—	2	10	7	—	35
73	—	—	—	—	—	1	—	1	1	—	—	1	1	—	—	1	—	—	—	—	30	—	—	1	2	—	19
74	—	1	1	—	—	—	—	—	—	—	—	—	—	1	—	—	—	—	—	—	7	—	1	—	18	—	26
75	—	—	—	—	2	4	—	—	5	—	—	—	—	—	—	—	—	—	—	—	12	—	2	2	10	—	231
76	—	—	—	—	—	—	—	—	2	—	—	—	—	—	—	—	—	—	—	—	7	—	—	—	1	—	52

Appendix 7 continued

Field No.	Cores Bl	Cores Fl	Cores Fr	Deb	Ch	Fl (Unb)	Bl (Unb)	Blt (Unb)	Fl (Br)	Bl (Br)	Blt (Br)	Bnt	Ret	T1	T2	T3	T4	T5	T6	T7	Bnt flint wt/g mean	Ph	RB	Med	P.med	Fab.A pres	RB	P.med mean wt/g
77+/78	—	—	—	—	—	—	—	—	—	—	—	—	—	—	—	—	—	—	—	—	—	—	—	—	—	—	—	61
79+/80	—	—	—	—	2	13	—	—	1	—	—	—	—	—	—	—	—	—	—	—	—	—	—	—	4	—	—	85
81	—	1	—	—	6	37	—	—	3	1	—	—	—	—	—	—	—	—	—	—	—	—	2	—	34	—	—	120
82	—	—	—	—	—	—	—	—	—	—	—	—	—	—	—	—	—	—	—	—	13	—	—	—	17	—	—	193
83	—	—	1	—	2	7	—	—	2	1	—	—	1	—	—	—	—	—	—	—	23	—	1	1	12	—	—	72
84	—	—	1	1	—	4	—	—	4	1	—	1	—	—	—	—	—	—	—	—	108	—	—	1	1	—	—	27
85	—	—	2	—	1	15	—	—	4	—	—	1	—	—	—	—	—	—	—	—	115	—	1	1	19	—	—	31
86	1	1	—	—	—	24	—	—	6	—	—	4	1	—	—	2	—	—	—	—	119	—	1	—	13	—	—	70
87	1	2	1	—	2	5	—	—	3	—	—	—	1	—	—	—	—	—	—	—	73	—	—	1	15	—	—	108
88	—	—	—	—	—	6	—	—	1	—	1	1	—	1	—	—	—	—	—	—	55	—	5	—	38	—	—	84
89+/90	—	—	—	—	—	9	—	—	4	—	—	—	—	—	—	—	—	—	—	1	65	—	1	1	58	—	—	97

Abbreviations

Bl = blade   Fl = flake   Fr = fragment   Deb = debitage   Ch = chip   Blt = bladelet   Bnt = burnt   Ret = retouched

1 = scrapers   2 = piercers   3 = knives   4 = fabricators   5 = arrowheads   6 = axe   7 = unclassified

Ph = prehistoric   RB = Romano-British   Med. = medieval   P.med = P.med   Fab.A pres = Fabric A present

Appendix 8 1982–87 Survey: Burghfield Area, all finds

Field No.	Cores Bl	Fl	Fr	Deb	Ch	Unbroken Fl	Bl	Blt	Broken Fl	Bl	Blt	Bnt	Ret 1	2	3	4	5	6	7	Bnt flint wt/g mean	Pottery Ph	RB	Med	P. med	Tile RB	A	Fab. A	P. pres. med wt/g
91	–	–	–	–	–	4	–	–	2	–	–	–	–	–	–	–	–	–	–	53	–	3	3	86	–	y	–	202
92+	–	1	–	–	–	20	–	–	13	1	1	–	2	–	–	–	–	–	7	47	3	2	19	127	y	y	–	204
93	–	–	–	–	–	–	–	–	–	–	–	–	–	–	–	–	–	–	–	–	–	–	–	–	–	–	–	–
94	2	1	–	–	–	19	1	–	27	1	1	2	–	–	–	–	–	–	–	146	–	13	14	76	–	–	–	145
95	1	2	1	–	–	16	–	–	19	–	1	1	–	–	–	–	–	–	–	75	–	1	4	56	–	–	–	183
96	–	–	–	–	–	16	–	–	5	–	–	2	–	–	–	–	–	–	–	161	1	4	–	55	–	y	–	283
97	1	6	3	2	1	22	1	–	31	–	2	1	10	–	–	–	–	–	–	89	1	–	1	24	–	–	–	66
98+	1	7	4	1	3	64	3	–	74	–	3	–	5	–	–	1	–	1	3	228	4	4	5	51	–	–	–	112
99	–	–	–	–	–	–	–	–	–	–	–	–	–	–	–	–	–	–	–	–	–	–	–	–	–	–	–	–
100	–	–	–	–	1	–	13	–	–	8	–	–	–	–	–	–	–	–	–	21	15	25	5	37	y	–	–	18
(10 m grid)																												
101a	–	–	–	–	1	14	–	–	2	–	–	2	–	–	–	–	–	–	–	130	4	–	8	45	–	–	–	201
101b	–	1	–	2	–	30	1	–	25	–	–	2	–	–	–	3	–	–	–	124	2	15	62	385	–	–	–	605
Total collection																												
102	–	–	–	–	–	5	–	–	3	1	–	1	–	2	–	–	–	–	–	164	25	7	1	18	–	–	–	65
103	–	–	–	–	–	11	–	–	2	–	–	2	–	–	–	–	–	–	–	233	–	–	2	82	–	–	–	49

See Appendix 7 for abbreviations

Appendix 9 1988–89 Survey, all finds

Field No.	Flint Cores Bl	Fl	Fr	Deb. Ch.	Flakes/Blades Unbroken Fl	Bl	Blt	Broken Fl	Bl	Blt	Brnt	Tools Ret	1	2	3	4	5	6	7	Mean wt/g	Brnt flint Ph.	Pottery RB.	Med. P. med.	Tile RB med.	Fab. A pres mean wt	P. med.	Tile	Fab. P.
104	–	7	5	–	124	1	–	23	1	–	23	12	–	–	–	1	–	1	–	19	–	–	2	–	60	–	y	73
105	–	2	1	–	61	–	–	2	–	–	6	–	–	–	–	–	–	–	–	34	–	–	–	–	14	–	y	55.5
106	–	4	2	–	48	1	–	14	–	–	7	3	–	–	–	–	–	–	–	27.5	–	–	–	–	25	–	y	79.5
107	–	3	–	–	57	–	–	15	–	–	2	2	–	–	–	–	–	–	–	30.5	–	–	2	–	55	–	y	65
108	–	–	1	–	36	1	–	12	–	1	8	2	–	–	–	–	–	–	–	19.5	–	–	–	–	37	–	y	65
109	–	1	–	–	54	–	–	22	–	–	2	2	–	–	–	–	–	–	–	120	–	–	–	–	20	–	y	64
110	–	2	–	–	96	–	–	28	–	–	3	2	–	–	–	–	–	–	–	187.5	–	–	–	–	21	–	–	64
111	–	4	–	–	19	1	–	9	–	–	2	–	–	–	–	–	–	–	–	161	–	–	2	–	22	–	y	87
112	–	3	3	–	111	–	–	34	–	–	6	–	–	–	–	–	–	–	–	50.5	–	–	–	–	44	–	y	87
113	–	9	3	–	100	–	–	29	–	1	7	–	–	1	–	–	1	–	–	58.5	–	–	1	–	259	–	y	181
114	–	3	2	–	60	–	–	10	–	1	3	2	–	–	–	–	1	–	–	138	–	–	52	–	82	–	y	291.5
115	–	1	–	–	8	–	–	3	–	–	3	–	–	–	–	–	–	–	–	208.5	–	–	2	–	20	–	y	287
116	–	2	–	–	35	–	–	10	–	–	1	–	–	–	–	–	–	–	–	88.5	–	–	2	–	49	–	–	125.6
117	–	4	2	–	140	–	–	25	–	–	19	–	–	–	–	–	–	–	–	228.5	4	–	–	–	210	–	y	159
118	–	–	–	–	29	–	–	7	–	–	3	2	–	–	–	–	–	–	–	251	–	–	–	–	19	–	–	170.5
119	–	4	8	–	51	2	–	51	–	–	24	2	–	–	2	–	–	–	1	117.5	–	2	–	–	70	–	y	223
120	–	–	–	–	37	–	–	14	–	–	2	1	–	–	–	–	–	–	–	115	–	–	–	–	41	–	y	126

Appendix 9 continued

Field No.	Flint Cores				Flakes/Blades Unbroken			Flakes/Blades Broken				Tools							Brnt flint Mean wt/g	Pottery Ph.	Pottery RB.	Pottery Med.	Pottery RB med. P.	Tile Fab. A pres	Tile P. med. mean wt
	Bl	Fl	Fr	Deb.	Ch.	Fl	Bl	Blt	Fl	Bl	Blt	Brnt	Ret	1	2	3	4	5	6	7						
121	–	–	–	–	–	9	–	–	5	–	–	1	–	–	–	–	–	–	–	–	14.5	–	–	48	–	132
122	–	2	–	–	–	64	–	–	8	–	–	1	3	–	–	–	–	–	–	–	35.5	–	3	131	y	90.5
123	–	1	1	–	–	39	–	–	7	–	–	5	1	–	–	–	–	–	–	–	44	–	10	22	–	96
124	–	2	2	–	–	9	–	–	–	–	–	1	1	1	–	–	–	–	–	–	28.5	–	1	9	y	203
125	–	1	–	–	–	23	–	–	7	–	–	2	1	1	–	–	–	1	–	–	60	–	3	30	–	92.5
126	–	4	2	–	–	49	–	–	14	–	–	1	1	–	–	–	–	–	–	–	89	–	–	37	y	143.5
127	–	1	–	–	–	13	–	–	6	–	–	–	–	–	–	–	–	–	–	–	86.5	–	–	38	y	107
128	–	1	–	–	–	10	1	–	1	–	–	–	–	–	–	–	–	–	–	–	64	–	–	31	y	221.5
129	–	1	–	–	–	48	1	–	23	–	–	4	–	–	–	–	–	–	–	–	65	–	–	766	–	154.5
130	–	1	8	–	–	92	–	–	33	–	–	3	–	–	–	–	–	–	–	1	44	–	–	70	y	140
131	4	2	2	–	–	60	2	–	12	3	–	9	2	–	–	–	–	1	–	–	99	–	3	30	y	59.5
132	–	–	–	–	–	–	–	–	–	–	–	–	–	–	–	–	–	–	–	–	88.5	–	–	10	y	32.5
133	–	–	–	–	–	–	–	–	–	–	–	–	–	–	–	–	–	–	–	–	56.5	–	–	21	y	122.5
134	–	–	–	–	–	–	–	–	–	–	–	–	–	–	–	–	–	–	–	–	143.5	–	–	19	–	38.5
135	–	–	–	–	–	–	–	–	–	–	–	–	–	–	–	–	–	–	–	–	74.5	1	–	26	y	96
136	–	–	–	–	–	–	–	–	–	–	–	–	–	–	–	–	–	–	–	–	62.5	–	–	23	y	81
137	–	5	3	–	–	27	1	–	13	–	–	4	–	–	–	–	–	–	–	–	86	–	3	40	y	138

For abbreviations see Appendix 7

118

Appendix 10: Summary of Archaeological Evaluations in the Survey Area

W99: Lower Way, Thatcham

NGR(SU)	Area (ha)	Topography	Geology
496672	2.5	floodplain	All.

The depth of deposits overlying the gravel varied between 0.53 m and 1.24 m and consisted of peat, tufa, and silts. Two old river channels were identified running parallel to the present course of the river leaving a gravel island between the two. No archaeological deposits were identified, although two fragments of burnt flint were recovered from the peat and a fragment of horse skull (New Forest pony size) from beneath the peat. There was evidence for a change in landuse from a fenland landscape, in which peat was forming, to agricultural use but the date at which this took place is unknown.

Lobb, S., 1985, Lower Way, Thatcham: archaeological evaluation, unpubl., Wessex Archaeology, Salisbury.

W100: Anslows Cottages, Burghfield

693700	20	floodplain and terrace	All./RG

At the edge of the floodplain, a channel containing a waterlogged timber structure and later Bronze Age pottery was identified with occupation features on the dry land to the south of the channel. Further ditches and post-holes were found on the gravel terrace, dating to the later Bronze Age and Romano-British periods. On the floodplain, several old river channels were identified and peat, clay and alluvial silts, up to 1.50 m in depth, overlay the gravel. Two ditches were sealed by the peat and were probably Romano-British in date.

Further large-scale excavation was carried out in advance of gravel extraction in the area of the Bronze Age occupation features and associated waterlogged timber structure. Additional timber structures were identified within the river channel dating to the Romano-British and Saxon periods.

Butterworth, C. and Lobb, S., 1986, Anslows Cottages: archaeological investigations 1985, unpubl., Wessex Archaeology, Salisbury.

W102: Elgar Relief Road, Reading

713724		floodplain	All.

On the northern bank of the Holy Brook a channel was identified some 4 m north of the line of the present bank. This channel was demonstrated to have been backfilled during the 19th century.

Hawkes, J., 1986, Holy Brook, archaeological excavations at Coley Park Farm and the Elgar Relief Road, Reading, 1985, unpubl., Wessex Archaeology.

W105: Bellwood, Newbury

493671	3.5	floodplain	All.

Gravel was sealed by up to 1.00 m of peat, reworked tufa, and silty clay. The peat in the centre of the site had been previously cut. No archaeological deposits were encountered. Large quantities of animal bone as well as a small number of fragments of ceramic building material and 2 sherds of 12th-century pottery were recovered from the tufa. A single sherd of pottery dating to the Romano-British period was found beneath the peat.

Lobb, S., 1986, Bellwood, Newbury: archaeological evaluation 1985, unpubl., Wessex Archaeology, Salisbury.

W130: Lower Way, Thatcham

498674	1.54	floodplain	All.

A major river channel filled with tufa was found to cross the site under the shallow bluff of the terrace edge. The higher ground had been disturbed by post-medieval and modern activity. Three worked flints were found unstratified reflecting the level of Mesolithic occupation in the surrounding area.

Mepham, L., 1986, Moorstream Cottage, Lower Way, Thatcham: archaeological evaluation, unpubl. Wessex Archaeology, Salisbury.

W131: Reading Business Park

700695	80	terrace	RG

Evaluation confirmed the presence of archaeological features in those areas where the air photos showed cropmarks and identified features and deposits over most of the remaining development area. Several phases of occupation were indicated — later Neolithic, later Bronze Age, Romano-British, and medieval. Further large scale excavation has been carried out in part of the site by the Oxford Archaeological Unit.

Dawson, R. and Lobb, S., 1986, Reading Business Park, Axiom 4: archaeological evaluation 1986, unpubl., Wessex Archaeology, Salisbury.

W143: Kennetholme Farm, Midgham

557662	14	terrace	RG

On the floodplain adjacent to the river, considerable deposits (over 3 m) of peat or mixed sand and re-deposited tufa were found to overlie the gravel. On the edge of the terrace, a buried soil (sand) was sealed beneath watermeadow deposits and contained flint flakes of Mesolithic date and burnt flint. One shallow feature was identified and contained worked flint. Further excavation of the Mesolithic deposits is required prior to gravel extraction.

Farwell, D., 1986, Kennetholme Farm, Midgham, Berkshire: Archaeological evaluation, unpubl., Wessex Archaeology, Salisbury.

W144: Smallmead Farm, Reading

| 698711 | 3 | floodplain | RG terrace |

On the floodplain, a large river channel filled with sands, silts, and organic deposits was encountered. Elsewhere the gravel was sealed by up to 0.80 m of clays and silts. At least two dry periods can be suggested by the two old land surfaces identified but these are undated. The features visible on air photographs on the higher ground to the south were not identified.

Barnes, I. and Lobb, S., 1986, Smallmead Farm, Reading: archaeological evaluation, unpubl., Wessex Archaeology, Salisbury.

W155: Enborne Gate Farm, Enborne

| 460664 | 2.1 | terrace | RG |

Evaluation identified ditches and pits dating to the Early Iron Age and Romano-British periods, although small quantities of worked flint suggest occupation in the prehistoric period in the near vicinity. Colluviation appears to have begun prior to the Iron Age period.

Barnes, I. and Lobb, S., 1986, Enborne Gate Farm, Newbury: archaeological evaluation 1986, unpubl., Wessex Archaeology, Salisbury

W164: Thames Valley Park, Reading

| 744742 | 35 | floodplain terrace and valley side | All./loam/RG/ RB |

Evaluation identified what was thought to be a man made ditch containing earlier prehsitoric worked flint on the higher ground above the floodplain; worked flints were also found unstratified over a wide area. The presence of a rectangular enclosure, visible on the air photographs, was confirmed and dated to the Late Iron Age, with a second phase of activity in the 2nd century AD. Features of this later phase were also found in the area surrounding the enclosure. On the floodplain the gravel was overlain by 0.20–1.50 m of alluvial silts containing a few pieces of worked and burnt flint. Further large-scale excavation has been carried out on the higher ground examining the worked flint scatter (subsequently dated to the Mesolithic period) and possible associated features, and the Iron Age and Romano-British activity. A watching brief and excavation was carried out on the floodplain and identified Mesolithic, later prehistoric, Romano-British, and medieval activity.

Barnes, I. and Lobb, S., 1987, Thames Valley Business and Country Park: archaeological evaluation, unpubl., Wessex Archaeology, Salisbury

Barnes, I., Hawkes, J. and Jenkins, V., forthcoming, *Excavations at Thames Valley Business Park, Reading*, Wessex Archaeology Report.

W165: Theale Industrial Site, Theale

| 650710 | 19.2 | floodplain | All. |

Gravel was overlain by 0.25–2.50 m of clay and silt deposits with layers of peat and tufa. Two old river channels were identified, one containing a timber stake which produced a C14 date of 1160±60 BP, AD 785–960 (1_) (HAR-8560). No other evidence for archaeological activity was recovered.

Butterworth, C., 1987, Theale, proposed industrial development: archaeological evaluation 1987, unpubl., Wessex Archaeology, Salisbury.

Butterworth and Lobb 1992

W169: Lower Farm, Greenham

| 501660 | 47.2 | floodplain/ terrace | RG |

Evaluation confirmed the presence of Romano-British features in some density in the eastern part of the site; analysis of this pottery suggests an initial occupation in the Late Iron Age with a major phase of occupation in the early Roman period. The presence of knapped flint from this area suggested the possiblility of occupation in the Mesolithic or Neolithic periods. In the western part of the site, features visible on aerial photographs were identified; the presence of the ditched field system was confirmed and a Romano-British date indicated, and the ring-ditch was dated by the Early– Middle Bronze Age pottery from the base of the ditch. The evaluation has been followed up by full scale excavation of the ring-ditch and watching brief in the surrounding area; the Romano-British site is to be preserved.

Butterworth, C. and Lobb, S., 1987, Lower Farm, Greenham: archaeological evaluation 1987, unpubl.,Wessex Archaeology, Salisbury.

W178: Whitehouse Public House, Newbury

| 482674 | 1.5 | floodplain | All. |

Gravel was overlain by 2.5 m of peat, tufa, and silts. No evidence for archaeological activity was found.

Smith, R., 1987, White House Public House, London Road, Newbury: archaeological evaluation, unpubl., Wessex Archaeology, Salisbury.

W182 Turnham's Farm, Tilehurst

| 65572 | 20 | valley side | PG/LC/RB |

Evidence for both prehistoric and Romano-British activity was recovered in the form of artefacts in two areas of the site and probably indicated associated settlement sites in the near vicinity.

Richards, J. and Thompson, N., 1987, Archaeological evaluation at Turnham's Farm, Tilehurst, Reading, unpubl., Wessex Archaeology, Salisbury.

W191: Bath Road, Woolhampton

| 561665 | 12 | floodplain terrace | RG |

Over most of the area gravel was overlain by alluvial deposits of tufa and silt and up to 0.75 m of silt loam. An old river channel filled with peat, tufa, clay, and silt was identified running parallel to the present course of the river close to the edge of the gravel terrace. One sherd of RB pottery was recovered from the subsoil in an area where the gravel was nearer the surface but there were no associated features.

Heaton, M. and Lobb, S.J., 1987, Bath Road, Woolhampton, Berkshire: archaeological evaluation, unpubl., Wessex Archaeology, Salisbury.

W224: Theale, White Hart meadow

| 647717 | 3.3 | floodplain | RG |

The gravel was overlain by alluvial clay and peat in places. The site has clearly been subjected to prolonged periods of flooding. The higher parts of the site may have formed small islands which may have been utilised by man, suggested by a pit and a few flint flakes which indicate an earlier prehistoric date (? Early Neolithic).

Chowne, P. and Farwell, C., 1987, White Hart Meadow, Theale, Berkshire: archaeological evaluation, unpubl., Wessex Archaeology, Salisbury.

W232: Ham Manor, Newbury

| 485673 | 2.5 | floodplain | All. |

Gravel was overlain by up to 1.22 m of peat, silt, and a layer of mixed tufa and silt indicating marshy conditions. Three pieces of undated (possibly medieval or later) worked timber were recovered (unstratified) from the tufa.

Lobb, S.J., 1987, Ham Manor, London Road, Newbury: archaeological evaluation, unpubl., Wessex Archaeology, Salisbury.

W239: Victoria Road, Mortimer

| 648648 | 1.5 | plateau | PG |

No evidence for the continuation of Grim's Bank as an earthwork was found. The boundary in this area was probably marked by the stream that passes through the site. No evidence for archaeological activity was found.

Trott, M.R., 1988, Victoria Road, Mortimer, Berkshire: archaeological evaluation, unpubl. rep., Wessex Archaeology, Salisbury.

W248: Midgham Bridge, Midgham

| 537663 | | floodplain | All. |

A Mesolithic blade was found in the tufaceous filling of a shallow river channel at the edge of the floodplain. The presence of the Roman Road which was was identified as a bank of loose sandy gravel (up to 0.44 m thick) was confirmed. Most of the site had shallow silty loam overlying the gravel but deep deposits of peat were identified adjacent to the canal and probably fill a large palaeo-channel.

Trott, M.R. and Lobb, S.J., 1988, Kennetholme Farm, west of the Brimpton road, Midgham: archaeological evaluation, unpubl., Wessex Archaeology, Salisbury.

W264: Crowfield Drive, Thatcham

| 511674 | 0.85 | terrace | RG |

Gravel was overlain by up to 0.50 m of silt subsoil and topsoil. No evidence for past activity was recovered.

Barnes, I., 1988, Crowfield Drive, Thatcham: Archaeological Assessment, unpubl. rep., Wessex Archaeology, Salisbury.

W280: Field Farm, Sulhamstead

| 636684 | 7 | n. facing slope | PG |

Previous information: amorphous cropmarks. Evaluation identified only 7 archaeological features, largely V-shaped ditches of an apparent field system of unknown date. Only two sherds of prehistoric pottery were recovered.

Barnes, I. and Lobb, S.J., 1988, Field Farm, Sulhamstead, Berkshire: archaeological evaluation, unpubl., Wessex Archaeology, Salisbury

W286: Mereoak Lane, Grazeley

| 708678 | 2.3 | floodplain terrace | RG |

Previously known cropmarks. Results: several phases of ditch cuttings, although no dating evidence. Two distinct environments are indicated by the ditch fills; the earlier ditches (?prehistoric) silted up in a dry environment while the later ditches were wetter. Evidence for periodic flooding, and most ditches are sealed by flood deposits.

Williams, P. and Lobb, S., 1988, Mereoak Lane, Grazeley, Berkshire: archaeological evaluation, unpubl., Wessex Archaeology, Salisbury.

W292: Dunston Park, Thatcham

| 523682 | 50.7 | s. facing slope rising from gravel terrace | RG/LC |

Other evaluations carried out by organisations in the survey area

Site	NGR (SU)	Topography	Geology	Reference
Hartshill Farm	532685	Plateau	PG	Miles & Collard 1986
Larkwhistle Farm, Brimpton	573627	Plateau	PG	Miles & Lange 1987
Burghfield Mill, Burghfield	676707	Floodplain	All.	Moore 1988
Moores Farm, Pingewood	688690	terrace	RG	Oxford Archaeol. unit, 1989
Holybrook Farm, Burghfield	711664	floodplain	All.	Hedges 1988
Butts Lake, Aldermaston	595666	floodplain		Ford n.d.

Very little previous information relating to a post-medieval mansion.

Several periods of activity were clearly identified, largely confined to the drier and freer draining soils of the site. Late Neolithic/Early Bronze Age pottery was associated with a small feature. Late Bronze Age/Early Iron Age pottery in small quantities and features were found over much of the site with two *foci* identified: in the north-west corner of the site, adjacent to a now dry valley, evidence for ironworking on a small-scale was recovered from a pit which was sealed by a deep colluvial soil which had accumulated in this period; in the south-east corner of the site, at the edge of the gravel terrace, a concentration of pits and post-holes were identified covering a large area. Further large-scale excavation in the southern area has revealed several round-houses with associated four-post structures and ditches. The second area of Bronze Age activity is to be preserved in an area of open space and various small-scale investigations and watching briefs are to be carried out during development.

Barnes, I., 1990, Dunston Park, Thatcham: excavation 1989, second interim report, unpubl.,Wessex Archaeology, Salisbury

Barnes, I. and Lobb, S.J., 1989, Dunston Park, Thatcham, Berkshire: archaeological evaluation, unpubl. Wessex Archaeology.

——, 1990, Dunston Park, Thatcham: excavation 1989, interim report, upubl. Wessex Archaeology.

Barnes, I., *et al.* 1995

W356: Diddenham Manor, Grazeley

702661	27	floodplain terrace	RG

Previous information: cropmark ditches in part of the area. Gravel was overlain by 0.4–0.6 m of yellowish clay loam subsoil and topsoil. Several ditches were identified but were undated and were interpreted as drainage and boundary ditches. Late Iron Age/early Roman pottery was recovered from one test pit indicting activity of that period in the vicinity.

Trott, M.R., 1990, Diddenham Manor Farm, Grazeley, Berkshire: archaeological assessment, unpubl., Wessex Archaeology, Salisbury.

W363: Wasing Estate, Woolhampton

570661	17	floodplain terrace

A substantial river channel, shown on an 18th- century map, was identified crossing the site, filled with mixed peat, silts and tufa. The gravel surface undulated across the site. Undated archaeological features were identified in areas where gravel was nearer the surface. Elsewhere the gravel was overlain by mixed loams and silts with reworked tufa. The previously noted cropmark features were not reidentified.

Butterworth, C.A., 1990, Wasing Estate, Woolhampton, Berkshire: archaeological evaluation, unpubl., Wessex Archaeology, Salisbury.

W365: Newbury Castle, Newbury

472674	0.85	floodplain terrace	RG

Gravel overlain by peat, clay, and silt layers indicating a marshy environment. Upper levels largely disturbed by post-medieval reclamation and buildings.

Adam, N.J. and Hawkes, J.W., 1990, Newbury Wharf, Newbury, Berkshire: archaeological assessment, March 1990, unpubl., Wessex Archaeology, Salisbury.

Bibliography

Andrews, P. and Crockett, A., 1996, *Three Excavations Along the Thames and its Tributaries, 1994: Neolithic to Saxon Settlement in the Thames, Colne, and Kennet Valleys*, Salisbury, Wessex Archaeology Report 10.

Anon., 1930–1938, 'Recent discoveries on Boxford Common', *Trans. Newbury Dist. Fld Club* 6, 103.

——, 1964, 'Archaeological notes from Reading Museum', *Berkshire Archaeol. J. 61, 96–109.*

Astill, G.G., 1978, *Historic Towns in Berkshire: an Archaeological Appraisal*, Berkshire, Archaeol. Comm. Publ. 2, 113.

——, 1979–80, 'Excavation at Grim's Bank, Aldermaston, 1978', *Berkshire Archaeol. J.* 70, 57–65.

Barfield, L.H. and Hodder, M.A., 1987a, 'Burnt mounds in the West Midlands: surveys and excavations', in Gibson, A. (ed.), *Midlands Prehistory*, Oxford, Brit. Archaeol. Rep. 204, 5–13.

—— and —— 1987b, 'Burnt mounds as saunas and the prehistory of bathing', *Antiquity* 61, 370–9.

Barnes, I., Boismier, W.A., Cleal, R.M.J., Fitzpatrick, A.P. and Roberts, M.R., 1995, *Early Settlement in Berkshire: Mesolithic–Roman Occupation Sites in the Thames and Kennet Valleys*, Salisbury, Wessex Archaeology Report 6.

Barnes, I., Butterworth, C.A., Hawkes, J.W. and Smith, L., forthcoming, *Excavations at Thames Valley Park, Reading, 1986–88*, Salisbury, Wessex Archaeology Report.

Barrett, J.C., 1973, 'Four Bronze Age cremation cemeteries from Middlesex', *Trans. London Middlesex Archaeol. Soc.*, 24, 111–34.

—— and Bradley, R., 1980, 'The later Bronze Age in the Thames Valley', in Barrett, J.C. and Bradley, R. (eds), *Settlement and Society in the British Later Bronze Age*, Oxford, Brit. Archaeol. Rep. 83, 247–71.

Barton, R.N.E. and Bergman, C.A., 1982, 'Hunters at Hengistbury: some evidence from experimental archaeology', *World Archaeol.* 14, 237–48.

—— and Froom, F.R., 1986, 'The long blade assemblage from Avington VI, Berkshire,' in Collcutt, S.N. (ed.), *The Palaeolithic of Britain and its Nearest Neighbours: Recent Trends*, 80–4.

Biddle, M., 1976, 'Hampshire and the origins of Wessex', in Sieveking, G., Longworth, I.H. and Wilson, K.E. (eds), *Problems in Social and Economic Archaeology.*

Boon, G.C., 1969, 'Belgic and Roman Silchester: the excavation of 1954–8 with an excursus on the early history of Calleva', *Archaeologia* 102, 1–82.

—— and Wymer, J.J., 1958, 'A Belgic cremation-burial from Burghfield (Cunning Man Site), 1956', *Berkshire Archaeol. J. 56, 46–53.*.

——, 1974, *Silchester: the Roman Town of Calleva*, Newton Abbot, David & Charles.

Bordes, F., 1961, *Typologie du Paléolithique Ancien et Moyen*, Bordeaux.

Bradley, R., 1978a, 'Colonisation and land use in the Late Neolithic and Early Bronze Age', in Limbrey, S. and Evans, J., *The Effect of Man on the Landscape: the Lowland Zone*, London, Counc. Brit. Archaeol. Rep. 21, 95–103.

——, 1978b, *The Prehistoric Settlement of Britain*, London, Routledge and Kegan Paul.

——, 1980, 'Subsistence, exchange and technology: a social framework for the Bronze Age in Southern England, c. 1400–700bc', in Barrett, J.C. and Bradley, R.J. (eds), *Settlement and Society in the British Later Bronze Age*, Oxford, Brit. Archaeol. Rep. 83, 57–76.

—— and Ellison, A., 1974, 'Rams Hill, Berkshire: a Bronze Age enclosure', *Current Archaeol.*, 4, 1974.

—— and ——, 1975, *Rams Hill: a Bronze Age Defended Enclosure and its Landscape*, Oxford, Brit. Archaeol. Rep. 19.

—— and Keith-Lucas, M., 1975, 'Excavation and pollen analysis on a bell barrow at Ascot, Berkshire', *J. Archaeol. Sci.* 2, 95–108.

—— and Richards, J., 1978, *Early Land Allotment in the British Isles — a Survey of Recent Work*, in Bowen, H.C. and Fowler, P.J. (eds), Oxford, Brit. Archaeol. Rep. 48.

—— and ——, 1979–80, 'The excavation of two ring ditches at Heron's House, Burghfield', *Berkshire Archaeol. J. 70, 1–7.*

—— 1980, Lobb, S., Richards, J. and Robinson, M., 'Two Late Bronze Age settlements on the Kennet gravels: excavations at Aldermaston Wharf and Knight's Farm, Burghfield, Berkshire', *Proc. Prehist. Soc.* 46, 217–95.

——, 1986, 'The Bronze Age in the Oxford area — its local and regional significance', in Briggs, G., Cook, J. and Rowley, T. (eds), *The Archaeology of the Oxford Region*, Oxford Univ. Dept. External Stud., 38–48.

Bryant, I.D., Holyoak, D.T. and Mosely, K.A., 1983, 'Late Pleistocene deposits at Brimpton, Berkshire, England', *Proc. Geol. Assoc.* 94 (4), 321–343.

Buckley, V., 1990, *Burnt Offerings: International Contributions to Burnt Mound Archaeology*, Dublin, Wordwell Ltd.

Butterworth, C.A. and Lobb, S.J., 1992, *Excavations in the Burghfield Area, Berkshire: Developments in the Bronze Age and Saxon Landscapes*, Salisbury, Wessex Archaeology Report 1.

——, 1990, *Wasing Estate, Woolhampton, Berkshire, archaeological evaluation*, unpubl. Wessex Archaeology report.

—— and Lobb, S.J., 1987, Lower Farm, Greenham, archaeological evaluation, Salisbury, Wessex Archaeology unpubl. report.

Care, V., 1979, 'The production and distribution of Mesolithic axes in Southern England,' *Proc. Prehist. Soc.* 45, 93–102.

Case, H., 1969, 'Neolithic explanations', *Antiquity* 43, 176–86.

Chadwick, P., 1981–2., 'Berkshire archaeological notes', *Berkshire Archaeol. J.* 71, 95–105.

—— and Hawkes S., 1986, 'The early Saxon period', in Briggs, G., Cook, J. and Rowley,T. (eds), *The Archaeology of the Oxford Region*, Oxford, Oxford University.

Charles, D., 1979, *Aspects of the chronology and distribution of Silchester Ware Roman Pottery*, Unpubl. undergrad. dissert., Univ. Reading.

Chartres, C., 1975, *Soil development on the terraces of the River Kennet*, unpubl. Ph.D. thesis, Univ. Reading.

Cheetham, G.H., 1975, *Late Quaternary palaeohydrology with reference to the Kennet Valley*, unpubl. PhD thesis, Univ. Reading

Churchill, D., 1962, 'The stratigraphy of the Mesolithic sites III and V at Thatcham, Berkshire, England', *Proc. Prehist. Soc.* 28, 362–70.

Cotton, M.A., 1947, 'Excavations at Silchester, 1938–9', *Archaeologia* 92, 121–67.

Cunliffe, B., 1984, 'Iron Age Wessex: continuity and change,' in Cunliffe and Miles, 1984, 12–45.

—— and Miles, D. (eds), 1984, *Aspects of the Iron Age in Central Southern Britain*, Oxford, Oxford Univ. Comm. Archaeol. Monog. 2.

Clarke, H., 1984, *The Archaeology of Medieval England*, London

Clinton, W.O., 1911, *A Record of the Parish of Padworth and its Inhabitants*

Cook, J., 1987, *Report on fieldwork around Undys Farm, Hungerford*, Ms Report, British Museum.

Cowell, R.W., Fulford, M.G. and Lobb, S., 1978, 'Excavations of prehistoric and Roman settlements at Aldermaston Wharf 1976–77', *Berkshire Archaeol. J.* 69, 1–35.

Dawson, R. and Lobb, S.J., 1986, *Reading Business Park: axiom 4, archaeological evaluation*, Salisbury, unpubl. Wessex Archaeology report.

Dickinson, T.M., 1977, 'British antiquity. Post-Roman and pagan Anglo-Saxon,' *Archaeol. Journ.* 134, 404–18.

Dimbleby, G., 1962, *The Development of British Heathlands and their Soils*, Oxford Forestry Memoir 23.

Entwistle, R., 1984, *Soil phosphate analysis and lithic scatters*, Reading, unpubl. undergraduate dissertation, Univ. Reading.

Evans, J.G., 1975, *The Environment of Early Man in the British Isles*, London, Paul Elek.

——, Limbrey, S., Máté, I. and Mount, R.J., 1988, 'Environmental change and land-use history in a Wiltshire river valley in the last 14000 years', in Barrett, J.C. and Kinnes, I.A. (eds), *The Archaeology of Context in the Neolithic and Bronze Age: Recent Trends*, 104–12, Sheffield, Dept. Archaeol. Prehist.

Farley, M., 1979, 'Flint flake dimensions in the British Neolithic', *Proc. Prehist. Soc.* 45, 322–23.

Farwell, D.E., 1986, *Kennetholme Farm, Brimpton: archaeological evaluation*, Salisbury, unpubl. Wessex Archaeology report.

Fasham, P.J. and Stewart, I.J., 1986–90, 'Excavations at Reading Abbey, 1985–6', *Berkshire Archaeol. Journ.* 73, 88–103.

Field, J., 1972, *English Field Names — a Dictionary*

Ford, S.D., 1976, 'Excavations in Newbury Town Centre, 1971–74, part 1', *Trans. Newbury Dist. Fld Club* 12 (5), 19–40.

——,1979, 'Excavations in Newbury Town Centre, 1971–4, part 2', *Trans. Newbury Fld. Club* 12 (5), 19–40.

Ford, S., 1977, *Flint distribution patterns on the Lower Kennet gravels*, unpubl. undergrad. dissert. Univ. Reading.

——,1987, *East Berkshire Archaeological Survey*, Dept. Highways and Planning, Berkshire County Council Occas. Pap., 1., Reading.

——1989, *Butts Lake, Aldermaston Wharf, Aldermaston, archaeological evaluation*, Reading, Thames Valley Archaeological Services unpubl. report.

—— 1990, *Cod's Hill, Beenham, Golf Course — archaeological evaluation*, Reading Thames Valley Archaeological Services unpubl. report.

Fox, G.E., 1892, 'Excavations on the site of the Roman city at Silchester, Hampshire', *Archaeologia* 53 (1), 263–88.

—— and St John Hope, W.H., 1890, 'Excavations on the site of the Roman city at Silchester, Hampshire, in 1893', *Archaeologia* 52 (2), 733–58.

—— and ——, 1894, 'Excavations on the site of the Roman city at Silchester, Hampshire, in 1893', *Archaeologia* 54 (1), 199–238.

Froom, F.R., 1963, 'The Mesolithic around Hungerford: parts I, II and III', *Trans. Newbury Dist. Fld Club* 11 (2), 62–87.

——,1965, 'The Mesolithic around Hungerford: parts IV and V', *Trans. Newbury Dist. Fld. Club 11* (3), 45–51.

——,1970, 'The Mesolithic around Hungerford: part VI', *Trans. Newbury Dist. Fld Club* 12 (1), 58–67.

——,1972a, 'Some Mesolithic sites in south-west Berkshire', *Berkshire Archaeol. Journ.* 46, 11–22.

——,1972b, 'A Mesolithic site at Wawcott, Kintbury, Berkshire', *Berkshire Archaeol. J.* 66, 23–44.

——,1976, *Wawcott III: a Stratified Mesolithic Succession,* Oxford, Brit. Archaeol. Rep. 27.

Fulford, M., 1982, 'Town and country in Roman Britain — a parasitical Relationship?' in Miles, D. (ed.), 1982, *The Romano-British Countryside. Studies in Rural Settlement and Economy,* Brit. Archaeol. Rep. 103 (ii), 19, 403–4, Oxford.

——,1984, *Silchester Defences 1974–80: with a Field Survey of Extra-Mural Settlement by Mark Corney,* London. Britannia Monog. 5.

——, 1985, *Guide to the Silchester Excavations. The Forum Basilica, 1982–4,* Dept. of Archaeology, Univ. Reading.

——,1987, '*Calleva Atrebatum:* an interim report on the excavations of the oppidum, 1980–86', *Proc. Prehist. Soc.* 53, 271–179.

——, 1989, *The Silchester Ampitheatre: Excavations of 1979–85,* Britannia Monog. 10.

—— and Sellwood, B., 1980, 'The Silchester Ogham Stone', *Antiquity* 54, 95–99.

—— and Startin, D.W.A., 1984, 'The building of town defences in earthwork in the 2nd century AD (workstudy: under six months' work?)', *Britannia,* 15.

Gates, T., 1975, *The Middle Thames Valley: an Archaeological Survey of the River Gravels,* Oxford, Berkshire Archaeol. Comm. Publ, 1, 1975.

Gaffney, V. and Tingle, M., 1989, *The Maddle Farm Project. An Intergrated Survey of Prehistoric and Roman Landscapes on the Berkshire Downs,* Oxford, Brit. Archaeol. Rep. 200.

Gelling, M., 1967, 'English place-names derived from the compound *Wicham*', *Medieval Archaeol.* 11, 87–104.

——,1973–76, *The Place-Names of Berkshire,* English Place-Name Society, 59–60.

——,1977, 'Latin loan-words in Old English place-names,' *Anglo-Saxon England* 6, 1–13.

——, 1978, 'The effect of man on the landscape: the place-name evidence in Berkshire', in Limbrey and Evans 1978, 123–5.

Gibbard, P.L., 1985, *The Pleistocene History of the Middle Thames Valley,* Cambridge; Univ. Press.

Gowlett, J.A.J., Hedges, R.E.M., Law, I.A. and Perry, C., 1987, 'Radiocarbon dates from the Oxford AMS system: Archaeometry datelist 5', *Archaeometry* 29 (1) 125–55.

Green, H.S., 1980, *The Flint Arrowheads of the British Isles,* Oxford, Brit. Archaeol. Rep. 75.

Hadcock, N., 1950, 'The earthwork at Ramsbury Corner, Buchlebury', *Trans. Newbury Dist. Fld Club* 9 (2–4), 24–5.

Harding, P., Gibbard, P.L., Lewin, J., Macklin, G. and Moss, E.H., 1987, 'The transport and abrasion of flint handaxes in a gravel-bed river', in Sieveking, G. and Newcomer, M.H, (eds), *The Human Uses of Flint and Chert: Papers from the Fourth International Flint Symposium,* Cambridge; Univ. Press, 115–26.

Hardy, W.K., 1937, 'Neolithic and other pottery from Enborne Gate gravel pit', *Trans. Newbury Dist. Fld. Club* 7, 1934–37, 127.

Hare, F.K., 1947, 'The geomorphology of a part of the Middle Thames', *Proc. Geol. Assoc.* 8, 294–339.

Harris, W.E., 1937, 'A Romano-British settlement at Thatcham Newtown', *Trans. Newbury Dist. Fld Club* 7, 1934–37 (2), 19–255.

——,1939, 'Belgic pottery at Thatcham Newtown', *Trans. Newbury Dist. Fld Club* 8 (2), 118.

Haslam, J., 1980, 'A Middle Saxon iron smelting site at Ramsbury, Wiltshire', *Medieval Archaeol.* 24, 1–68.

Hatherly, J.M. and Cantor, L.M., 1979/80, 'The medieval parks of Berkshire,' *Berkshire Archaeol. J. 70, 67–80.*

Hawkes, S.C., 1986, 'The early Saxon period,' in Briggs, G., Cook, J. and Rowley, T. (eds), *The Archaeology of the Oxford Region,* Oxford, Univ. Dept Extra-Mural Stud., 64–108.

Hawkes, J.W., 1991, 'Excavations on the site of Reading Abbey Stables, 1983', *Berkshire Archaeol. Journ., 73,* 66–88.

—— and Fasham, P.J., forthcoming, *Excavations on Reading Abbey Waterfront Sites 1979–1988,* Salisbury, Wessex Archaeology Report 5.

——, forthcoming, in Barnes *et al.,* forthcoming

Healy, F., 1993, 'The excavation of a ring-ditch at Englefield by John Wymer and Paul Ashbee, 1963', *Berkshire Archaeol. J.* 74, 1991–3, 9–26.

——, Heaton, M.J. and Lobb, S.J., 1992, 'Excavations of a Mesoloithic site at Thatcham, Berkshire', *Proc. Prehist. Soc.* 58, 41–76.

Heaton, M.J. and Smith, R.J.C., 1990, 'The excavation of a ring-ditch at Lower Farm, Greenham, Berkshire', Salisbury, Wessex Archaeology unpubl. report.

Hedges, J., 1974, 'The burnt mound at Liddle Farm, Orkney,' *Curr. Archaeol.*, 4, 251–3.

——, 1975, 'Excavations of two Orcadian burnt mounds at Liddle and Beaquoy', *Proc. Soc. Antiq. Scot.*, 106, 81

Hedges, J.W., 1988, *Archaeological assessment, Holybrook Farm, Berkshire*, Oxford, Oxford Archaeological Unit unpubl. report.

Hinton, D.A., 1981, 'Hampshire's Anglo-Saxon origins,' in Shennan and Schadla-Hall, 1981, 56–65.

Hodder, M.A., 1990, 'Burnt mounds in the English West Midlands,' in Buckley 1990, 106–11.

Holgate, R., 1986, 'Mesolithic, Neolithic and earlier Bronze Age settlement patterns south-west of Oxford (arieal survey and fieldwork),' *Oxoniensia* 51, 1–14.

——, 1988, *Neolithic Settlement in the Thames Basin*, Oxford, Brit. Archaeol. Rep. 194.

—— and Start, 1985, BAJ (can't find this ref.)

Holyoak, D.T., 1980, *Late Pleistocene sediments and biostratigraphy of the Kennet Valley, England*, unpubl. Ph.D. thesis, Univ. Reading.

Jacobi, R.M., 1979, 'Early Flandrian hunters in the south-west,' *Proc. Decor Archaeol. Soc.* 37, 48–93.

——, 1981, 'The last hunters in Hampshire', in Shennan, S.J. and Schadla-Hall, R.T. (eds), *The Archaeology of Hampshire*, Hampshire Fld. Club and Archaeol. Soc. Monog. 1.

——, 1982, 'Later hunters in Kent: Tasmania and the earliest Neolithic,' in Leach, P.E. (ed.), *Archaeology in Kent to AD 1500*, London, Counc. Brit. Archaeol. Rep. 48.

——, 1987, 'Lessons of context and contamination in dating the Upper Palaeolithic,' in Gowlett, J. and Hedges, R., (eds), *Archaeological Results from Accelerator Dating*, 81–86.

Jarvis, M.G., Hazeldon, J. and Mackney, D., 1979, *Soils of Berkshire*, Soils Survey Bull. 8, Harpendon.

Jarvis, R.A., 1968, 'Soils of the Reading District', *Mem. Soil Surv. Gt Brit.*, Harpenden, Soil Survey.

Johnston, J., 1983–85, 'Excavations at Pingewood,' *Berkshire Archaeol. J.* 72, 17–52.

Johnston, D., 1985, 'Munificence and municipia: bequests to towns in classical Roman law,' *J. Roman Stud.* 75, 105–25.

Joyce, J.G., 1881, 'Third account of excavations at Silchester', *Archaeologia* 46 (2), 344–65.

Karslake, J.B.P., 1910, 'Note on discoveries in the other entrenchment,' in St. John Hope and Stephenson 1910, 330–2.

——, 1914., 'Report on excavations at Silchester', *Proc. Hampshire Fld Club Archaeol. Soc.* 7, 43–4.

Kemp, B.R, 1967–68, 'The Mother Church of Thatcham,' *Berkshire Archaeol. J.* 63.

Lambrick, G. and Robinson, M., 1979, 'Iron Age and Roman riverside settlements at Farmoor, Oxfordshire,' Oxford, *Oxfordshire Archaeol. Unit Rep.* 2.

Leadman, I.S., 1887, *Domesday of Inclosures*, Royal Historical Soc.

Le Patourel, J., 1968, 'Documentary evidence and the medieval pottery industry,' *Medieval Archaeol.* 12, 101–26.

Lobb, S., 1978, 'Brimpton — excavation and watching brief', *Berkshire Archaeol. J. 69, 37–44*.

——, 1978, 'Excavation of two ring ditches at Burghfield, by R.A Rutland', *Berkshire Archaeol. Journ.* 70, 9–20.

—— and Richards, J., 1982, 'Berkshire: Newbury, Cheap Street,' in Young, S. and Clark, J., (eds), 'Medieval Britain in 1981', *Medieval Archaeol.* 26, 171–2.

——, 1985, 'Excavations of two ring ditches at Burghfield by R.A. Rutland,' *Berkshire Archaeol. J.* 70, 9–20.

——, 1991, 'Excavations and observations at Brimpton 1978–79,' *Berkshire Archaeol. J.* 73, 43–54.

——, 1994, 'Excavation at Crofton causewayed enclosure,' *Wiltshire Archaeol. Natur. Hist. Mag.*, 88, 18–25.

—— and Morris, E.L., 1994, 'Investigations of Bronze Age and Iron Age features at Riseley Farm, Swallowfield,' *Berkshire Archaeol. J.* 74, 37–69.

—— and Mills, J., 1994, 'Observations and excavations in the Pingewood area — Bronze Age, Roman and medieval features,' *Berkshire Archaeol. Journ.*, 74, 85–95.

——, Mees, G. and Mepham, L., 1991, 'Meales Farm, Sulhamstead: archaeological investigation of Romano-British and medieval features 1985–87,' *Berkshire Archaeol. J.* 73, 54–66.

Lyne, M.A.B. and Jefferies, R.S., 1979, 'The Alice Holt/Farnham (Surrey) Roman pottery industry,' London, *Counc. Brit. Archaeol. Res. Rep., 30*.

Maclanghlan, H., 1851, 'Silchester', *Archaeol. J. 8, 227–43*

Manning, W.M., 1974, 'Excavations of Late Iron Age, Roman and Saxon sites at Ufton Nervet, Berkshire, 1961–63,' *Berkshire Archaeol. J.* 67, 1–61.

Meany, A.L., 1964, *A Gazetteer of Anglo-Saxon Burial Sites*, London.

—— and Hawkes, S.C., 1970, *Two Anglo-Saxon Cemeteries at Winnall, Winchester, Hampshire*, Soc. Medieval Archaeol., Monog. Ser. 4.

Mellor, M., 1980, 'Late Saxon pottery from Oxfordshire: evidence and speculation,' *Medieval Ceram.* 4, 17–27.

Mepham, L., 1992, 'Pottery; fired clay; worked bone objects; worked timbers, and other vessels,' in Butterworth and Lobb, 1992, 108–15, 116–27.

Miles, D., 1982, 'Confusion in the countryside: some comments from the Upper Thames Region,' in Miles, D. (ed.), *The Romano-British Countryside, Studies in Rural Settlement and Economy,* Oxford, Brit. Archaeol. Rep. 103, 53–79.

—— and Lange, J., 1987, *Archaeological assessment, Larkwhistle Farm South, Brimpton Common, Berkshire,* Oxford, Oxford Archaeological Unit unpubl. report.

—— and Collard, M., 1986, *Bucklebury, Hartshill Copse, archaeological evaluation,* Oxford, Oxford Archaeological Unit unpubl. report.

Mook, W.G., 1986, 'Business meeting: recommendations/resolutions adopted by the 12th International Radiocarbon Conference', *Radiocarbon* 28, 799

Moore, J., 1988, *Archaeological evaluation, Mill Road North, Burghfield, Berkshire',* Oxford, Oxford Archaeological Unit Report.

—— and Jennings, D., 1992, *Reading Business Park: a Bronze Age landscape, Thames Valley landscapes: the Kennet Valley, vol. 1.,* Oxford, Oxford Archaeological Unit.

Newman, C. and Lovell, J., 1992, *Field Barn Farm, Beenham, Berkshire, archaeological evaluation,* Salisbury, Wessex Archaeology unpubl. report.

O'Neil, B.H. St J., 1943, 'Grim's Bank, Padworthy, Berkshire,' *Antiquity* 17, 188–95.

——,1944, 'The Silchester region in the fifth and sixth centuries AD,' *Antiquity* 18, 113–22.

—— and Peake, H.J.E., 1943, 'A linear earthwork on Greenham Common, Berkshire,' *Archaeol. J.* 100, 177–87.

Oxford Archaeological Unit, 1989, *Archaeological assessment, Burghfield: Moore's Farm, Pingewood,* Oxford, Oxford Archaeological Unit unpubl. rep.

Palmer, R., 1976, 'Interrupted ditch enclosures in Britain: the use of aerial photography for comparitive studies,' *Proc. Prehist. Soc.* 42, 161–86.

——,1978, 'Causewayed enclosure at Crofton, (Great Bedwyn),' *Wiltshire Archaeol. Natur. Hist. Mag.,* 70–1.

Palmer, S., 1875, 'On the antiquities found in the peat of Newbury,' *Trans. Newbury Dist. Fld Club.* 2, 123–53.

Parrington, M., 1978, *The Excavation of an Iron Age Settlement, Bronze Age Ring-Ditches and Roman Features at Ashville Trading Estate, Abingdon, Oxfordshire, 1974–6,* London, Oxford Archaeol. Unit Rep. 1; Counc. Brit. Archaeol. Rep., 28.

Peake, H., 1931, *The Archaeology of Berkshire,* London.

——,1935, 'The origins of the Kennet peat,' *Trans. Newbury Dist. Fld Club* 7, 934–37.

—— and Crawford, O.G.S., 1922, 'A flint factory at Thatcham, Berkshire', *Proc. Prehist. Soc. E. Anglia* 3, 499–514.

Peake, J.E. and Coghlan, H.H., 1932–35, 'Further work on Boxford Common,' *Trans. Newbury Dist. Fld Club* 7, 12–14.

Piggott, C.M., 1936, 'An early settlement at Theale, Reading, Berkshire,' *Trans. Newbury Dist. Fld Club* 7, 146–49.

—— and Senby, W.A., 1937, 'Early Iron Age site at Southcote, Reading', *Proc. Prehist. Soc.* 3, 43–57.

Pitts, M., 1978, 'Towards an understanding of flint industries in Post-glacial England,' *Inst. Archaeol. Bull.* 15, 179–99.

Rashbrook, C., 1983, *A discussion of the pottery found at Hamstead Marshall, near Newbury, Berkshire,* unpubl. undergrad. dissert. Univ. Reading.

Richards, J.C., 1978, *The Archaeology of the Berkshire Downs: an Introductory Survey,* Reading.

——, 1984, 'The excavation of a Late Bronze Age settlement and ditch at Beedon Manor Farm, Berkshire,' in Catherall, P.D, Barnett, M. and McClean, H. (eds), *The Southern Feeder. The Archaeology of a Gas Pipeline.*

——, 1985, 'Scouring the surface: approaches to the ploughzone in the Stonehenge environs', *Archaeol. Rev.* 4, 27–42.

——,1990, *The Stonehenge Environs Project,* London, HBMCE Archaeol. Rep. 16.

Rivet, A.L.F., 1964, *Town and Country in Roman Britain,* London.

—— and Smith, C., 1979, *The Place-Names of Roman Britain,* Cambridge.

Robinson, M.A., 1978, 'A comparison between the effects of man on the environment of the first gravel terrace and floodplain of the Upper Thames Valley during the Iron Age and Roman periods,' in Limbrey and Evans 1978, 35–43.

Robinson, M., 1984, 'Landscape and environment of central southern Britain in the Iron Age,' in Cunliffe and Miles, 1984, 1–11.

—— and Lambrick, G., 1984, 'Holocene alluviation and hydrology in the upper Thames basin,' *Nature* 308, 809–14.

Rocque, 1761, *A Topographical Survey of the County of Berkshire in 18 Sheets.*

Rodwell, W.J., 1981, *The Archaeology of the English Church*, London.

Roe, D., 1978, *A Survey of the Palaeolithic and Mesolithic Periods in Berkshire*, Berkshire Archaeol. Soc. Occas. Pap. 1.

Royal County of Berkshire Planning Department, 1982, *Minerals Subject Plan*.

——, 1984, *Review of Berkshire's Structure Plans*, Consultation Document.

Shennan, S.J., 1981, 'Settlement history in East Hampshire', in Shennan and Schadla-Hall, 1981, 106–21.

——, 1985, *Experiments in the Collection and Analysis of Archaeological Survey data: the East Hampshire Survey*, Dept. of Archaeol. and Prehist. Univ. Sheffield.

Sheridan, R., Sheridan, P. and Hassel, P., 1967, 'Excavation at Greenham Dairy Farm, Newbury, 1963,' *Trans. Newbury Dist. Fld Club* 11 (4), 66–73.

Shrubsole, O.A., 1907, 'On a tumulus containing urns of the Bronze Age, near Sunningdale, Berkshire, and on a burial place of the Bronze Age at Sulham, Berkshire,' *Proc. Soc. Antiq.* 21, 303–14.

Slade, C.F., 1971–2, 'Excavations at Reading Abbey 1964–1967', *Berkshire Archaeol. J.* 66, 65–116.

——,1975–76, 'Excavations at Reading Abbey 1971–3', *Berkshire Archaeol. J.* 68, 29–70.

Smith, I., 1965, *Windmill Hill and Avebury*, Oxford.

Smith, W.G., 1916,'Notes on the Paleaolithic floor near Caddington,' *Archaeologia* 67, 49–74.

Stevens, J., 1894, 'The discovery of a Saxon burial place near Reading,' *Journ. Brit. Archaeol. Assoc.* 50, 150–7.

St. John Hope, W.H., 1909, 'Excavations on the site of the Roman city at Silchester, Hampshire, in 1905', *Archaeologia* 60 (1), 149–68.

——, 1909, 'Excavations on the site of the Roman city at Silchester, Hampshire, in 1908', *Archaeologia* 61, 473–86.

—— and Stephenson, M., 1910, 'Excavations about the site of the Roman city at Silchester, Hampshire in 1909,' *Archaeologia* 62, 317–32.

Taylor, C.C., 1978, 'Aspects of village mobility in medieval and later times,' in Limbrey and Evans 1978, 126–34.

——, 1983, *Village and Farmstead*, London.

Thomas, C., 1981, *Christianity in Roman Britain to AD 500*, London.

Thomas, M.F., 1957, *River terraces and drainage patterns in the Reading area*, unpubl. MA thesis, Univ. Reading.

——,1961, 'River terraces and drainage development in the Reading area,' *Proc. Geol. Assoc.* 72, 415–36.

Timby, J., 1985, 'The pottery', in Fulford, 1985.

Underhill, F.M., 1937, 'Notes on recent antiquarian discoveries in Berkshire, part 1,' *Berkshire Archaeol. J.* 41, 3.

Underwood, C., forthcoming, 'Pottery', in Fasham, P.J. and Hawkes, J.W., *Excavations on Reading Waterfront Sites, 1979–88*, Salisbury, Wessex Archaeology Report 5.

Vince, A., 1980, *Bartholomew Street, Newbury. A Preliminary Report on the Archaeological Excavations of 1979*, Newbury.

——, Fasham, P.J. and Hawkes, J.W., 1981–2, 'Excavations at Reading Abbey 1979 and 1981', *Berkshire Archaeol. Journ.* 71, 33–55.

—— forthcoming, 'Excavations at Nos 143–5 Bartholomew Street, 1979', in Vince, A.J., Lobb, S.J., Richards, J.C. and Mepham, L., *Excavations in Newbury, 1979–1990*, Salisbury, Wessex Archaeology Report.

Wade-Martins, P., 1975, 'The origins of rural settlement in East Anglia', in Fowler, P.J., *Recent Work in Rural Archaeology*, Bradford on Avon.

Wainwright, G. and Longworth, I., 1971, *Durrington Walls: Excavations 1966–1968*, London, Rep. Res. Comm. Soc. Antiq., London 29.

Waton, P.V., 1982b, 'Late Devensian and early Flandrian vegetation changes in southern England', in Bell, M. and Limbrey, S. (eds), 1982, *Archaeological Aspects of Woodland Ecology*, Archaeol. Reps International Series 146, 75–92.

Watson, P., 1982a, 'Man's impact on the Chalklands: some new evidence', in Bell and Limbrey 1982.

Wessex Archaeology, 1993, *The Southern Rivers Palaeolithic Project, report No. 1, 1991–92. The Upper Thames Valley, the Kennet Valley, and the Solent Drainage System*, Salisbury, unpubl. Wessex Archaeology report.

Whittle, A., 1977, *The Earlier Neolithic of Southern England and its Continental Background*, Oxford, Brit. Archaeol. Rep. 35.

Wilkey, C., 1977, *Ufton Nervet: an archaeological survey of a parish in Berkshire*, unpubl. undergraduate dissertation, Univ. Reading

Wilkinson, 1985, *A Palaeolithic study of the Theale area near Reading*, Reading, unpubl. undergraduate dissertation, Univ. Reading.

Wood, R., 1959, 'The Early Iron Age camp called Grimsbury Castle near Hermitage, Berkshire', *Berkshire Archaeol. J.* 57, 74–82.

Woodward, P., 1978, 'Flint distributions, ring ditches and Bronze Age settlement patterns in the the Great Ouse Valley', *Archaeol. J.* 135, 32–56.

Wymer, J.J., 1962, 'Excavations at the Maglemosian site at Thatcham, Berkshire, England', *Proc. Prehist. Soc.* 28, 329–61.

——,1964, 'Notes from Reading Museum', *Berkshire Archaeol. J.* 61, 99–100.

——,1966, 'Excavations of the Lambourn Long Barrow', *Berkshire Archaeol. J. 62, 1–16.*

——,1968, *Lower Palaeolithic Archaeology in Britain.*

——,(ed.), 1977, *Gazetteer of Mesolithic sites in England and Wales,* London, Counc. Brit. Archaeol. 20.

——, 1978, 'The Mesolithic period in Berkshire', in Roe 1978.

——, 1987, 'The Palaeolithic period in Surrey', in Bird, J. and Bird, D.G. (eds), *The Archaeology of Surrey to 1540,* Guildford, Surrey Archaeol. Soc., 17–29.

Index

by Lesley and Roy Adkins

Entries are largely in alphabetical order, but within subentries, periods such as Late Bronze Age and Iron Age are given in chronological order whereever practical. Microfiche tables are referred to as Mf1–36.

Abbey
  burnt flint Table 15
  pottery 44, 45, Table 16
Able Bridge
  burnt flint Table 13
  flints 34, Table 13
  phosphate survey Table 13
  air/aerial photographs 3, 5, 64, 68, 69, 84, 88, 101, 102, 103, Fig. 3
  1976–77 survey 12, 13, 103, Mf.1
  field systems 81
  of later Bronze Age sites 79
  on plateau gravels 12, 13
  recommendations 109
  ridge and furrow survey 13, 109
Aldermaston
  later Bronze Age pottery 19
  Romano-British site 20
  Saxon site 93
  late Saxon town 96, Fig. 18
  medieval
    borough 6, 96, 98
    house (The Hornets) 20
    minster church 96
    park 98
  village 65
Aldermaston Bridge (pottery) Table 16
Aldermaston parish 65
  flint clusters Table 1
  Inclosure awards 12
Aldermaston Wharf, Beenham
  Late Bronze Age site 81, Fig. 15
  Iron Age site Fig. 16
  Romano-British building/villa 11, 90, 93, Fig. 17
  economy 82
  field system 84, 90
  flints 14
  plough damage 11
  pollen evidence 81
  pottery 28, 49
Allotment Gdns (pottery) Table 16
alluvium 7, 66, Table 4
  accumulation/development 77, 79, 82, 89, 96, 101
  burnt flint 48, 63
  date 17
  flint densities 16, 17, 33, 34, 47, 100, Tables 2–3
  medieval sites Table 9
  Mesolithic flints beneath 75
  pottery 20, 21, 22, 40, 44, 101, Tables 5–6, 8, 10–11, 17
  pre-Roman 88
  Romano-British sites Table 7
  tiles 45
Amners Farm, Burghfield 30
  burnt flint 48, Table 20
  cropmarks 48, Tables 13, 20
  phosphate survey Table 13
  post-medieval tile 53, Mf.28
Anslows Cottages, Burghfield

Late Bronze Age site 69, 81, 118, Fig. 15
  Romano-British ploughsoil 88
  Saxon site 93
  multi-period site 118, Table 12
  alluvium 77, 79, 82
  burnt flint 40, 63
  evaluation 69, 118
  excavations 26, 69, Table 12
  gravel extraction 118
  pottery 28, 51
  radiocarbon dates 93
  watermeadow 93
archive 14, 27, 29, 33, 57, 61
Arundells Copse
  flint 33, 37, Table 14
  pottery Table 16
auger surveys/augering 52, 54, 58–61, 69, 102, Figs 9–11
Avenell's Cottages, Thatcham (colluviation) 73
Avington VI (Upper Palaeolithic knapping floor) 72, 73

Back Lane (Meso flint) 34
Bagshot Beds 94, 101, Table 4
  burnt flint Table 4
  churches 98
  enclosures 84
  flint densities 16, 17, 33, Tables 2–3
  phosphate analysis 30
  pottery 19, 20, 21, 40, 44, Tables 5–6, 8, 10–11, 17
  Romano-British sites 89
  tiles 45
Banks Farm, Thatcham (medieval pottery/site) 22, 65
  barrows 5, Fig. 14
  Early Bronze Age 78
  geology/topography 78
  see also ring-ditches
Basingstoke Road
  pottery 43, 44, 45, Table 16
  tiles Table 18
Bazetts Plantation (burnt flint/flints) Table 15
Beenham
  Romano-British villa 93
  Saxon cremation 92
  medieval pottery 23
  flints 23
  Inclosure awards 12
  parish 65, Fig. 19
  ring-ditch 77, 78, Fig. 14
  see also Aldermaston Wharf, Cod's Hill
Beenham Grange (Farm)
  burnt flint Table 15
  flints 34, Tables 13–15
  phosphate survey Table 13
  post-medieval tile Table 13
Bellwood, Newbury (flood deposits, pottery) 68, 88–9, 118
Berkshire Minerals Local Plan 10
Berkshire Replacement Structure Plan 66
Blacklands Copse (burnt flint) 29
Boot Farm
  burnt flint 40, 63, Table 15

flints 33, Tables 14–15
phosphate survey Table 13
tiles Table 18
Borough Hill (Camp) possible hillfort 6, 85, Fig. 16
boroughs (medieval) 6, 96, 98, 101
Breaches Gully
    pottery 44, Table 16
    tiles Table 18
Brick Kiln Wood *see* Shaw
bricks (post-medieval) 29
    see also tiles
Brimpton
    Middle Bronze Age site 79
    Iron Age site 84, Fig. 16
    Romano-British
        sites 20
        tiles in church 45, 90
    late Saxon site 96
    medieval mill (possible) 20
    medieval sites/settlement 20, 44 burnt flint Table 4
    charter 93
    flints Table 4
    hollow-way (Water Lane) 20
    Inclosure awards 12
    pottery
        later Bronze Age 19
        Saxon 93
        medieval 14, 20, Table 4
    village 65
    see also Mill Field
Brimpton Common (burnt flint/flints) Table 15
Brimpton Manor Farm
    cropmark enclosure 47
    lava stone 47
    pottery Table 16
Bronze Age 5
    cremation cemetery Table 12
    sites 37
    see also Early Bronze Age, Late Bronze Age, later
        Bronze Age, pottery, ring-ditches
Bucklebury
    Romano-British villa 90
    late Saxon site 96
    parish 65
    royal manor 6
Bucklebury Common 7, 12
    ancient woodland 10
Burghfield
    flint 34
    Inclosure awards 12
    late Saxon site 96
    moat 14
    ring-ditches 77, 78, Fig. 14
    see also Amners Farm, Anslows Cottages, Burghfield
        area, Field Farm, Heron's House, Knight's Farm,
        Pingewood
Burghfield area
    flints 47–8, Table 19, Mf.20–2
    location Fig. 2
    phosphate analysis 30
    Saxon settlement 93
    survey 24–6, Fig. 6
    tiles 29, 53, Table 23, Mf.25
    see also burnt flint, pottery
Burghfield parish 94
    flint clusters 16, Table 1
Burghfield Road
    pottery (RB) 47

tiles Table 23, Mf.28
whetstones 47
Burghfield village (north of)
    pottery 51, 52, 53
    tiles 53
burnt flint 17–18, 27, 28, 29, 30, 37–40, 48, 56–7, 111–17,
    Tables 4, 13, 15, 20, 25, Mf. 13, Mf. 32
Burghfield area 28, 48, 63, Table 20, Mf. 23
    by geology/topography 37, 48, 56, 63, 64, Tables 4, 15,
        20, 25
    from industrial workings 81
    from peat 118
    function 63
    mapping 102
    near water 37, 56, 63, Tables 15, 20, 25
    survey comparisons 63, 64
Burnt House Ground (field name) Table 4
burnt mounds 18, 37–40, 63
Bury's Bank, Greenham (name) 14
Bussock Camp (hillfort) 6, 85, Fig. 16

Cable Factory
    burnt flint Table 15
    flints 33, Table 14
    phosphate survey Table 13
    pottery 40
Calleva Field Research Group (fieldwalking) 89
Carbins Wood Lane (flint) 34, Table 14
castles (medieval) 6, Fig. 19
chalk 7, 22, Table 4
    flint densities 16–17, 34, 62, Table 2–3
    pottery Tables 5–6, 8
Church Cottages (phosphate analysis) 30, Table 13
churches (medieval) 6, 96, 98–9, 100, Fig. 19
Cod's Hill, Beenham (Late Bronze Age site) 81
Cold Ash (burnt flint, flints, pottery) 17, Table 4 Colthrop
    burnt flint 40
    phosphate survey Table 13
    pottery 40, 45, Table 16
    tiles Table 18
Colthrop Manor
    flint 33, Tables 13–14
    medieval site 65
    phosphate survey Table 13
    pottery 43, 45, 64
    tiles 45, 64
Cooper's Farm
    burnt flint 81
    Late Bronze Age,
        ironworking 81, 82, 85
        pottery 82
        site 81, Fig. 15
Copyhold Farm (burnt flint, tiles) Table 15
cremation burials/cemeteries 79, 81, 84, 86, 89, 90, 92, Fig. 15,
    Table 12
Croft Cottages (burnt flint, flints, pottery) 33, Tables 14–15
Crookham Common (ditch) 29
Crookham (Iron Age site) 84
cropmarks 5, 48, Fig. 3
    Iron Age 6
    Late Iron Age 84
    Romano-British 6, 86
        pottery 45
    on clayey soils 12
    destroyed 27
    evaluations 66
    fieldwalking 22, 23, 27, 45, 51, 106
    phosphate survey Table 13

on plateau gravels 13
ring-ditches 52
on river gravels 101
see also enclosures

deforestation 10
see also woodland
Denton's Pit (Palaeolithic finds) 70, Fig. 12
Deverel-Rimbury *see* pottery
documentary evidence/research 5, 12–14, 20, 46, 96, 100
Domesday 10
hundreds 6, 96
manors 97
Donnington (Castle)
burnt flint 56, Table 25
castle 6
flints 54–6, 75, Tables 24–5
tiles Table 27, Mf.36
Donnington parish
flint clusters Table 1
ring-ditch 103, 106
Dunston Park, Thatcham
economy 82
evaluation 68, 69, 120–1
excavation 68
fieldwalking 54, 68
Late Bronze Age
ironworking 69, 121
site 68, 81, 121, Fig. 15
multi-period site 121

Earley (early Saxon cemetery) 92, 93
earlier Neolithic 5
see also Early Neolithic, Neolithic
earlier prehistoric *see* flint
Early Bronze Age
barrows 78
burnt mounds 63
settlements 78–9
see also Late Neolithic/Early Bronze Age, pottery
Early Iron Age 14, 100, 102
see also Iron Age
Early/Middle Bronze Age *see* pottery
Early Neolithic 62, 73, 75–7, 100, 102
see also flint, Neolithic
early prehistoric *see* flint
earthworks 5, 14, 27, 30, 60, 92, 105, Mf.1
on air photographs Fig. 3
damage 11
few survive 5, 6
of ridge and furrow 6
survey recommendations 109
in woodland 14, 27, 29, 105
see also moats, Grim's Bank
Eling (RB villa) 90
Enborne Gate/Enborne Gate Farm, Enborne
Late Neolithic site 77
Saxon site 93, Fig. 18
burnt flint Table 25
evaluation 119
flints 54, 56, 70, Table 24
pottery 65, Tables 25–7
ring-ditches 77
tiles 57, Tables 25, 27, Mf.36
Enborne (medieval site) 65
Enborne parish 103
Estate maps 12
enclosures
Late Bronze Age 6

Iron Age Table 12
Middle Iron Age 84
Late Iron Age 69, 84, 88, 119
Late Iron Age/Romano-British Table 12
Romano-British 69, 88
of 18th/19th centuries 10
post-medieval 48, 53, Table 20, Mf.28
as cropmarks 20, 22, 23, 30, 47, 53, 65, 84, 89, 101,
103, 107, Table 20, Mf.28
with external bank 29
Padworth 13, 14, 84, 105
see also hillforts
Englefield
flints 72–3, 77
ring-ditches 77, 78, Fig. 14
environmental evidence/data 3, 5, 14, 17, 69, 79, 82, 88
Early Neolithic 75–7
Middle Bronze Age 79
Iron Age 85
Romano-British 88, 89, 90
Saxon 93
from river gravels 70, 101
recommendations 109
Eocene Beds 7, 12, 13
estate maps 12, 20, 97, 99, 108
evaluations 1, 26, 27, 66–9, 101, 118–21, Fig. 11

faunal remains 5, 70, 82
Ferrises
burnt flint Table 15
flints 33, Tables 14–15
pottery 44, Table 16
field boundaries 12, 53, 81, 97
Field Farm, Burghfield
Mesolithic site Fig. 13
Late Neolithic occupation 63
Middle Bronze Age cremation cemetery 79, 81, Fig. 15
later Bronze Age site Fig. 15
Late Bronze Age site 82
Saxon cemetery 93, Fig. 18
post-medieval tile Table 20, Mf.28
multi-period site Table 12
burnt flint 48, Table 20
cropmark enclosures 48, 53, Table 20
cropmarks 48
excavations 28, 48, 52, 53, 63, 75, 77, Table 12
flints 47, 48, 63, 75, Table 19–20
phosphate analysis/survey 30, Table 13
pottery 28, 40, 49, 52, 75, 77, 79, 82, Tables 20–1
radiocarbon date 78
ring-ditches 78, 79, Fig. 15
Field Farm, Sulhamstead 68, 120
field names 12–14, 65, 97, 104–5, Tables 4, 13–16, 18, 20, 24–6,
Mf.28, Mf.36
field systems 81, 101
later Bronze Age 81
Late Bronze Age 84
Iron Age 84
Middle Iron Age 84, 90
Late Iron Age 90
Romano-British 119, Table 12
ridge and furrow 6
fieldwalking 1, 12, 13, 14
appraisal 22–3
Burghfield area 27, 28, Figs 6–7
detailed survey 27
extensive survey 26–7
recommendations 109
see also cropmarks

fishponds 6, 96
flint/worked flint 14–17, 27, 28, 30–7, 54–6, 57, 106, 111–17,
    Tables 1, 13–15, 24–5, Mf.2
    Palaeolithic 47, 54, 70–2, Mf.22
    Mesolithic 14, 15–16, 28, 34, 37, 73, 75, 118, Fig. 13,
        Table 12, Mf.3
    Late Mesolithic 75
    early prehistoric 18, Table 20
    earlier prehistoric 28, 33, 37, 47, 48, 62, 63, Tables 14,
        19
    Neolithic 34
    Early Neolithic 14, 15, 16, 75, Fig. 14
    Late Neolithic 62, 77–8, Fig. 14
    Late Neolithic/Early Bronze Age 14, 16, 77
    Neolithic/Early Bronze Age 15, 16, Mf.4
    Early Bronze Age 77, 78–9
    later prehistoric 33–4, 47, 62, Tables 14, 19
    later Bronze Age 14, 16, 63, 79
    arrowheads 34, 56, 75, 78–9, 114, Fig. 14, Mf.12, Mf.31
    availability/sources 16, 54, 56, 75, 77
    axes 62, 77–8, 114, Fig. 14, Mf.12, Mf.22, Mf.31
        ground 47, 56, 63, 75
    beneath alluvium 75
    blades 28, 54, 63, 75, 111–17, Tables 1, 24, Mf.9,
        Mf.20, Mf.30
        Palaeolithic 72
        earlier prehistoric 33, 47, 62, Tables 14, 19
        Mesolithic 15, 16, 28, 37, 62, 120
        later prehistoric 34, 47, Table 14
    Burghfield area 47–8, Table 19, Mf.20–2
    burnt unworked see burnt flint
    cores 28, 48, 56, 111–17, Table 24, Mf.11, Mf.21
        Palaeolithic 47
        earlier prehistoric 33, 47, 62, 73, Table 14
        Mesolithic 15
        Late Neolithic 63
        Late Neolithic/Early Bronze Age 77
        later prehistoric 34, 62, Tables 14, 19
    from cropmarks 23
    fabricators 33, 34, 47, 56, 114, Mf.12, Mf.31
    flakes 14, 28, 33, 54, 56, 62, 111–17, Table 4, Mf.10, Mf.12,
        Mf.20, Mf.22, Mf.30–1
        Palaeolithic 47–8, 54
        earlier prehistoric 33, 47
        Mesolithic 15
        Late Neolithic 63
        Late Neolithic/Early Bronze Age 77
        later prehistoric 33, 34, 47
    geology/topography see separate entry
    handaxes 70, 72
    knapping 33, 37, 62, 72, 73
    knives 33, 34, 56, 114, Mf.12, Mf.31
    piercers 33, 34, 56, 114, Mf.12, Mf.31
    from ring-ditches 17, 22
    scrapers 33, 34, 47, 56, 62, 72, 114, Mf.12, Mf.22, Mf.31
    survey comparison 62–3
    tranchet axes 33, 34, 62
floodplain 5, 11, 19, 22, 37, 43, 44, 54, 58, 62, 65, 66, 69, 70, 75,
    77, 84, 88, 93, 100–1, 107, 108, 110, 118, Fig. 12, Tables 1,
    14, 16
    gravel extraction 10
    gravels 7
    terrace 6, 15, 16, 19, 40, 63, 64, 65, 66, 78, 88, 89, 100,
        101, 107, 108, Fig. 12, Table 16
        pottery 18, 19
Fodderhouse Copse (pottery) 44, Table 16
forestry 10–11
Forest of Windsor 10, 97
Frilsham (RB villa) 90

Fronds Farm
    burnt flint Table 15
    flints 33, 40, Tables 14–15
    lava stone 47
    pottery 40, 43, 47, Tables 15–16
    tiles 65, Table 18
fulacht fiadh 18

geology/topography 7, 12, Fig. 4
    Iron Age sites 84–5
    Romano-British sites/settlements/villas 64, 88, 89, 90,
        100
    medieval
        churches 98–9, 100
        parks 101
        settlement 98, 100
    post-medieval settlements 65
    barrows 78
    burnt flint 37, 48, 56, 63, 64, Tables 15, 20, 25
    flint densities 16–17, 33, 34–7, 47–8, 54, 62, 100, 101,
        Tables 1–3, 14, 19, 24
    moated sites 98
    parishes 97
    phosphate analysis/survey 30, Table 13
    ring-ditches 78
    see also pottery, tiles
geophysical survey (recommendations) 109
gravel extraction 3, 5, 10, 11, 24, 26, 84, 92, 101, 118
    at Meales Farm 89
    in Burghfield area 24–6
    destruction of sites 27
    evaluations 66
    on plateau gravels 12
Grazeley parish 103
Green Farm
    burnt flint Table 20
    Palaeolithic flake 47–8
    phosphate analysis 30, Table 13
    pottery 51, Table 20
Greenham
    Inclosure awards 12
    Romano-British burials 90
    see also Lower Farm
Greenham Dairy Farm (Mesolithic site) 3, 73, Fig. 13
greensand (building material) 46, 53
greenstone (building material) 46
Grim's Bank 6, 14, 85–6, 96, 120, Figs 16, 18
    dating 92
    evaluation 68
    survey recommendations 109 Grimsbury hillfort 6,
        85, Fig. 16
Grovelands (Farm), Palaeolithic finds 70, Fig. 12

Hall Place Farm
    burnt flint Tables 13, 15
    flints Table 15
    phosphate survey Table 13
    pottery Table 15
Hamstead Marshall 72
    handaxes 70
    Romano-British kilns 29, 89
Hartshill Copse (LBA site) 81, Fig. 15
Hartshill (Farm)
    Bronze Age features 37
    Late Bronze Age site Table 15
    medieval pottery Table 13
    burnt flint 37, 40, Table 15
    evaluation 68, 121
    flints 33, 37, Tables 14–15

phosphate analysis/survey 30, Table 13
pottery 37, 40, 44, 45, Tables 15–16
Hartshill Farm, Bucklebury
    Late Bronze Age site 68
    Romano-British pits 68
    burnt flint 68
    evaluation 69
    flints 68
Haywards Farm, Theale (Mesolithic site) 75, Fig. 13
Henwick Lane
    pottery 63
    tiles Table 27, Mf.36
Henwick Manor Table 27, Mf.36
Henwick (tiles) 58
Hermitage (RB villa) 90
Heron's House, Burghfield
    cremation/burial Fig. 15
    ring-ditches 78, 79, 81
hillforts 6, 30, 85, 105, 13, Fig. 16
hollow-ways 13, 14, 20, 105
Hungerford (Palaeolithic flints) 72

Inclosure awards 12
Inclosure maps 12, 105
Inclosures 97, 99
Iron Age 82–6, Fig. 16
    coins Fig. 16
    cropmark enclosures 48, 101
    enclosures Table 12
    evidence scarce 5
    field systems 84
    oppidum (at Silchester/*Calleva*) 6, 85, Fig. 16
    round-houses 85
    sites/settlements 19, 84–6, Fig. 16, Mf.6
    see also Early Iron Age, hillforts, Grim's Bank, Late
        Iron Age, Middle Iron Age, pottery
iron objects 27

Jacob's Green (medieval site) 65

Kennetholme/Kennetholme Farm, Midgham
    burnt flint Table 15
    evaluation 75, 118–19
    fieldwalking 54
    flints 34, 75, Table 14–15
    gravel extraction 118
    Mesolithic site Fig. 13
    pottery 44, Table 16
Kiff Green
    burnt flint 40, Tables 13, 15
    flints Tables 14–15
    phosphate survey Table 13
    pottery 40, 44, 47, Tables 13, 15–16
    whetstones 47
Knight's Farm, Burghfield
    Middle Bronze Age site 81
    Late Bronze Age site 81, Fig. 15
    excavations 79
    field system 81
    flints 14, 79
    pottery 28, 40, 49, 79, 82
    radiocarbon date 82, 84

Lane End (burnt flint, flints) 33, Tables 14–15
Late Bronze Age 100
    burials 81–2
    enclosure 6
    field systems 84
    ironworking 69

round-houses 81
sites 28, 68, 69, 81–2, Table 15
see also Bronze Age, later Bronze Age, pottery
Late Bronze Age/Iron Age *see* pottery
Late Iron Age
    cropmark sites 84
    enclosures 69, 84, 88, 119
    field system 90
    linear earthworks 6
    settlement/sites 88, 100
    Silchester 3
    see also pottery
Late Iron Age/Romano-British enclosures Table 12
Late Neolithic 78, 101
    sites 77
    see also flint, later Neolithic, pottery
Late Neolithic/Early Bronze Age 77–9, 100, 101
    see also flint, Late Neolithic, later Neolithic
later Bronze Age 79–82, 86, Fig. 15
    settlement/sites 14, 48, 52, 79–82, 85, Fig. 15, Mf.5
    see also flint, Late Bronze Age, pottery
later Neolithic ring-ditches 5
    see also Early Bronze Age, Neolithic
later prehistoric *see* flint
lava stone (quern) 46, 47
Lea Cottage
    burnt flint Table 15
    flints 33, Tables 14–15
    tiles Table 18
limestone (building material) 46, 53
linear earthworks 6
loess 7
London Clay 19, Table 4
    burnt flint 37
    churches 98
    flint densities 16, 17, 33, 37, 47, 48, 54, Tables 2–3
    medieval parks 97
    moated sites 98
    parishes 94
    phosphate analysis 30
    pottery 20, 21, 40, 44, 49, 52, Tables 5–6, 8, 10–11, 17,
        22 tiles 45, 53
Lower Farm, Greenham
    Late Iron Age/Romano-British site 88, Fig. 17
    Romano-British site 69
    evaluation 66, 69, 88, 119
    ring-ditch 69, Fig. 14
Lower Henwick Farm
    burnt flint 56, Table 25
    flints 54, 56, Table 25
    tiles Table 27, Mf.36

Maddle Farm Project/Survey 64, 86
Manor Ash Moats
    burnt flint 40, Table 15
    earthworks 27
    flints 33, Tables 14–15
    medieval
        manor house 46
        moated site 30, 44–6, 65, Table 13
    phosphate analysis/survey 27, 30, Table 13
    pottery
        Romano-British 40, 45, Table 16
        medieval 45–6
        post-medieval 46
    tiles 65, Table 13
        medieval 29, 45–6
        post-medieval 46, Table 15
manors/manor houses *see* medieval

manuring 18, 20, 22, 44, 45, 46, 57, 58, 64, 65, 86, 89
Marshall's Hill, Reading (Bronze Age site) 5–6, 82, Fig. 15
Meales Farm, Sulhamstead
    Romano-British site 89, Fig. 17
    RB/med site Table 12
    medieval
        manor 44
        pottery 29, 43, 44, 51
    excavations 44, Table 12
    gravel extraction 89
medieval
    boroughs 6, 96, 98, 101
    castles Fig. 19
    churches 96, 98–9, 100, Fig. 19
    common fields 7
    house (The Hornets) 20
    manors/manor houses 44, 46, 94, 96, 97, Fig. 19
    mills 96
    moats/moated sites 6, 14, 29, 30, 44–5, 46, 96, 98, 103,
        Fig. 19, Table 13
    open fields 12, 21, 65, 97, 98, 99, 101
    parishes 94, 98, Fig. 19
    parks 97–8, 101
    pottery see separate entry
    scheduled monuments 5
    settlements/sites 12, 19, 20, 22, 44, 108, Table 9, Mf.8
        pattern 64, 65
    strip estates 90
    tiles see separate entry
    towns 5, 96, 96–7, Fig. 19
    villages 6, 65
Mesolithic 5, 73–5, 100, 102, Fig. 13
    sites 3, 62, 68, 69, 73–5, 101, Fig. 13
        sealed by peat 100
    see also flint
Middle Bronze Age
    burnt mounds 63
    cremations/cremation cemeteries 79, 81, Fig. 15
    ring-ditches 78
    sites/settlements 79–81
    see also Bronze Age
Middle Iron Age 102
    enclosure 84
    field systems 84, 90
    sites/settlements 84, Fig. 16
    see also Iron Age
Middle/Late Iron Age sites 28
    see also pottery
Midgham see auger survey, Kennetholme
Midgham Green (enclosure) 29
Midgham parish (estate maps) 12
Mill Field, Brimpton 14, 105, 108
    pottery 40, 47, Table 16
    tiles Table 18
    whetstones 47
mills 20, 65, 96, 105
millstone grit quern fragments 53
Minerals Local Plan 24, 54
moats/moated sites see medieval
Moores Farm, Pingewood
    evaluation 69, 121
    Middle Bronze Age site 79
Mortimer
    Grims Bank evaluation 68
    handaxe 70
Mortimer Common (barrows) 78
Mortimer parish (enclosure) 103
mounds 13, 14, 30
    see also barrows

Mousefield Farm
    flints Table 24
    tiles Table 27, Mf.36

Neolithic 102
    evidence scarce 5
    see also earlier Neolithic, Early Neolithic, flint, Late
        Neolithic, later Neolithic, pottery
Neolithic/Early Bronze Age see flint
Newbury
    Romano-British
        cemetery 90
        coin hoards 90
        sites/villa 86, 88, 90, Fig. 17
    medieval 96
        borough 6, 98
        pottery 29, 43, 51, 97
        town 96, Fig. 19
    castle 6, 121
    excavations 3, 5
    fieldwalking 54
    ridge and furrow 13
    see also Bellwood

Oakwood Farm (pottery) Table 16
open fields
    medieval 12, 21, 65, 97, 98, 99, 101
    post-medieval 97
oppidum (Silchester, *Calleva*) 6, 85, Fig. 16
Oxford (medieval pottery) 29, 43

Padworth
    enclosure 13, 14, 84, 105
    medieval pottery 20
    pillow mound 14, 105
    strip parish 97
palaeo-channels 61, 120
    see also river channels
Palaeolithic 3, 5, 70–3, 101, Fig. 12
    environmental evidence 3
    working floors 72
    see also flint
Pangbourne
    Romano-British kiln, villa 89–90
    Saxon spearhead 92
parishes 97
    by geology 97
    medieval 94, 98, Fig. 19
    see also individual parishes
Park Farm (burnt flint/flints) 54, Table 15
parks (medieval) 97–8, 101
peat 7, 61, 66, 68, 73, 88–9, 100, 118, 120, Fig. 10
    accumulation/development/formation 75, 88, 93, 96,
        101, 118
    cutting 10
    radiocarbon dating 81
Pennant sandstone quern fragments 46
phosphate survey/analysis 27, 30, 54, Table 13
pillow mound (Padworth) 14, 105
pilot auger survey see auger survey
Pingewood, Burghfield
    Bronze Age ring-ditch Table 12
    Middle–Late Bronze Age site 79, Fig. 15
    Middle–Late Iron Age cremations 84
    Romano-British
        field system Table 12
        site 88, Fig. 17
    post-medieval tile Mf.28
    burnt flint 53, Table 20

cropmark enclosures 30, 51, 53, Mf.28
cropmarks 52
environmental evidence 88
excavations 49, 52, Table 12
fieldwalking 27
flints 47, Table 19
phosphate analysis/survey 27, 30, Table 13
place name 93
pottery 43, 49, 51, 52, 53, Table 21
tiles Table 23
see also Moores Farm
place names 3, 14, 98, 104–5
    Saxon evidence 92, 93–4, 96
    of medieval parks 97
plant remains 5
plateau gravels 7, 10, 12, 30, 70, 101–2, Table 4
    Early Neolithic axes 78
    Bronze Age use 82
    earlier Bronze Age barrows 78
    Late Bronze Age sites 81
    Iron Age hillforts 6, 85
    Romano-British settlement/sites 88, 89, 90
    medieval
        churches 98
        moated sites 98
        parks 97–8
        use 65
    air photographs 12, 13
    burnt flint 56, Table 4
    cremation cemeteries 81
    cropmarks 13
    evaluations 66
    fieldwalking 27
    flint densities 16, 17, 33, 34, 62, Tables 2–3
    gravel extraction 10, 12
    pottery 18, 20, 21, 40, Tables 5–6, 8, 10–11, 17
    Rocque's map (1761) 97
    woodland 13
ploughing 18, 34, 63, 103
Pond Farm (hillfort) 6, 85, Fig. 16
post-medieval
    brick 29
    cropmark enclosures 48, 53, Table 20
    open fields 97
    scheduled monuments 5
    settlements 65, 98, 99
    see also pottery, tiles
post-Romano-British linear earthworks 6
    see also Saxon
pottery 18–22, 27, 28–9, 40–5, 57, Tables 5–6, 8, 11, 16–17, 26
    prehistoric 22, 40, 49, 57, 68, 111–17, Tables 15–17, 20–2, 25–6, Mf.14, Mf.24, Mf.33
        with burnt flint 37, 56
        distinguish from RB pot 28
        distribution 40, 44, 49, 52 with RB pot 51
        survey comparisons 63–4
    Neolithic 18, 107
    Early Neolithic 75
    Late Neolithic 29, 77
    Neolithic/Early Bronze Age Mf.4
    Beaker 77
    Bronze Age 49, 64
    Early Bronze Age 18
    Early/Middle Bronze Age 49
    Deverel-Rimbury 18, 79
    later Bronze Age 18, 19, 40, 79, 101, 107, 118, Mf.5
    Late Bronze Age 17, 28, 37, 40, 49, 57, 64, 82
    Late Bronze Age/Iron Age 18, 19
    Iron Age 19, 28, 64, 101, Fig. 16, Table 5, Mf.6

Early Iron Age 84, 85
Middle Iron Age 64, 84
Middle/Late Iron Age 40, 84
Late Iron Age 19, 64, 84
Roman 28
Romano-British 18, 19, 28, 40, 57, 88, 89, 111–17, Tables 15–16, 26, Mf.7, Mf.15, Mf.33
    beneath peat 68, 88–9, 118
    Burghfield area 49–51, 52, 53, Tables 21–2
    with burnt flint 37, 40, Tables 20, 25
    with cropmarks 45
    distribution 44
    by geology/topography 21–2, 40, 52, 89, 101, 107–8, Tables 6, 16, 17, 22
    kilns 89–90
    with lava stone 47
    from manuring 44, 89
    with medieval pot 51
    medieval pot comparisons 20–3, 43, 44, Tables 10–11
    phosphate levels comparison 30, Table 13
    production 89–90
    survey comparisons 63–4
    with tiles 45, 64
    with whetstones 47
Saxon 18, 92, 93
late Saxon 93, 96
Saxo-Norman 18
medieval 14, 18–19, 20–2, 23, 29, 40–3, 57, 68, 111–17, Fig. 19, Tables 11, 13, 16, Mf.8, Mf.16, Mf.33
    Burghfield area 51, 52, 53, Tables 21, 22, Mf.26
    with burnt flint 17, 37, 56, Tables 4, 15, 20, 25
    distinguish from RB pot 28
    distribution 44, 45, 64–5
    by geology/topography 20–2, 52, 108, Tables 8, 10–11, 16–17, 22
    from manuring 44, 64
    from Newbury 97
    with post-med pot 45, 52, 53, 57
    with post-med tiles Mf.28
    with RB pot 21, 51, Table 10
    RB pot comparison 44
    with stone 46
    survey comparisons 63–5, 68
    with tiles 45–6, 53, 57, Table 27
post-medieval 27, 29, 40, 43–4, 45, 46, 49, 108, 111–17, Tables 15–17, 25–7, Mf.17, Mf.34
    Burghfield area 51–3, Tables 21–2, Mf.27
    distribution 44, 45, 57, 65
    with post-med tiles 57, Mf.28
undated 28
    Burghfield area 28, 49–53, 64, 65, Tables 21–2, Mf.24, Mf.26–7
    by geology/topography 18, 19, 20–2, 40, 44, 52–3, 64, 101, 107–8, Tables 5–6, 8, 10–11, 16–17, 21–2, 26
    from cropmarks 22, 23
    in manuring 18, 20, 22, 44, 45, 57, 64
    Silchester 29
    survey comparisons 63–5
prehistoric *see* pottery

querns 46, 53

radiocarbon dates 73, 75–7, 78, 84
    Early Neolithic 75–7
    Middle Bronze Age 79
    Late Bronze Age 82
    Romano-British 86

Saxon 92, 93
calibration 6
peat 81
Ramsbury Hillfort 6, 85, Fig. 16
  flint 33
  name 14
  phosphate analysis/survey 30, Table 13
  pottery 44, Table 16
Rams Hill 14, 85
Reading 24
  Neolithic axes 78
  Romano-British
    coin hoards 90
    settlement/sites 86, 88, 100, Fig. 17
  Roman port 86
  Saxon settlement 92, 93
  late Saxon
    revetments 93
    town 96, Fig. 18
  medieval
    Abbey 3, 6, 96
    borough 6, 98
    castle motte 6
    minster church 96
    pottery 29, 43, 51, 97
    town 96–7, Fig. 19
  evaluations 66
  excavations 3, 5
Reading Beds 7, 56, Table 4
  flint densities 54, Tables 2–3
  pottery Tables 5–6, 8
Reading Business Park
  Late Bronze Age sites 69, 118
  Romano-British site 69, 118
  multi-period site 118
  cropmarks 118
  evaluations 66, 68, 118
  excavations 69
  see also Smallmead Farm
Replacement Berkshire Structure Plan 10
ridge and furrow
  on air photographs 13
  field systems 6
  of plantations 14
  survey 109
ring-ditches 79, 81, 103, 106, Fig. 14
  Late/later Neolithic 5, 77, Fig. 14
  Bronze Age 78, Table 12
  Early Bronze Age 79
  as cropmarks 52
  flint densities 17, 22
  geology/topography 78
  see also barrows
Riseley Farm, Swallowfield
  Iron Age
    enclosures 84, Fig. 16
    pottery 84
    site 84, 85
  Romano-British enclosure 88
  multi-period site Table 12
  excavations 24, Table 12
river channels 40, 58, 59, 68, 69, 79, 81, 88, 93, 118, 119, 120,
  Tables 12, 20
  see also palaeo-channels
river gravels (terraces) 12, 101
  Mesolithic sites 101
  Romano-British sites/villas 101, Table 7
  medieval settlement/sites 98, Table 9
  aerial photography 3

barrows 78
burnt flint 48, Table 4
cropmarks 101
fieldwalking 27
flint densities 16, 17, 33, 34, 47, 54, Table 2
moated sites 98
open fields 21, 98, 99, 101
parishes 94
pottery 19, 20–1, 22, 40, 44, 52, Tables 5–6, 8, 10–11
see also floodplain terrace, terraces
Rocque's map (1761) 98
  county boundary 92
  of Enborne 57
  of Midgham Green 29
  of Pingewood 51
  plateau gravels 97
  of Woolhampton 65
Roman
  Roads 45, 64, 85, 86, 88, 89, 92, 93, 94, 103, 104, 105,
    106, 120, Fig. 17
  town of Silchester (Calleva) 3, 6, 85, 86, 88, 89, 90,
    Fig. 17
    fieldwalking 89
  see also pottery, Romano-British, tiles
Romano-British 5, 86–92, Fig. 17
  burials 90, Fig. 17
  cemeteries 86, 94
  coins/coin hoards 86, 90, 92, Fig. 17
  cremation burials 86, 89
  cropmark enclosures 101, Table 20
  enclosures 69, 88
  estates 90
  field systems 119, Table 12
  kiln 29
  linear earthworks 6
  pottery see separate entry
  sites/settlements 14, 18, 19–20, 22, 28, 64, 69, 86–92,
    94, Fig. 17, Table 7, Mf.7
  strip estates 90
  villas 86, 90, 93, 100, 101, Fig. 17
  see also pottery, Roman, tiles
Rookery Copse
  burnt flint Table 15
  flints 33–4, 75, Table 14
  phosphate survey Table 13
round-houses 85, 121
royal estates (Saxon) 6
royal manors 6, 96

sandstone whetstones 46
sarsen quern fragments 53
Saxon
  boroughs 6
  cemeteries 92, 93
  climatic deterioration 93
  coins 92
  evidence scarce 5
  inhumation cemetery Table 12
  place name evidence 92, 93–4, 96
  revetments 93
  royal estates 6
  royal manors 96
  settlement 92–7, Fig. 18
  Silchester 92
  stake 68
  timber revetments 93
  timbers 93, Table 12
  towns 5, 96–7, Fig. 18
  wells 14

see also pottery
Saxo-Norman *see* pottery
scheduled ancient monuments 5, 6, 10, 11, 109, Fig. 3 Shaw
    Brick Kiln Wood 57, Table 27, Mf.36
    flints 54, 56, Table 24
    Romano-British kilns 89
    tiles 57, 58, Table 27, Mf.36
Sheffield deserted settlement (Trash Green) 52, 53, 99
Shortheath Lane, Sulhamstead
    excavations Table 12
    Middle Bronze Age cremations 79, Table 12, Fig. 15
Silchester
    Late Iron Age 3
    Roman road to Cirencester 45
    Roman town (*Calleva*) 3, 6, 85, 86, 88, 89, 90, 100,
        Fig. 17
    pottery production 89
    Saxon period 92
    cropmarks 13
    fieldwalking 89
    place name 93
    pottery 29, 51
    see also oppidum
Skinners Green (tiles) 58
slag 27
Smallmead Farm, Reading (evaluation) 27, 119
    see also Reading Business Park
Smallmead/Smallmead Farm
    later Bronze Age settlement 48, 52
    Late Bronze Age
        field system 81
        site 79, 81, 82, Fig. 15
    Saxon logboat coffin 92
    burnt flint Table 20
    excavations 28–9, 48, 52, 79
    flints 47
    gravel extraction 92
    pottery 49, 51, 52, 53, 64, 79, Table 21
    radiocarbon dating 92
    tiles 53
Snelsmore Common 79
    clearance horizon 81
    environmental evidence 77
    woodland
        clearance 85
        regeneration 96
soils 7
    see also geology
soil samples *see* phosphate survey
Southcote Manor (excavations) 3
Southcote (Middle Iron Age site) 84, Fig. 16
Speen 86
    late Saxon site 96
    medieval village 6
    see also Spinis
Speen parish (flint clusters) 16, Table 1
Spinis (RB settlement) 86, 93, 100, Fig. 18
spring line 7, 19, 33, 37, 89, 101
stone
    axes 77–8
    fragments 28
    non-local 46–7, 53
Stratfield Mortimer parish 94
strip fields 12
Structure Plan 54
Sulham (MBA cremations) 79
Sulhamstead
    Inclosure awards 12
    parish 97

enclosure 103
    see also Field Farm, Meales Farm, Shoreheath Lane
surface collection *see* fieldwalking
surveys
    1976–77: 1, 7, 12–23, 62, 62–4, 68, 103–8, Fig. 2,
        Tables 1–11, Mf.1–8
        recommendations 109
    1982–87: 1, 7, 24–53, 62–5, 111–15, Figs 2, 6–7, Tables
        12–18, 20–1, 23, Mf. 9–29
    1988–89: 1, 3, 7, 54–61, 62-3, Figs 2, 8, Tables 24–7,
        Mf.30–6
    comparison 62–5
    location Fig. 1
Swallowfield parish 94
    see also Riseley Farm

terraces (river gravel terraces) 47, 52, 53, 56, 62, 70–2, 75, 77,
    78, 81, Fig. 12, Tables 1, 16, 19, 21, 28
    see also floodplain terrace, river gravels
Thames Valley Park, Reading
    evaluation 66, 69, 119
    excavations 69
    flints 75
    multi-period site 69, 119
    pottery 40, 51
    woodland clearance 77
Thatcham
    Palaeolithic 3
    Mesolithic sites 3, 62, 68, 73, 75, Fig. 13
    Romano-British
        site/villa 64, 90
    late Saxon town 96, Fig. 18
    medieval
        borough 6, 96, 98
        parks 98
        pottery 22
        town 96, Fig. 19
    cropmark enclosures 103
    Inclosure awards 12
    manors 96, 97
    minster church 94, 96
    radiocarbon dates 73
    see also Avenell's Cottages, Banks Farm, Dunston
        Park
Thatcham Newtown (Romano-British settlement/town) 86–8,
    90–2, 94, 100, 108, Fig. 17
Thatcham parish 65
    flint clusters Table 1
Thatcham Sewerage Works (Mesolithic site) 3
Theale Ballast Hole Fig. 14
    cremation burial (MBA) 79
    Saxon site 93, Fig. 18 Theale/Theale Green
    Palaeolithic 3
    Romano-British villa 90, Fig. 17
    Saxon
        revetment 93
        stake 68
        cropmarks 3
        fieldwalking 3
        ring-ditches 17
        worked flint 3
tiles 45, Tables 13, 25
    Roman/Romano-British 27, 29, 45–6, 57, 64, 88, 89,
        111–17, Table 18, Mf.15
    Burghfield area 53, Table 23, Mf.25
    kilns 89
    medieval 27, 29, 45, 46, 57, 65
    see also Fabric A

post-medieval 27, 37, 46, 56, 57–8, 111–17, Tables 13,
    15, 20, 27, Mf.36
    Burghfield area Mf.28
    with burnt flint 56, Table 25
    distinguish from RB tile 29
    distribution 46, 53, 65
  Fabric A 111–17, Mf.18
  geology/topography 45, 46, 53, Tables 18, 27, Mf.36
  from manuring 45, 58
Tithe Apportionment 93, Table 4
Tithe awards 12
Tithe maps 12, 13, 97, 106
topography *see* geology
Trash Green
    tiles 53
    see also Sheffield

Ufton medieval park 98
Ufton Nervet
    Iron Age site 84, Fig. 16
    LIA/RB
    enclosures 84, 88, Fig. 17
    Romano-British site 90
    Saxon site 93, Fig. 18
    late Saxon site 96
    barrows 78
    earthworks 105
    estate maps 12
    flints 17, 34, Table 1
    parish 97
        survey 3–5
    pottery 28, 96
    ring-ditches 78, 103, 106

valley sides *see* Bagshot Beds, London Clay, plateau gravels

Wallingford
    late Saxon town 96
    medieval town 97
Wash Common barrows 78
Wasing 72
    cropmark enclosure 22
    handaxe 70
    medieval settlement 44
    moat 14
    pottery 22, 107
Wasing Estate, Woolhampton
    evaluation 68, 121
    fieldwalking 68
    pottery 68
Wasing Lower Farm
    burnt flint Table 15
    cropmark enclosures 89
    cropmarks Table 13
    flints 30, 33, 34, 62, 73, Fig. 13, Tables 13–15

mill 105
moat 103
phosphate survey Table 13
pottery 40, 44, 45, 47, Tables 13, 15–16
Romano-British site 89
tiles 45, 64, 65, Table 18
whetstones 47
Wasing mound 105
Wasing parish 103, 107, 108
    estate maps 12
Wasing Wood (mound) 30
watching briefs 68
    recommendations 110
watermeadows 10, 60, 66, 93, 118
Wawcott
    Mesolithic sites 3, 73, 75
    radiocarbon dates 73, 75
Webbs Lane
    flint 33, 34, Table 14
    phosphate survey Table 13
    pottery Table 16
whetstones 46–7, 53
Wickham
    Burghfield 14, 104
    Woolhampton 14, 104
Woodcock
    burnt flint Table 15
    flints 33, Table 15
    lava stone 47
    phosphate survey Table 13
    pottery 44, 47, Table 16
woodland 10, 11, 97, Fig. 5
    Devensian 72
    Middle Bronze Age 79
    ancient 10, Fig. 3
    boundaries 29
    clearance 17, 77, 88, 101
    earthworks 14, 27, 29, 105
    management of sites 110
    on plateau gravels 13
    regeneration 77, 96
    survey 12, 14, 27, 29–30, 109, Fig. 2, Mf.1
    see also Brick Kiln Wood
Woodspeen (site of *Spinis*) 86
Woolhampton 59, Fig. 9
    Romano-British site 20
    medieval mill 65
    gravel terraces 70
    parish 65, 107
    scheduled ridge and furrow earthworks 6
    village 65
    see also Wickham
Woolhampton Park (pottery) 44, Table 16
worked flint *see* flint